57 **Governmentality, Biopower, and Everyday Life**
Majia Holmer Nadesan

58 **Sustainability and Security within Liberal Societies**
Learning to Live with the Future
Edited by Stephen Gough and Andrew Stables

59 **The Mythological State and its Empire**
David Grant

60 **Globalizing Dissent**
Essays on Arundhati Roy
Edited by Ranjan Ghosh & Antonia Navarro-Tejero

61 **The Political Philosophy of Michel Foucault**
Mark G.E. Kelly

62 **Democratic Legitimacy**
Fabienne Peter

63 **Edward Said and the Literary, Social, and Political World**
Edited by Ranjan Ghosh

64 **Perspectives on Gramsci**
Politics, Culture and Social Theory
Edited by Joseph Francese

65 **Enlightenment Political Thought and Non-Western Societies**
Sultans and Savages
Frederick G. Whelan

66 **Liberalism, Neoliberalism, Social Democracy**
Thin Communitarian Perspectives on Political Philosophy and Education
Mark Olssen

67 **Oppositional Discourses and Democracies**
Edited by Michael Huspek

68 **The Contemporary Goffman**
Edited by Michael Hviid Jacobsen

69 **Hemingway on Politics and Rebellion**
Edited by Lauretta Conklin Frederking

70 **Social Theory in Contemporary Asia**
Ann Brooks

71 **Governmentality**
Current Issues and Future Challenges
Edited by Ulrich Bröckling, Susanne Krasmann and Thomas Lemke

72 **Gender, Emotions and Labour Markets - Asian and Western Perspectives**
Ann Brooks and Theresa Devasahayam

73 **Alienation and the Carnivalization of Society**
Edited by Jerome Braun and Lauren Langman

74 **The Post-Colonial State in the Era of Capitalist Globalization**
Historical, Political and Theoretical Approaches to State Formation
Tariq Amin-Khan

75 **The Psychology and Politics of the Collective**
Groups, Crowds and Mass Identifications
Edited by Ruth Parkin-Gounelas

The Psychology and Politics of the Collective

Groups, Crowds and Mass Identifications

Edited by Ruth Parkin-Gounelas

Routledge
Taylor & Francis Group
NEW YORK LONDON

First published 2012
by Routledge
711 Third Avenue, New York, NY 10017

Simultaneously published in the UK
by Routledge
2 Park Square, Milton Park, Abingdon, Oxon OX14 4RN

Routledge is an imprint of the Taylor & Francis Group, an informa business

Library of Congress Cataloging-in-Publication Data

The psychology and politics of the collective : groups, crowds, and mass identifications / edited by Ruth Parkin-Gounelas. -- 1st ed.
p. cm. — (Routledge studies in social and political thought ; 75)
Includes bibliographical references and index.
1. Social groups. 2. Social psychology. 3. Group identity. 4. Individuality. 5. Collective behavior. 6. Online social networks. I. Parkin-Gounelas, Ruth, 1950–
HM716.P793 2012
302.3—dc23
2011040462

ISBN: 978-0-415-51026-4 (hbk)
ISBN: 978-0-203-12322-5 (ebk)

Typeset in Sabon
by IBT Global.

Printed and bound in the United States of America on sustainably sourced paper by IBT Global.

Contents

Introduction

Ruth Parkin-Gounelas

> It is a curious subject to enquire into the due medium between individuality and concert. On the one hand, it is to be observed that human beings are formed for society. Without society, we shall probably be deprived of the most eminent enjoyments of which our nature is susceptible. In society, no man possessing the genuine marks of a man can stand alone . . . On the other hand, individuality is of the very essence of intellectual excellence. He that resigns himself wholly to sympathy and imitation can possess little of mental strength or accuracy.
>
> (Godwin 756–57)

The subject of the relationship between the individual and the social group is no less "curious" today than it was in the 1790s when William Godwin was writing. How could it be otherwise, with something so fundamental to the human condition which is simultaneously obvious yet elusive? For all his quaintly anachronistic faith in the enduring "excellence" of the individual,[1] Godwin understood very well, and in ways that are of particular relevance today, that periods of radical social and cultural upheaval call for an equally radical assessment of the individual-group relationship. Poised as he was on the crest of the first wave of industrial expansion, he was acutely sensitive to the way this relationship tests out the inter-implication of the historically specific and the universal. On the one side, in his day, were the historical forces of capitalism (the above passage is from Book VIII, "Of Property") and the high idealism of the French Revolution, of which he was a prominent champion. On the other were the universals of "Justice," "Morals" and "Happiness" of his book's title, which he followed eighteenth-century philosophy in putting at the centre of his discussion. In taking on afresh such old and intractable questions as these, as well as other related ones like the conflicting claims of cognition and affect (which as Enlightenment Romantic he was also well placed to tackle), Godwin gave a scope to his "curious" topic that subsequent periods, with their more rigid dichotomies, have rarely been able to match.

To move from the late eighteenth to the early twenty-first century is to be struck by the ways in which radical philosophy today has returned to these very same questions, but this time against the grain of Godwin's founding faith in individualism. Over two centuries of colonial imperialism committed to notions of both personal and national identity and individuality (what one post-colonial theorist has called "the consolations of self-identical community" [Ghandi 30]) have changed the ideological landscape irrevocably, as have the increasing commodifications of global capitalism and the uniformities of bureaucratised social life (Mouffe 308–9).[2] In the mean time, psychoanalysis has irrefutably demonstrated that the individual is always already other-directed, inhabiting what Jacques Lacan called a "transindividual reality" whose operations, via speech/discourse, are those of history (*Écrits* 214).[3] The implications of this dyadic relationship, brought more explicitly into the political arena by the Frankfurt School in the middle of the last century, have become particularly insistent in our own post-communist, post-industrial age.

For Fredric Jameson, a prominent advocate of the deposition of the individual as an outmoded product of modernity, "depersonalisation and desubjectification" are not to be regarded in negative terms (the "alienation" described by Adorno and Horkheimer). Following Lacan, Jameson calls for a move away from the obfuscations of the centred subject to make way for new liberating rituals of praxis—Rilke's "not I, but the wind that blows through me!" (Jameson, *Singular* 133–35). An increasing number of voices have come to join Jameson's. The political task of our generation, Giorgio Agamben argues in *The Coming Community*, is to eschew old identity models with their "senseless form of individuality" and construct a "community . . . without subjects" composed of people with a "common . . . singularity" (65). A radical democracy, for Ernesto Laclau, demands consensus among a plurality of social actors, a primary constitutive diversity of the collective will, where concepts such as class or ethnic identity are not unified and essential but transient and contingent. And for Alain Badiou, we need to refuse the logic of the primordial bond, which gave rise to the bureaucratic state, so that mass movements can become the site for the political "event." Like Laclau's, Badiou's is what he calls a "praxiological" model (as opposed to either a constructivist or a transcendental one), where "the event blocks its *total* [totalitarian] singularisation by the belonging of its signifier to the multiple that it is" (*Being and Event* 182). With Badiou's "multiple being," Agamben's "common singularity" and Laclau's "collective subject," moving beyond individualism has come to mean opening up possibilities of understanding and action that may make us better equipped to deal with a new planetary humanity.

Within the context of shifting social bonds in global culture, this volume brings together debates on the left from a range of disciplines (political philosophy, psychoanalysis, social psychology, and media and cultural studies) in the attempt to configure new meanings of identity, community and collective action. Discontent with liberal-capitalist models of individualism has led analysts from different fields to re-think the meaning of the group in contemporary information societies, pondering such questions as whether the role of the masses is open to retrieval, whether the high technology of a globalised market economy is congruent with democracy, the fate of multiculturalism, the relative claims of the cognitive and the affective, the relevance of identity models in a culture mediated by images and what happens in a crowd. In the aftermath of the great mass movements of the twentieth century—Marxist-Leninism, Mao—we are confronted by what Badiou calls the "great enigma" of the last century: why, he asks, did "the subsumption of politics, either through the form of the immediate bond (the masses), or the mediate bond (the party), ultimately give rise to bureaucratic submission and the cult of the State?" (*Metapolitics* 70). A site of semantic ambiguity in the post-communist vacuum being rapidly filled by digitally-mediated forms of collectivity, the group/mass raises crucial questions to do with sovereignty, agency and the biopolitical—as well, and underlying all these, as with the significance of affect, both within the group and towards others outside it.

Long ignored by cultural and political theory, affect has in recent years become increasingly prominent in discussions of political expression and collective behaviour. With affective investment in social categories being channeled away from party or church loyalties towards new social movements and global internet networks, a new set of terms and tools is needed, one capable of drawing on a multi-disciplinary approach which questions the old divides of history-body or sociology-biology. Emphasis on our shared affect, the contributors to this book demonstrate, has suddenly become imperative to counter today's atomistic modernity . It has taken us many decades to distance ourselves from the horrors of totalitarian crowds, where passion was marshalled to effect forms of submission (concentration camps, the Gulag) unparallelled in human history. It is worth remembering, for example, the ways in which Wilhelm Reich's *Mass Psychology of Fascism*, which argues that fascism is "the expression of the irrational structure of mass man" (Reich xxiii), was taken up by the counterculture in the 1960s, hurled at police during protests. Work by social psychologists such as Stephen Reicher (of which his essay on "Crowds, Agency and Passion" in this volume is a characteristic example) has done a great deal in recent years to restore dignity and agency to collective action. Put differently, it could be said that what is at stake here is the task of re-thinking the significance of "com-passion," to use Jean-Luc Nancy's term. What he has in mind is not a compassion that feeds on itself, a form of self-pity, but rather "the contagion, the contact of being with one another" in the turmoil of antagonistic togetherness. Com-passion, he writes, "is not altruism, nor is it identification; it is the disturbance of violent relatedness" (*Being* xiii).

We don't need to be reminded that the biggest obstacle humans face in organising their lives collectively is the bedrock of aggression. According to psychoanalysis, "civilisation" by its very nature involves "discontent" or melancholia, in that loving thy neighbour means turning the death drive inward, against ourselves, in the form of a punishing super-ego ("thou shalt not"). Evolutionary theory has emphasised how our survival as a species has been dependent on our capacity to bond as a group, for which empathy, shared intentions, is a fundamental prerequisite. (In his chapter in this book, Holger Briel analyses the "swarm intelligence" being created by today's bloggers.) Like other primates, however, we've also inherited the tendency to *intra*-group hostility, competition for control over territory and mates, in particular since the arrival of the concept of property with the establishment of sedentary communities in the Neolithic period. Much has been written in recent decades about the role of community as a bulwark against fragmentation or social exclusion, from communitarian ethics to Derrida's "politics of friendship." And yet (as Derrida well understood) it may be equally important to remember that for the maintenance of social bonds, aggression has always been as important as love. The Furies or Eumenides at the end of Aeschylus's *Orestia* trilogy call on the Athenians to unite and avoid civil war—by not only having "one common will for love," but also learning to "hate with one strong heart" (Aeschylus 274). As Slavoj Žižek puts it, it is as if truly "authentic" community can function only in conditions of permanent threat (*Violence* 23).[4] Bonding *within* the group necessarily means establishing a conflictual relation to another group; culture is by definition both collective (what we share with others) and particular (exclusive of other cultures). Postmodern identity or single-issue politics bears the trace of the cult of individualism in its emphasis on the specificity-individuality of the group—racial, gender, class *difference*, what distinguishes one group from another, as opposed to what all humans have in common. It is one of the main contentions of this book that investigating the relation between the individual and the group necessarily entails a reconceptualisation of the dichotomy sameness-difference.

Taxonomies of the collective continue to proliferate in the attempt to accommodate changing social bonds—from new social movements and Badiou's "evental site" to blogospheres and twitter communities. The logic of the bond itself, in Badiou's well-known paradox, needs to be resisted: the social is more appropriately understood as the "*un*binding" which it nonetheless prohibits. In this regard Agamben's *Coming Community* (1990) invites closer examination as a text equivalent, perhaps, to Godwin's *Enquiry* in its uncompromising drive to break with the past. Citing Badiou's "unbinding," Agamben sets out to describe a future community not of "essences" (*what* something is) but of cohabiting "existences" (*that* something is), an external "as-suchness" which, in Heideggerian vein,[5] he calls "whatever subjectivity [which] has no identity":

> if instead of continuing to search for a proper identity in the already improper and senseless form of individuality, humans were to succeed in belonging to this impropriety as such, in making of the proper being-thus not an identity and an individual property but a singularity without identity, a common and absolutely exposed singularity—if humans could, that is, not be-thus in this or that particular biography, but be

> only *the* thus, their singular exteriority and their face, then they would for the first time enter into a community without presuppositions and without subjects, into a communication without the incommunicable.
>
> Selecting in the new planetary humanity those characteristics that allow for its survival, removing the thin diaphragm that separates bad mediatized advertising from the perfect exteriority that communicates only itself—this is the political task of our generation. (*Coming* 65)

Agamben's "coming community" challenges the doxa on another count as well, by refusing the distinction between the particular and the universal. Social sciences models of the 1980s, along with the constructivist approach of post-structuralism, failed to account for what is common to all human subjects. It is a "false dilemma," Agamben argues, "that obliges knowledge to choose between the ineffability of the individual and the intelligibility of the universal" (*Coming* 1). After all, he reminds us, the human face is both common and "proper" (individual, particular); "common nature and singularity . . . change roles and interpenetrate" (20): "It is whatever face, in which what belongs to common nature and what is proper are absolutely indifferent" (19)—in the same way that the human word is neither the appropriation of what is common (language) nor the communication of what is particular to each of us. Dangerous for the way it is all too readily co-opted into the service of a dominant culture to justify imperial expansion, universality is as "impossible" as it is necessary, as Ernesto Laclau puts it (Laclau, *Populist* 115).

Laclau's intervention in this volume lays out the main points of reference of this debate, drawing on the changing terms of his engagement with psychoanalysis and political philosophy since his (and Chantal Mouffe's) seminal work on hegemony and socialist strategy in the 1980s. For Laclau, the tension between particularity and universality is irresolvable. As he puts it in this volume, differences achieve (discursive) identity only if one of them "divides its own identity between its original particularity and its role of representing an (absent) totality which is incommensurable with its own particularism." This representation of absolute/impossible totality is what he calls the hegemonic or empty signifier. It is for this reason, he argues, that we should be concentrating not on the particularisms themselves (class, race, gender, etc.) but on the logics capable of articulating these plural demands in wider political identities. Hence his insistence on the specific logic of equivalence, in order "to start the construction of the 'people' as a global subject confronting power." A radical democracy, then, will necessarily involve a struggle over the universal as the site of competition where different groups attempt (temporarily) to give to their particularisms the function of a universal representation. The point here, as Žižek has put it, is that universality is not a neutral container of particulars but rather the "battle itself, the struggle leading from one particular formation to another" (*Parallax* 30).

* * * *

The particular and the universal, the individual and the mass, the local and the global: a psychology or a politics that focuses on one side of the dichotomy at the expense of the other is doomed to sterility. This impossible necessity of thinking the one in relation to the other lies at the core of the Marxist-Freudian project. Although Freud founded psychoanalysis on the theory of the libido, he was soon (in the second decade of the twentieth century) to move towards object relations, placing the dyadic rather than the monadic model at the core of his thinking about the self as implicated in the other, and by extension in the group or symbolic order (the Lacanians' "Big Other"). Freud's "Group Psychology" essay of 1921 provides the point of departure for several of this book's authors (Laclau, Merck, Reicher, Politi), proving itself to be as foundational as it is vitally in need of revision. The essay's recent re-translation as "Mass Psychology and Analysis of the 'I'" offers a timely opportunity to re-position the debates it has stimulated, to return to the historical and political implications of "die Massen" elided in James Strachey's original English translation.

The first thing that strikes you on reading Freud's essay today is his refusal to shy away from the difficulties of the subject. Surveying other theories of mass psychology, Freud (like Godwin) felt daunted by the task, by the "total contradictions" ("Mass" 33) in the evidence, both that of others and his own, which made the topic seem unworkable. He writes:

> If, bearing in mind the mutually supplementary descriptions of authors writing about mass psychology, one casts a general look at the life of the individual person today, one may, faced with the complications that emerge here, be discouraged from offering a comprehensive account. Each individual is a component of many masses . . . has a share in many mass minds (those of his race, his class, his religious community, his nationality, etc.) and may also beyond that rise to a certain amount of independence and originality. ("Mass" 84)

The next thing you notice is the contradictions in Freud's own arguments, at least according to the terms of today's debates. That an individual should "rise" to independence of the mass ("raise himself above them" in Strachey's translation) (Freud, "Group" 161), suggesting the superiority of the former over the latter, has led some contemporary crowd theorists to dismiss Freud's views as reductive, complicit with Gustave Le Bon's notorious view of the crowd as irrational, irresponsible and credulous. There is plenty of evidence in the essay for Freud's support of Le Bon's interpretation of the crowd, which he at one point calls "brilliant" ("Mass" 84), citing the French social psychologist's view that the crowd (at least the "short-lived" crowd, as opposed to more permanent groups like the army and the church) brings out the "primitive" in humans, or that "a man descends several rungs in the ladder of civilization" ("Mass" 25; Le Bon 13) when he joins a crowd, terms that chime with the hierarchical ascriptions of late nineteenth-century anthropology.

Freud spends the first two chapters of his essay summarising Le Bon, however, only to state at the beginning of the third chapter that although the emphasis is warranted because of Le Bon's attention to the unconscious factors involved in group behaviour, what he says has been said many times by others and, more importantly, a great deal of evidence to the contrary needs to be brought into play. To illustrate this, he cites the "higher"—heroic or altruistic—actions of which the mass is clearly capable, as well as the role played by the group in the production of language, folklore, etc. What seems to be happening here in Freud's equivocal acknowledgement of Le Bon may have something to do with the anxiety of influence, an anxiety common among the Freud circle at this period, which is the subject of Mandy Merck's chapter in this book. It is also the case, however, that the concept of the mass tends to act as an elastic ideological container, pulled in all directions to accommodate changing political and psychological prerequisites. This is no less the case today than it was at the beginning of the last century. If Freud's anxious vacillations between fear of the mass and a more measured recognition of its creative potential may also have had something to do with the Russian Revolution, as Jina Politi argues in her chapter here, today the concerns have more to do with contested scientific questions about the relationship of body ("nature") and history. After Freud, and as the twentieth century progressed, theories of the rational, self-contained individual came to dominate social psychological discourse, accompanied by an increasing reluctance to investigate intra-group affective responses. That trend has now begun to reverse, with recent theorists exploring what Nigel Thrift calls the complex biocultural "'disposition' . . . by which masses of people and things become primed to act" (Thrift 220). Like many of the authors in this volume, Thrift attempts to answer questions such as the following: "What would the study of affect look like if it did not focus on the subject and subjectivity?"; "How do political formations generate affect?"; and "To what extent is affect a political form in itself?" (222).

The contemporary preoccupation with group affect has led commentators back to Freud's controversial discussion (via Le Bon) of the "contagion" of emotion in a crowd—that (as he put it) not only is our affectivity "extraordinarily enhanced" in the group, but also there is "no doubt" that the tendency exists in us "of succumbing to a particular affect when we become aware of a sign of that affective state in someone else" (Freud, "Mass" 39–40). Much scientific attention has been paid in the past decade to the discovery of the existence of mirror neurons in the frontal and parietal lobes of the brain, which have been proved to trigger a mimetic response to others so that the motor system of one person "resonates" with that of another (Gallese; Damasio 115–16). When we observe someone performing a particular action (for example clapping, or reaching for a nut), researchers have discovered, concurrent visual and motor circuits in the brain are activated in the same way, as if we were doing the same thing ourselves. Neuroscientists of affect such as Antonio Damasio, Joseph LeDoux and Jack Panksepp stress the evolutionarily-shared nature—across species—of "affective consciousness" (Panksepp 580), a term that is being used increasingly to avoid earlier assumptions that affect excludes cognition. The "affective turn" taking place across the political, economic and cultural disciplines draws on these findings to express, as Michael Hardt puts it, a "new ontology of the human" (Hardt, "Foreword" xii), which follows Spinoza in postulating a correspondence between body and mind as well as a continuum between reason and the passions,[6] undermining the ancient (and Le Bonian) distinction between the rational individual and the irrational crowd.[7]

Another line of exploration of the specific mechanisms for the transmission of affect in groups focuses on human endocrinology, specifically on "pheromones," "airborne chemical signs that are released by an individual into the environment and which affect the physiology or behavior of other members of the same species" (Brennan 180n53).[8] Research so far has been mainly on other animals, and researchers stress the importance of acknowledging the ability of the individual to resist contagion in groups. But as Teresa Brennan puts it in a recent book entitled *The Transmission of Affect*,

> The nature of the internal resistance [to the idea of group contagion] can only be grasped in a context where the transmission of affect is acknowledged. Research on hormones supports the realization that the environment, especially the environment in the form of other people, changes human endocrinology, not the other way around. It also changes the affects accompanying the hormones. That otherwise good science holds back from this conclusion testifies to the power of the illusion of self-containment. (Brennan 73)[9]

After over two generations of antipathy to Le Bon, an increasing understanding of our own "primitive" or animal constitution is beginning to make some (although not the political) aspects of his theory less preposterous after all. In this regard, the way forward was pointed by the British psychoanalyst Wilfred Bion in his work on group experiences and dynamics in the 1940s–1950s. Using a Kleinian model, he challenged the view that the group is incapable of intellectual activity (which he analysed as "work group" activity) yet at the same time acknowledged the importance of involuntary intra-group emotions ("basic assumption" activity). For the latter Bion also used the term "valency" taken from physics to refer to the power of combination of atoms (Bion 175), thus avoiding the negative connotations associated with words like "suggestion" and "contagion."

Contemporary scientists from a variety of fields have followed suit in exploring a wide range of evidence for the transmission of intensity from one body to another in group activity.[10]

These theories need to be tested in relation to those from within the social psychology of crowd theory today. Stephen Reicher, whose work has been influential in challenging ahistorical and essentialising claims about crowd behaviour, is unwilling to entertain theories that undermine human agency in groups. Agreeing in his chapter in this volume that crowds are "indeed passionate affairs," Reicher is nonetheless wary of psychoanalytic or biological explanations of group affect, instead recommending an approach dependent upon what he calls "the triad of social identity, collective practice and social being." Georges Lefebvre wrote in his iconic post-war study of the French Revolution that it is perhaps only in the crowd that people become the subjects of history; far from losing agency in the crowd, the crowd is one of the few occasions when we gain (collective) agency. However, although Freud was wrong in many of his conclusions, Reicher argues here, social scientists are equally wrong to carp at his failings when his is "the only voice in town" on the subject of affective investment in crowds. Reicher's chapter calls for new questions to be asked about how we invest in groups, offering examples from observation of how human agency in groups is always played out against specific socio-historical determinants. Our task, he concludes, is to understand spontaneous sociality in terms other than the outmoded view of crowd action as de-socialised.

Like Reicher, Jina Politi attacks the Taine- Le Bonian view of crowds as unruly, lacking in judgment and manipulable by wily demagogues, a view which has served to shift the blame for violence onto the masses and legitimated repression. The violence that should be attended to, she argues, is institutional violence, the practices of repressive state apparatuses (or, we might add with Žižek [*Violence*19], of an unbridled market economy and ruthless financial speculation) rather than individual violence. Grappling with the complex nuances of Freud's mass psychology, Politi also shares Reicher's scepticism of Freud's view of crowds as vertically structured (through common identification with a leader) and draws attention to the way Freud's familial (Oedipal) model prevented him from addressing crucial questions to do with what came to be known as public space: the socio-economy, class and labour. Freud's characteristic bourgeois anxiety after the Russian Revolution mirrors that of Wordsworth, a century earlier, who came to prefer a "crowd of golden daffodils" to the rebellious crowds of the French Revolution. Unlike the social and political theorists of the crowd that proliferated from the late nineteenth century, she points out, literature (at least since Shakespeare's *Coriolanus)* has tended to represent the masses as the product of specific historical moments marked by social transformations.

In her chapter, for her part, Mandy Merck explores the way Freud's conceptualisations of leadership and the group grew out of the fraught rivalries over intellectual property and originality in the Vienna Psychoanalytic Society in the period immediately preceding the writing of his essay on group/mass psychology. A few months before, one of the group's members, Victor Tausk, had committed suicide—not long after he had presented his paper on schizophrenic delusions of intellectual influence. Amidst an atmosphere of paranoia which included accusations of plagiarism, Freud pondered in his essay "how much the individual thinker or writer owes to the stimulation of the group in which he lives." Freud, it seems, resented what he saw as Tausk's intrusions into his own intellectual projects and at the same time feared being influenced himself by the work of others. Reading "Group Psychology" in the light of Tausk's discussion of the "influencing machine," this chapter considers its effective acknowledgement of the impossibility of escaping intellectual influence. This is a question Merck finds relevant in today's academic environment, dependent as it is upon the individually-oriented star system favoured by the Research Evaluation Framework (formerly the Research Assessment Exercise) in the UK. In an age in which myths of originality have been subjected to systematic academic critique, she argues, it is ironic that the academic system which supports these theories is structured to promote the originality of the individual thinker rather than the productivity of group thought.

Several of the chapters in this book select a specific historical moment to test out taxonomies of the individual-mass relationship in the post-war period. In her chapter on "Globality, the Totalitarian Mass and National Belonging," Effie Yiannopoulou outlines the post-war fear of the totalitarian mass through an investigation of the fascist attempt to impose a uniformity that ignores the messy heterogeneity of any collective practice and along with it "the regenerative estrangement" foundational to any progressive politics. One response to these totalitarian "arrests" (arrested discursive and subjective mobility) was the formulation by Hannah Arendt of a politics of togetherness based on an "anti-communitarian" logic, one that is structured around the conflictual coexistence of heterogeneous viewpoints made possible through respect for the spaces of division within the collective and a retreat from the "common." This was the moment, in other words, when the problems inherent in a mass collectivity premised on the fixity of the bond and self-identical subjectivity became acutely apparent. (It is also worth remembering that in addition to pre-figuring Badiou's "unbinding," Arendt was also early in calling for a "participatory democracy" as the most productive outcome of the revolutionary movements of the first half of the twentieth century [Arendt, *Violence* 22]).[11] It was within this context of the re-assessment of modes of belonging that avoid the nation-state, Yiannopoulou argues, that we can read Rebecca West's anxious concern with treason as that which undermines national boundaries, as well as the emergence at the time of global Englishness.

Like Yiannopoulou, Josiane Paccaud-Huguet uses Giorgio Agamben's concept of *homo sacer* to explore the biopolitical dimension of the post-war mass under the surveillance of "expert" administration of *zoe* (bare life) in the name of democratic rights. Confronting "the 'nomos' of the camp," both essays suggest, has been a central challenge for radical politics in a post-Nazi as well as a post-colonial era. Paccaud-Huguet's chapter explores representations of the gay community under late capitalism in Will Self's novel *Dorian: An Imitation* (2002), which depicts the way new identificatory models, this time with a society of mass enjoyment, result in simply another version of the bureaucratic administration of bare (bodily) life. Re-formulating Freud's model of both vertical and horizontal modes of identification in a group via Lacan's distinction between the big and small other, Paccaud-Huguet explores contemporary culture's search for identification not with others but with an "alternative (Imaginary) me." Here, Imaginary relations (what Self calls "the looks thing") triumph over the Symbolic ties which regulate kinship and whose function is to provide a viable relation between the sexes or between generations; the dweller of the camp (in Self's novel, the luxury camps like gay California, etc.) is not a citizen but a human being deprived of a symbolic body. What has come loose, she concludes, is the fragile binding among the Imaginary body (the image), the Real body (the flesh) and the Symbolic body (the name, the social signification).

Cultural representations of group or crowd action are also explored by Sean Homer in his chapter on "The Masses as a 'Vanishing Mediator:' Class and Politics in Dušan Kovačević's *The Professional*." Homer is interested in the way contemporary Balkan cinema curiously *erases* evidence of crowd protests in the decade preceding the disintegration of the former Yugoslavia (in 1991), in spite of the historical fact that hundreds of thousands of students and workers across the republic were repeatedly out on the streets in support of strikes and peace movements. Using Fredric Jameson's concept of the "vanishing mediator," he demonstrates how representations of street protests in *The Professional* (2003) are always mediated through television screens or shown in sepia colours, as if a relic of a bygone age, and thus function as a traumatic point in the narrative, a point that cannot be integrated into its overall symbolic network. This observation resonates with other accounts in this volume of the way collective action has often been nervously conflated with hard-line communism in post-war (or post-communist) Europe. Homer also draws on Badiou's notion of the "particularity of the masses" and the impossibility of representing their "pure multiplicity." Rejecting Sartre's glorification of the identificatory transparency of the mass movement ("group-in-fusion") at moments of revolutionary transformation, Badiou (like Arendt) argues that it is the very *inconsistency* of the mass which constitutes its political status. The mass movement, Homer concludes, is the unrepresentable at the heart of historical presentation.

Le Bon's claim in 1895 that his was "the ERA OF CROWDS"[12] was countered a few years later by Gabriel Tarde that he regarded it instead as "the age of the public," defined as a "collectivity . . . of physically separated individuals whose cohesion is entirely mental" (qtd. in Laclau, *Populist* 44–45). New forms of human aggregation, made possible by the printing press—the so-called Fourth Estate—were to characterise the future. A century later, however, the emergence of the "Fifth Estate" (the internet and other digital information and communication technologies) has demonstrated that the collectivities of the future are decidedly *not* fated to be entirely mental. As global revolts from Seattle to the Arab Spring have shown, "publics" can now be quickly mobilised onto the streets from the isolation of individual homes and offices; social networks, in fact, are making it easier than ever to rally individuals to collective physical action. There is a wider context to this as well. As Michael Hardt and Antonio Negri (along with many others) have argued recently, network forms of information, communication and cooperation, the primary axes of post-Fordist "immaterial labour," are taking place on the biopolitical terrain, directly producing "new subjectivities and new forms of life" (Hardt and Negri 82–83).

Recent events have starkly illustrated two of the central arguments tested out in this volume. The first, of Ernesto Laclau, is that mass movements tend to aggregate around empty signifiers ("democracy," "freedom") whose content is filled from a range of different, often conflicting demands. In the cases of Tunisia, Egypt, Bahrain and Libya, the calls for the overthrow of long-term regimes have been hard to trace to a single source of discontent. The second is the thesis of Reicher and Politi, that mass uprisings or demonstrations involve forms of participation not necessarily dependent on leadership (though there is still a large body of work, particularly from psychoanalysis, which would contest this view).[13] Much of this perception may be traced to shifting definitions of the human which elide the singular-plural distinction in ways I have referred to above. As Deleuze and Guattari wrote over thirty years ago, "the statement [is] always collective even when it seems to be emitted by a solitary singularity like that of the artist" (*Kafka* 83)—or, we might add, of the leader. Thus like language, behaviour can never ultimately be located in individuals. Deleuze and Guattari link Kafka with a project of deterritorialisation in ways relevant to the spatial dislocations and contractions brought about by communications and media technologies in a global economy. As it emerges from the essays by Yiannopoulou, Gratale, Rehling and Briel, which all explore the complexities of territorial belonging and non-belonging in relation to changing modes of subjectivity, proprietary convictions are ultimately as problematic in relation to matters of space as they are for those of language and behaviour in a globally connected society.

In a famous television debate on CBC Network in 1968, Marshall McLuhan and Norman Mailer disagreed about the effects of the new mass-mediated environment on human interaction and the potentially "totalitarian" (Mailer's word) effects of information technology. Now, over forty years later (and after the work of Serge Moscovici and many others in the past couple of decades), several of the authors in this book re-assess this debate in terms of the media's function in global culture and the role of mediating mechanisms and institutions in shaping mass psychology. Nicola Rehling, for example, reads the Madeleine McCann case as an example of the use by the British popular press of a rhetoric of inclusion involving a collective "we" with a common affective and ethical base. This strategy, she states, depends on establishing clear national and class borders, allowing the press to construct and solidify a community of readers and fulfil its self-appointed role as purveyor of normative familial and gender values. Fundamental to this rhetoric are codes of "individualizing identification" (of readers with each other as well as with the McCann family), eliding the collective forces behind crimes like child-snatching (such as the opportunities for human trafficking provided by global capitalism and the market-driven EU "freedom of movement"). The construction of the imagined community of nation and the need to re-narrativise Britain can be read as part of a reaction to its erosion by global networks. While feverish online discussions and DIY media creations on the topic of Madeleine McCann might not exemplify Habermas's invigorated public sphere, an extended democratic space or empowered citizenship, Rehling concludes, such participation certainly refutes any notion of mass media audiences as passive consumers.

It is a frequently cited paradox that our globally-connected society has led to the increased isolation of each of us before our individual screens. Some argue that the internet has raised as many borders as it has destroyed, with nation-states and global institutions acting in new regulatory ways and so-called e-democracy inaugurating new forms of injustice. These dangers are assessed by Holger Briel in his chapter on blogging. There is no doubt, he contends, that the phenomenon is re-shaping writing and reading practices—in ways perhaps similar to the novel in the eighteenth century, which also made personal narratives more public than ever and contributed further to the spread of capitalism. Blogging's de-bordering effect on human subjectivity (today's "distributed identities") he views as part of the postmodern dissolution of extended, sited narrative, leading to an interactive culture based on links or threads of connection. In addition peer-to-peer file sharing has sparked off an important debate about intellectual property and property rights as a whole, forcing media owners to rethink their sales strategies and producing a culture change from hoarding to sharing, from ownership to "cloud participation." This virtual collectivity is thus doing away with the culture of collect*ing*; with the arrival of Web 2.0 and its philosophy of social networking, we have begun moving into a cloud of ever-changing, ever-present and mutually-owned content. While most blogs are perhaps not the harbingers of a culture many might wish for, Briel writes, their potential for effecting radical social change is indisputable, creating as they do something akin to a swarm intelligence,[14] where the overall entity of many individuals develops a mind of its own. For an animal group, he reminds us, such swarm behaviour may be a matter of life and death.

Increased global communication is having some odd effects, in many Western countries transforming politics towards internet groups with special interests, "instant communities, worlds gathered around products and production processes" (Thrift 23)—micro-trends, narrower affiliations rather than traditional groups of class, race or gender. (This latter phenomenon was closely researched by polling advisors in the last American elections in the attempt to understand the new dynamics of American social life.) The conflict between the opposing claims of the global and the local is explored here by Joseph Gratale in his chapter on "Geographies of Cultural Globalization and Cosmopolitanisms of the Future," where he returns to Zygmunt Bauman's question: "after the nation-state—what?" A post-national politics capable of confronting the simultaneity of the particular and the universal, Gratale contends, is necessary to break up the fixity and homogeneity of the national unit which has been responsible for so much violence in modern history. Warning against the celebratory tone of certain globalist discourses, Gratale nevertheless finds the model of identity as fluid and plural helpful as a way of thinking about our late modern interconnectedness. Using Arjun Appadurai's notion of "scapes" to describe disjunctive and non-isomorphic forms of global flow, he challenges the old (geographically bounded) concept of "society" as well as the model of global imperialism which suggests a uni-directional flow of culture (from a developed centre to a developing periphery). A "cosmopolitan consciousness," he concludes, will be better able to negotiate the diversity and otherness of the other. Gratale's essay calls yet again for the impossible necessity for planetary humanity to unbind the bonds which perpetually work to fix us into units of totalising sameness.

* * * *

Twenty years ago, an influential volume entitled *Who Comes After the Subject?* (1991) presented a series of debates pre-figuring many of those in this book. Against the long tradition of Western thought that postulated the solitary or monadic individual as the fundamental form of human authenticity, that volume followed a trajectory of radical thought from Marx, Nietzsche, Freud and Heidegger in raising questions as to "who" may be its successor. One voice from within seems to have been tuned to a slightly different tonality in questioning the "singularity" of the "who." Replying to Jean-Luc Nancy, Jacques Derrida said:

> The singularity of the "who" is not the individuality of a thing that would be identical to itself, it is not an atom. It is a singularity that dislocates or divides itself in gathering itself to answer to the other, whose call somehow precedes its own identification with itself. (Cadava, Connor and Nancy 100)

Derrida's demand (via Levinas) that we embrace the heterogeneity of the other, that we "put ourselves there where the disparate itself *holds together*" (Derrida, *Specters* 29), has been enormously influential in contemporary thought.[15] Constituted as it is by interpellation (the other's call), the subject can not be "liquidated," he replied to Jean-Luc Nancy, but can only ever be re-inscribed. The terms of this re-inscription have become particularly apparent in the two decades following this book, a period marked, as I have noted, by a plethora of converging voices. Within the last decade, in particular, the perception has gathered that the ethical and political challenges of our time demand an awareness of the inter-implication of singularity and plurality.[16] To re-think the human (which is also increasingly involving the need to re-think the "inhuman" in other than negative terms), the refrain of cultural particularities (cultures, nationalities, gender differences, etc.) is no longer adequate. Indeed, as Badiou and Žižek concur in a recent dialogue, postmodern multiculturalism is a "reactionary refrain" that needs to be challenged at every level (Badiou and Žižek 75).[17] Another way of putting this would be to say that in an age which has (mostly) rejected communism, there is an urgent need to return to the communitarian basis of its project beyond a climate of reactionary unease. In the vacuum left by the demise of communism, the call of the collective, our being-in-common, is more important than ever before.

The human subject has a history characterised by experiments in different forms of grouping, both private and public, small-scale and large. From the primal horde to the modern nuclear family, from the Athenian *polis* to virtual internet communities, such experiments have been provisional and historically contingent and will no doubt continue to be so. But our own age, with its post-industrial explosion of increasingly-virtual private spaces, demands the same radical re-theorisation of the individual-group relation as that deemed important by Godwin during the industrial revolution. The essays in this volume take up this challenge, each in its own singular (yet always plural) way.

NOTES

1. Godwin's faith in individualism led him to notoriously absurd extremes. For him most forms of human co-operation, even such daily activities as eating with others, are "pernicious" (*Enquiry* 758).
2. Mouffe's argument here, one followed closely by many contributors to this volume, is that what the left needs now in this climate of rampant capitalism and bureaucratised social life is a "postindividualistic concept of freedom" which would presuppose a true "*pluralism of subjects*" (308–9).
3. Lacan's views on the crowd, which underlie the chapters by Paccaud-Huguet, Homer and Laclau in this book, are discussed again at the beginning of the Epilogue.
4. This threat is orchestrated, Žižek continues, "in the best 'totalitarian' manner by the inner circle . . . In a proto-Hegelian way, the external threat the

community is fighting is its own inherent essence" (*Violence* 23). The lesson of all totalitarianisms, he writes further on, is that "the fight against the external enemy sooner or later always turns into an inner split and the fight against the inner enemy" (113). For a description, after Hobbes, of fear as the basic supposition of the social covenant, see Esposito 20–40.

5. For an assessment of Heidegger's influence on contemporary community theory, see Ruth Parkin-Gounelas, "Helping Yourself to Heidegger."
6. For an attempt to read debates among neuroscientists of affect within a cultural and psychoanalytic context, see Ruth Parkin-Gounelas, "From Burke to Neuroscience."
7. Serge Moscovici argued that this phenomenon (of individual rationality and mob irrationality)

   > is universally confirmed by public records. According to Solon, a single Athenian is a wily fox but a group of Athenians is a flock of sheep. Frederick the Great trusted each of his generals as individual [*sic*] yet he described them as fools when they were gathered together in a council of war. And we are indebted to the Romans for this most apt and universal of proverbs: . . . *senators are all good men, the Roman senate is a noxious beast.* (qtd. in Laclau, *Populist* 29)

8. Brennan is quoting from a 1998 article in *Nature* by Kathleen Stern and Martha McClintock.
9. See also Tristram D. Wyatt, *Pheromones and Animal Behaviour.*
10. Inter-disciplinary studies of consciousness have been focusing on yet another set of findings. In a recent book entitled *Braintrust: What Neuroscience tells us about Morality* (Princeton UP, 2011), philosopher Patricia S. Churchland draws on neuroscience to emphasise the role of the peptide oxytocin, as well as related neurochemicals, in solidifying the bond of empathy between mother and infant, and by extension between the individual and other members of the group.
11. Arendt writes:

    > The one positive political slogan the new movement [of the 1960s] has put forth, the claim for "participatory democracy" that has echoed around the globe and constitutes the most significant common denominator of the rebellions in the East and the West, derives from the best in the revolutionary tradition—the council system, the always defeated but only authentic outgrowth of every revolution since the eighteenth century. But no reference to this goal either in word or substance can be found in the teachings of Marx and Lenin, both of whom aimed on the contrary at a society in which the need for public action and participation in public affairs would have "withered away," together with the state. (*Violence* 22–23)

12. The full context of Le Bon's claim is: "While all our ancient beliefs are tottering and disappearing, while the old pillars of society are giving way one by one, the power of the crowd is the only force that nothing menaces, and of which the prestige is continually on the increase. The age we are about to enter [at the turn of the twentieth century] will in truth be the ERA OF CROWDS" (4).
13. Both Bion and Lacan follow Freud in insisting on the processes of identification in operation in all group behaviour, that sovereignty (analysed by Lacan in terms of both the "master signifier" and the analyst as "subject supposed to know" [invested with the power of knowledge]) is integral to all intersubjective and signifying practices. See also n3 here. A nuanced explanation of the role of the leader is offered by Ernesto Laclau in the interview in this book. This entails understanding what Freud described as identifications resulting

from only a small separation between ego and ego ideal, so that a leader may be selected as one of the brothers, as it were, rather than the totemic father of the primal horde. This model of identification, Laclau explains here, "makes possible a far more democratic vision of the role of the leader."

14. For the use of the term "swarm intelligence" in cognitive and computational processes, see Kennedy and Eberhart; also Hardt and Negri 57 and 91–93.
15. For a wonderful theorisation and history of the other or foreigner, from Homer to the present, see Kristeva, *Strangers*, especially Ch. 8: "Might Not Universality be . . . Our Own Foreignness?"
16. This awareness is played out in Jean-Luc Nancy's own work before and after the interview with Derrida in *Who Comes After the Subject?* See in particular his *The Inoperative Community* and *Being Singular Plural.*
17. For a fuller discussion of this phenomenon, see Vertovec.

Part I

Psychoanalysis and the Group

1 Brother Animal's Long Tail
Sigmund Freud, Victor Tausk and Intellectual Influence

Mandy Merck

AN OPEN QUESTION

Sigmund Freud's "Group Psychology and the Analysis of the Ego" is no testament to the wisdom of crowds. It begins by endorsing Gustave Le Bon's description of the credulous, emotional and exaggerated thinking of social groups and ends with a summary of the neurotic impulses argued to stimulate the formation of religious and philosophical communities. "Great decisions in the realm of thought and momentous discoveries," the essay proclaims, "are only possible to an individual working in solitude" (111). But, in a brief qualification of this argument, Freud goes on to concede society a few accomplishments—folklore, folk music and "language itself." Moreover, he allows, "it remains an open question . . . how much the individual thinker or writer owes to the stimulation of the group in which he lives, and whether he does more than perfect a mental work in which the others have had a simultaneous share" (111).

Freud had reason to pose this question. "Group Psychology" was begun in the winter of 1919–20, after one of the periodic crises that beset his movement. In July 1919, Victor Tausk, a psychiatrist and prominent member of the Vienna Psychoanalytic Society, committed suicide. Tausk was an extremely able intellectual, who had practised law and worked as a writer and journalist before a breakdown precipitated by the failure of a love affair prompted him to contact Freud. So impressed was Freud with the younger man that he not only encouraged him to study psychoanalysis but arranged and contributed to the financial support for his medical training as well.

By 1909 Tausk was appointed an Associate of the Vienna Society, frequently offering papers and later giving public lectures on psychoanalysis—the only member besides Freud to do so in Vienna. In 1912 he became an intimate friend, or possibly even a lover, of Lou Andreas-Salomé, who had arrived in the city to pursue her own study of psychoanalysis. Salomé's journal of the period discusses Tausk at length, declaring him of all Freud's followers "the most unconditionally devoted to Freud and at the same time the most prominently outstanding" (57). But the two men were often at odds, and Salomé observes that

> any independence around Freud, especially when it is marked by aggression and display of temperament, worries him and wounds him quite automatically in his noble egotism as investigator, forcing him to premature discussion . . . he longs in his heart for the peace of undisturbed research which he enjoyed . . . until the founding of his school. (Andreas-Salomé 97–98)

That Freud's early research was conducted in peaceful solitude is certainly disputable, and the later conflicts within his school have become notorious. He anxiously sought to control the development of psychoanalysis, and he greatly valued his own eminence as its founder. In this he was often supported by his followers, who backed their man against his rivals in order to win Freud's favour as well as to ensure that their faction prevailed. Tausk himself was deployed to see off the formidable Jung at the Munich Congress of 1913. "Clever and dangerous," Freud remarked of Tausk at the time; "he can bark and bite" (Andreas-Salomé 169). But if Freud sought the support of his disciples against the apostasy of rivals like Jung, he resented their intrusion into his own theoretical projects, particularly their development of his unpublished observations. In a milieu in which new hypotheses were constantly circulating in discussion, not least in the confidences of the consulting room, there were frequent contests over authorship and attribution. Freud's devoted friendship with Wilhelm Fliess concluded with an angry exchange of this kind. During an analytic session with the young psychologist Hermann Swaboda, Freud mentioned Fliess's unpublished theory of cellular bisexuality (arguing that in our derivation from male and female zygotes, human beings are physically bisexual). Swaboda then repeated it to his friend Otto Weininger, who promptly developed the notion into a book-length study. When Fliess protested this "misuse of someone else's property" (Masson 463), Freud defensively replied that Krafft-Ebing and his predecessors had also investigated bisexuality, and that he was endeavoring for Fliess's sake to avoid the topic "as far as possible" (Masson 464) in his forthcoming "Three Essays on the Theory of Sexuality." But after a few days' reflection Freud wrote to Fliess admitting that his disclosure of his theory revealed his own desire to "rob you of your originality" (Masson 466) and he offered him the proofs of the "Three Essays" to alter if necessary. His final letter in their correspondence recommended withholding ideas prior to their publication, but it was not a rule Freud always observed himself.

After Freud had confided the fundamentals of the unwritten *Totem and Taboo* to Salomé, he was particularly unnerved to hear Tausk (who was already complaining that Freud appropriated *his* ideas) lecturing on "The Father Problem" a few weeks later. During the talk Freud anxiously passed her a note asking if Tausk "knew all about it already?" (Andreas-Salomé 114). Salomé assured Freud that she had not disclosed his theories, and Tausk's lecture actually focused on primitive matriarchy rather than parricide; but she soon concluded that he did have a serious father problem. In a sad farewell to their relationship, an entry in her journal of August 1913 laments "the whole tragedy of Tausk's relation with Freud":

> he will always tackle the same problems, the same attempts at solution, that Freud is engaged in. This is no accident, but signifies his "making himself a son" as violently as he "hates the father for it." As if by thought transference he will always be busy with the same thing as Freud, never taking a step aside to make room for himself. (166–67)

Tausk spent the war years as an army psychiatrist, publishing in 1916 papers on soldiers' psychoses and the psychology of the deserter. Afterwards he returned to Vienna, and, although still no closer to Freud, he again received some assistance from him in patient referrals and teaching appointments. At the January 6, 1918, meeting of the Vienna Psychoanalytic Society, the ill-fated analyst read the paper that would become his best-known contribution to psychoanalytic literature. Its subject was intellectual influence.

"On the Origin of the 'Influencing Machine' in Schizophrenia" concerns a conviction widespread among psychotics that their mental activity is under the control of a distant apparatus operated by an enemy. Tausk did not purport to discover this symptom, which entered psychiatric history with the case of James Tilly Matthews, an English tea merchant and self-appointed peace emissary to France during the Napoleonic Wars. After shouting "Treason" from the visitors' gallery during a debate in the House of Commons, Matthews was sent to London's "Bedlam," Bethlem Royal Hospital. There he invoked, as sufferers typically do, the new technology of his time to claim that he was being controlled by a device he called the "air loom," by whose "pneumatic chemistry" a gang of spies was siphoning magnetic fluid into his skull. Reviewing the general features of such claims, Tausk writes that patients characteristically describe a machine that transmits and removes "thoughts and feelings by means of waves or rays or mysterious forces"—a "suggestion-apparatus" (Tausk 187). When the machine made his early twentieth-century patients see images, he notes that it was typically compared to "a magic lantern or cinematograph" (187) in its production of two-dimensional images on a picture plane, an observation—from one of the few early psychoanalysts engaged by moving pictures—that has survived in the theorisation both of paranoia and of the cinema.[1] (Contemporary delusions of this type include being influenced by a chip planted in one's brain, being a character in a computer game and—as a repeated theme—control via the internet.)[2]

Tausk also notes that the influencing machine is often said to produce physical reactions, notably "erections and seminal emissions, that are intended to deprive the patient of his male potency" (187). The operator of the machine is similarly characterized as male, exclusively so in Tausk's view, "predominantly physicians by whom the patient has been treated" (187). But it is Tausk's discussion of two women patients that distinguishes his psychoanalytic contribution to the literature on this condition. His first example is a patient cited earlier by Freud, "Emma A," who believed that her eyes were being twisted out of position by the influence of a deceitful lover, who had "made her as evil as himself" (190). Here Tausk echoes Freud's argument that Emma unconsciously identified with her persecutor, projecting her sense of inner change outward onto an external cause. Such an identification is wonderfully demonstrated in Tausk's second case study, that of his own patient Natalija A, a former philosophy student who maintained that she was under the influence of an electrical machine operated by her rejected suitor, a college professor.

Natalija A's influencing machine was unusually anthropomorphic: she detailed its resemblance to a woman's body, with a coffin-shaped trunk containing batteries and lined with silk or velvet. The limbs were drawn on the lid, but she could not see the head. A blow to this mechanical double was felt in the corresponding place in her own body. At first manipulation of the machine's genitalia caused Natalija to experience arousal, but when the machine lost its genitalia, she lost all sexual sensation. She attributed this persecution to the professor's jealousy. He had, she claimed, first tried to charm her relatives by suggestion, but when that failed he employed the machine to control all those close to her, including her physicians, who consequently misdiagnosed her ailments. "On her third visit," Tausk writes, "she became inaccessible and only stated that the analyst, too, was under the influence of the apparatus, that he had become hostile to her, and that they could no longer understand each other" (195).

Natalija's vivid description of the influencing machine as an unacknowledged projection of her own body led Tausk back to infancy, when an absence of ego boundaries encourages the child to believe that others know its thoughts. Here, among several citations of Freud, he notes his observation during the initial discussion of this paper that this belief

> has its source in the process of learning to speak. Having obtained its language from others, the infant has also received thoughts from them; and the child's feeling that others know his thoughts as well as that others have "made" him the language and, along with it, his thoughts, has therefore some basis in reality. (215n5)

Natalija's sexual characterisation of the machine (the trunk pregnant with its batteries, the soft skin of its lining, the absence of a ruling head, the arousal which it seems to turn on and off uncontrollably) linked it to the pre-genital stage in which "the entire body is a libidinal zone" seeking a return to the womb. "Such fantasies," Tausk observes, are also evident in the wishes of the extremely infantile neurotic who desires "to creep completely into the genital from which he came, refusing to content himself with any lesser satisfaction" (212).

The intimations of the *unheimliche* with which Tausk concludes his paper were not the only ones in this affair. His ability to channel Freud's ideas, "as if by thought transference," would be declared uncanny by Freud in the months to come (Roazen 170). Even more uncannily, the lure of the mother's womb, the sinister professor, the mechanical woman, displaced eyes, the power of thought and the phenomenon of doubling would all find their way into Freud's own study of strange coincidences published almost two years after Tausk's lecture.[3] And to this list of coincidences I will add one more, that of another conflict between Freud and a different disciple eight years earlier, in the summer of 1910, when he abruptly withdrew from a planned collaboration with Sandor Ferenczi. Here again, the question of influence arose, this time because Ferenczi refused to let Freud literally dictate to him their supposedly co-authored text, but also because the study in question was of Daniel Paul Schreber, the German jurist whose own father complex manifested itself in paranoid delusions of divine dictation. In her entertaining account of this episode, Pamela Thurschwell notes that in his commentary on Schreber's autobiography, Freud anxiously asserts that he had already "developed my theory of paranoia before I became acquainted with the contents of Schreber's book," as though he might be accused of plagiarising the author (Thurschwell 161; Freud, "Psycho-Analytic Notes" 79). Influence seems to seep everywhere in this affair, since key elements of the Schreber case—notably Freud's argument that the divine rays that plagued Schreber were actually "projections outward of libidinal cathexes" ("Psycho-Analytic Notes" 78)—also feature in Tausk's interpretation of the influencing machine.

That paper was the last Tausk would read to the Vienna Society. At a time when training analyses were becoming the norm, and apparently troubled by his failure to sustain relationships with women, he asked Freud for analysis. Freud declined, later explaining to a pupil that, if he analyzed Tausk, "he would never be able to publish another line without Tausk's thinking Freud had stolen it" (Roazen 78). In his stead, he nominated Helene Deutsch, another psychiatrist who was embarrassingly junior to Tausk in years and analytical experience. Deutsch was being analyzed by Freud, and the triangular transference that ensued, in which Tausk's incessant remarks about Freud were passed on by Deutsch in her analysis, lasted three months—until Freud insisted that she choose between them. Deutsch terminated her analysis with Tausk at the end of March. In July, after an allegedly impotent tryst with his fiancée (a former patient whom—according to Kurt Eissler [*Victor* 91]—he had seduced, gotten pregnant and very reluctantly consented to marry), Tausk committed suicide. On the night in question he went home, wrote out his bequests and farewells (including a letter to Freud professing his admiration and lack of resentment), tied a noose around his neck and shot himself.

This "overkill," as it has been unsurprisingly described, was potentially scandalous for a movement that purported to cure psychological distress. To avert criticism, Freud published with Tausk's paper on the influencing machine a highly complimentary obituary, attributing his suicide to the rigours of the war. But in a letter to Salomé he confided: "I do not really miss him; I had long taken him to be useless, indeed a threat to the future." The personal nature of this threat was spelled out in Freud's valedictory phrase: "he fought out his day of life with the father-ghost" (Roazen 140). In her reply Salomé readily concurred with Freud's description of Tausk as a threat "to you as also to the cause" of psychoanalysis, despite, as she carefully added, his advocacy of it "with such enthusiasm and sincerity" (Roazen 144). At the end of their relationship she had remarked in her diary on the "irreconcilable contradictions" between Tausk's "maternal" sensitivity and the aggression that led Freud to call him a "beast of prey," describing his travails as "the struggle of the human creature. Brother-animal. You" (Andreas-Salomé 167–68).

In 1969 Paul Roazen took Salomé's tender epithet (or not so tender, if we recall the bark and the bite) as the title for a biography of Tausk that was highly critical of Freud. The ensuing reaction yielded Francois Roustang's excellent study *Dire Mastery*, on the difficulties that the phenomenon of the transference presents to professional psychoanalytic institutions. It also spawned (the word is deliberate) the analyst Kurt Eissler's obdurately non-psychoanalytic commentary on the affair, *Talent and Genius*. As secretary of the Sigmund Freud Archives and his ardent apologist, Eissler wrote 400 pages asserting the derivative character of Tausk's research and the originality of Freud's: Tausk may have coined the term "ego boundary," but Freud had identified structural changes in the ego five years earlier. Tausk's theory of the influencing machine as a projection of the patient's body was indebted to Freud's interpretation of the imagined camera in "A Case of Paranoia Running Counter to the Theory of the Disease" (1915). If Tausk was first to use the term "identity" in psychoanalysis, it was not in the correct sense. Tausk may have published his essay on melancholia before Freud's, but Freud had been discussing the idea for at least as long. And so on.

Genius, argues Eissler, in a not very original invocation of Thomas Kuhn, discovers paradigms. Talent merely recombines and modifies them. Tausk may have penned the occasional eloquent phrase but this is "as far as talent can go" (Eissler, *Talent* 274). Confessing his desire "to glorify the genius," Eissler does not hesitate to pursue the broader political implications of his argument. It may be contrary to "the American democratic tradition," he avers, but "the development of culture and civilization depends on more than the huge numbers of people who keep society going . . . Mankind would still be living in caves . . . had there not been the few who were able to 'unthink' the world as it was" (250–51). Nor does he refrain from an explicitly male characterisation of these few. Quoting Freud's own address on receiving the Goethe prize, he endorses his observation that "the individual's attitude toward genius depends on his attitude towards his parents, and particularly toward the father." In an unapologetic gendering of genius, the filial Eissler seizes on Freud's own imagery of fertilisation when discussing creativity to elaborate its paternal function, claiming that the mental activity of such individuals is "so intensely charged with energy that it becomes equivalent to physical genital discharge . . . an almost uninterrupted stream of creations of the highest quality" (Eissler, *Talent* 263; Freud, "Address" 212). To Eissler, Freud's work is truly seminal.

The homoerotic implications of all this are too obvious to miss. Working forward chronologically, we could start with Freud's romantic relation to Fliess, the theorist of cellular bisexuality, whose ending Freud described (to Ferenczi, shortly after he aborted *their* attempt at collaboration) as an "overcoming" of homosexual "need . . . I have succeeded where the paranoiac fails" (Santner, *Own Private* 19). The paranoiac alluded to is Schreber, whose spectacular delusions of sexual abuse and emasculation by no less than the Creator were traced by Freud to his repressed homosexual desire for his father in a logic of negation recapitulated as "I do not *love* him—I *hate* him, because HE PERSECUTES ME" (Freud, "Psycho-Analytic Notes" 101). As Eric Santner has wonderfully elucidated, Freud's fascination with this case reflects his preoccupation with both intellectual influence and "same-sex passion" (Santner, *Own Private* 21). From it we move on to Tausk's account of the influencing machine as a classically paranoid projection of the patient's own ambivalent object love, and the notable way that the analyst encloses his two case studies of women with discussions of the machine's power "to deprive the patient of his male potency" and the male neurotic's identification of himself as a giant genital, specifically "the penis of the father" (212). A year after Tausk reads this paper, Freud begins to write "Group Psychology," in which he will famously compare the group's affection for its leader with being in love, in love with the primal father. Finally, when Paul Roazen dares to disturb the father's shrine, Kurt Eissler replies with his "glorification" of genius, comparing its fruits to "physical genital discharge" (Eissler, *Talent* 263) in an eerie echo of Tausk's description of the influencing machine's stimulation of "erections and seminal emissions . . . intended to deprive the patient of his male potency" (Tausk 187).

If this were an exercise in queer theory, I might posit the existence of "paradigm paranoia," a symptom of homophobic male intellectual societies in which repressed same-sex longings are inverted into accusations of plagiarism as castration. But much as Freud, and the history of psychoanalysis in general, is implicated in this symptomology, there is also the countervailing impetus, the one that leads him to admit his desire to steal his colleagues' ideas and to interrupt "Group Psychology" to wonder "how much the individual thinker or writer owes to the stimulation of the group in which he lives" (Freud, "Group" 111). Posed so soon after Tausk's final paper and his death, the question acknowledges less the influence of any particular idea than the idea of influence itself, influence that Freud had to acknowledge if he was to assert the psychological unity of the group.

THE AUDIT CULTURE

Forty years have elapsed since *Brother Animal* versus *Talent and Genius*. After subsequent exposés by the likes of Jeffrey Masson, Mikkel Borch-Jacobsen and Frederick Crews, we may have become indifferent to the succession of scandals and recuperations in matters Freudian, but do we still operate within the evaluative purview endorsed by Eissler? The word "genius" is long out of fashion, and "talent" has given way to "cultural capital," but in their place new terms and practices of intellectual distinction arise. Surveying one such, the academic "star system" in the humanities, the literary scholar Jeffrey Williams argues that it represents a positive change in intellectual authority, one preferable to the dire mastery of the patrilineal senior professor of old. Where he (inevitably he) held sway over his inherited domain of junior faculty and graduate students, today's stars rise without such patronage, to be judged instead by advancing, or better yet, creating a field. (Queer theory and postcolonial studies are the two examples offered.) Such scholars are mostly employed in the US research universities which, since the 1960s, have expanded to establish a much larger market for intellectual prestige. This is acquired by one's standing in research, the index of which is name recognition, most gloriously that name's adjectification. For "Freudian" read Williams' examples, "Butlerian, Derridean, Bhabhaesque" (J. Williams 385). These much cited figures are argued to have no scholarly fathers, nor indeed any progenitors. "Whose student was Andrew Ross? Judith Butler? Cornel West?" Jeffrey Williams asks (378). Dismissing Butler's complaint that this culture "draws attention away from my work and puts it on my person" (MacFarquhar 6–7), Williams pronounces celebrity and citation inevitable academic practices, celebrity bolstering university ranking and advertising value, citation functioning as a basic tool of intellectual attribution and classification as well as one of the few rewards in a lamentably low-paid profession. The influence of such practices on academic employment and promotion is too assumed to merit more than brief acknowledgement, while the possibility of a negative effect on research is not even considered.

Here I should explain the perspective from which I survey this issue. Since 1986, university departments in the United Kingdom have been subject to regular national audits of their research. Under the 1986, 1992, 1996, 2001 and 2008 versions of this procedure, the Research Assessment Exercise (RAE), individual academics were asked to submit four works of research—books, articles or, in the case of creative practitioners, annotated works such as films or musical compositions—published since the previous exercise for evaluation by appointed panels of subject experts. Their ratings—of university departments as aggregates of their members' ratings—have had a major influence on the amount of government funding directed to them. To the dismay of the UK academic union, a football-style transfer market has arisen in which prolific publishers are lured from their departments with offers of increasingly higher salaries and fewer teaching and administrative duties, while less prolific ones are refused permission to be submitted for evaluation at all, with a consequent reduction of their chances for promotion or research funding in the future. And there are further concerns: the rigidity of the RAE dating system creates vast queues for British book and journal publishers in the final years of the audit period. Projects likely to take a long or unpredictable time to complete are more hazardous than ever. As the anthropologist Marilyn Strathern has complained, "In research, time must be set aside for all the wasteful and dead-end activities that precede the genuine findings. Both require otherwise non-productive periods. Yet there is almost no language in the audit culture to talk about productive non-productivity" (318). In addition to worries over a project's duration, attempts to anticipate the subject panelists' criteria affect the choice of what publications to submit and therefore what research to conduct. Thus a philosopher at Liverpool University declared to a *Guardian* journalist in 2005 that feminist topics seemed far too risky for the Philosophy panel and she planned to submit work on metaphysics instead (MacLeod 3).

But if the RAE has been controversial, it has also proved contradictory, since it was conceived as a Thatcherite initiative to drive both productivity and selectivity in academic research in order to limit public expenditure and increase the universities' contribution to the economy. In regard to the first objective, a 2006 editorial in the *British Medical Journal* enthused:

> Overall, UK research tops the world league for papers per dollar expended and citations per dollar expended, and it is fourth ranked for papers per researcher . . . delivering 9% of the world's research effort for 4.5% of the world's research expenditure. (Hobbs and Stewart 983)

Conversely the Scottish cultural theorist Andrew Ross, to cite one of Jeffrey Williams' notables, complained in 2007 that the RAE's "rigid quotas . . . mean that most British academics spend their time churning out superfluous publications with no end in sight" (Schueller and Dawson 117). As for selectivity, the same *BMJ* article observed that "the proportion of total funding to the top tenth of researchers in the UK increased from 47% in 1980–1 to 57% in 1997–8" (Hobbs and Stewart 983). But this tendency may undermine research productivity, as educationalist Paul Hare warned in 2003:

> the RAE system has resulted in an increasing concentration of public research funding, with barely 20 institutions receiving the lion's share of the funding, the weakest receiving very little. This concentration effect has been exacerbated by ever more stringent constraints on the total research money available to the Funding Councils to allocate to institutions. Yet there is at best very limited evidence that bigger research units are more productive (despite popular—and official—opinion to the contrary). (58)

Faced with the contradiction between a state-mandated proliferation of research and equally mandatory limits on expenditure, the Higher Education Funding Council for England (HEFCE) raised the bar for the 2008 audit. The previous rating scale had ranged from a rare starred 5 for departments whose aggregate submissions were deemed more than 50% "internationally excellent" down through several levels. (3b represented more than 50% departmental submissions of "national excellence".) From 2008 each submitted publication was individually rated on a tighter four-point scale on which research of "international excellence" counted only 3, and a new designation—"world-leading"—topped the bill. When the expert panels nevertheless rewarded the highly disciplined researchers with many 3s and 4s (17% of the work submitted was judged "world-leading") and distributed these widely between institutions, previously high-funded universities complained of grade inflation. Proponents of the RAE claimed that these ratings demonstrated its stimulation of excellent research, but this militated against selectivity. HEFCE responded by setting aside an extra £20 million to cover shortfalls at leading institutions and ring-fencing the previous proportion of funds flowing to science, technology, engineering and mathematics. The total allocation for the humanities was commensurately adjusted downwards. In other words, the assessment was selectively ignored.

And there was a further problem: evaluating four publications of several thousand UK academics—monographs tend to score more points in the humanities, while the sciences prefer articles in leading journals—is an extremely expensive operation.

So a new system of evaluation was piloted for the next exercise, one which would replace the difficult and disputable processes of peer evaluation with quantifiable measures, notably the number of citations an individual publication generates. This was already an established mode of evaluation in the sciences, but again it was not without controversy. Surveying statistical graphs in which a minority of much-noted publications rapidly subsides to a "long tail" of rarely cited ones, the proponents of bibliometrics argued that amputation was the most efficient way of directing resources to cited researchers. But the problems with this method were already obvious: research is cited for different reasons, as evidence of reading, point of departure, object of attack, blatant self-advertisement. Scientists publish shorter articles in greater numbers than scholars in other fields, whose work is consequently cited less. And even in the sciences the claims for bibliometrics are challenged by a notorious example of citation failure, in which a 1967 paper on elementary particle physics failed to receive any citations until its first single one in 1970 and three more in 1971. In 1972 it received 65 citations and in the following year it received 165. In 1979 its author, Steven Weinberg, received the Nobel Prize in Physics and his 1967 paper eventually became the most cited in the discipline. In another notable example, a prominent geneticist undertook two collaborations with a less known biochemist. In one of them his name was listed first, in the other his collaborator's was listed first, but both were genuinely shared efforts. The article listing the more prominent name first received 50 % more citations.

Interestingly, the latter case has been widely circulated, not by a scientist or an educational theorist, but by the business columnist of the *New Yorker* in a work of popular economics (here illustrating another factor in citation generation). In stated opposition to the nineteenth-century sociology on which Freud drew, James Surowiecki argues for the productivity of group thinking. His most powerful example is the discovery of the SARS virus, an effort orchestrated by the World Health Organization in eleven research laboratories around the world. Responding to the emergency that began with the death of 305 Chinese from an unidentified respiratory disease in February 2003, the laboratories cooperated by trading virus samples, daily teleconferencing and web posting interim results. By April 16 of that year they had conclusively identified the virus. As Surowiecki stresses, there was no principal investigator in this project. Each partner group had "the freedom to focus on what it believed to be the most promising lines of investigation, and to play to its particular analytical strengths, while also allowing the labs to reap the benefits—in real time—of each other's data and analyses" (160–61). Surowiecki's *The Wisdom of Crowds* is one of several contemporary arguments for a new understanding of group dynamics and their economic consequences in modern information societies. In his study of internet sales in *The Long Tail*, Chris Anderson points out that the old economic wisdom that 20% of the products account for 80% of sales has been abandoned in the digital marketplace. Analysis of the demand curve of entertainment media downloads demonstrates the financial benefits of selling not only hit records and bestselling books but also the vast number of less popular products, the "niche" items, that "when aggregated, make up a significant market" (Anderson 10).

It may seem strange that an audit of academic research aimed at making it more economically productive would proceed against the logic of both knowledge accumulation and commercial success in the new information economy, but the Higher Education Funding Council of England remains a striking exception to the evidence for group intelligence. Thus it took HEFCE two years of reviewing research results from 22 universities, one interim report, two subsequent reports on data collection and outcomes, one final report and a consultation to conclude that "citation information is not sufficiently robust to be used formulaically or as a primary indication of quality" (HEFCE 1). Among their discoveries were the variations in citation between disciplines, the distorting effect of negative citations, the lack of citations for recent publications, and the difficulty presented by scholars with the same name. For the next research audit, now titled the Research Evaluation Framework (REF) and scheduled for 2014, peer evaluation of submitted scholarship will remain the major means of assessment, counting 65%. The economic, social or cultural benefit of particular research projects follows at 20%, with the "research environment" of the submitting department coming last, at 15%.

During HEFCE's most recent deliberations, the drive to selectivity took on a radical new impetus, as the Conservative-led government withdrew almost all public funding from university teaching, to be replaced by fees of up to £9,000 per year, made available as loans to a limited number of aspiring students. Several departments, and possibly entire universities, face closure. With less publicity, much research funding has also been withdrawn, even in the supposedly protected fields of science, technology, engineering and mathematics. In 2010, the government cut infrastructure budgets in the national research councils by half. By 2011 British scientists were directed to apply to private sources for 50% of the costs of routine equipment ranging from test tubes to computers. Researchers were urged to share expensive facilities such as PET scanners, while the Science and Technology Facilities Council stopped funding telescopes in the northern hemisphere. "The inevitable outcome," claims David Phillips, president of the Royal Society of Chemistry, will be "fewer research departments in the UK" (Sample).

HEROIC MYTHS

Reflecting on the contest over intellectual "priority and originality" between Tausk and Freud, Francois Roustang comments on what has long been known in literary criticism as "the anxiety of influence."[4] "The question: who invented this idea—me or someone else? cannot be dissociated from the questions: have I heard it elsewhere and, without realizing it, have I reproduced or repeated it? Have I been influenced? Do others transmit their ideas to me?" (92) In Roustang's interpretation the fear of being plagiarised masks the fear of its opposite, being influenced by another. (Again, Freud's thought illustrates this inversion, with his dismissal of the superstitious belief in thought projection in "The 'Uncanny'," contradicting his lifelong fascination with telepathy.) "Group Psychology" sets out to explain mental influence, complaining that the conventional term for it—"suggestion"—"will soon come to designate any sort of influence whatever" while being itself "exempt from explanation" (Freud, "Group" 118). To illustrate this lack of grounding Freud cites the theological conundrum of Saint Christopher, who in legend carried the infant Christ to safety across the flood: "Christopher bore Christ; Christ bore the whole world; Say, where did Christopher then put his foot?" (118n2).

The solution "Group Psychology" proposes to the origin of influence is the libido, specifically the erotic impulses that are converted into the function of the ego, identification, and the ego ideal, idealisation. Thus, the boy grows up to salute his general and identify with his fellow soldiers or "loves Christ as his ideal and feels himself united with all other Christians" (167). But, as Freud briefly acknowledges, identification and idealisation are not always separate processes—surely one reason why rivalry so frequently threatened hierarchy in his own relations with the other pioneers of psychoanalysis. Far from stabilising social ties, libidinal currents often run in conflict. One of the most telling passages in his essay argues that the ego may rebel against the strictures of the ego ideal and the guilt that it imposes. Conversely, it may identify with it in a manic "mood of triumph and self-satisfaction, disturbed by no self-criticism" (165). Socially, the tension between the ego and the ego ideal is discerned in the periodic transgressions of the carnival. Psychologically, it is said to power the mania that oscillates into the depressive misery of melancholia, "in which the ego ideal, in an excess of sensitiveness, relentlessly exhibits its condemnation of the ego in delusions of inferiority and in self-depreciation" (165). The explicit allusion is to Freud's 1917 "Mourning and Melancholia," but it is made in the aftermath of Tausk's fatal descent from competitive identification to suicidal abjection.

Any attempt to ground these libidinal ties in prehistory is bound to be as circular as the cosmology of the Christ bearer, since the patriarchal creator, the father of the primal horde, is merely an invention, "the lie of the heroic myth" (170). But if the creator himself is a creation, how can Freud resolve the question of creativity? In place of God, the postscript to "Group Psychology" offers us a secular creator, the first epic poet. Driven by his longing for a primal father, he invents two of them, the totemic father-monster and the hero who slays him and becomes the first ego ideal. In Freud's description, the poet who creates the myth of the heroic individual who emerges from the group *is* the heroic individual who emerges from the group. In effect, he creates himself:

> The poet who had taken this step, and had in this way set himself free from the group in his imagination, is nevertheless able . . . to find his way back to it in reality. For he goes and relates to the group his hero's deeds which he has invented. At bottom this hero is no one but himself. (170)

But again, Freud's attempt to heroicise the creative intellectual is confounded by the influence of the group. Not only must the epic poet return to it to relate his hero's deeds (storytelling requires an audience) but, as a footnote reveals, the deeds in question are not his sole invention, but that of "legends, myths, fairy tales" (170n2), the folklore that Freud had previously acknowledged as one of the few contributions of the group to "creative genius in the field of intelligence" (111). However much he criticises the group mind in this essay, Freud's own logic demonstrates the impossibility of the author without influence, isolated from "the stimulation of the group in which he lives" (111), not to mention its lore and language.

To say this, of course, is to say nothing original, particularly in an era in which myths of origins are subject to constant deconstruction—except, perhaps, when it comes to the deconstructionists' own scholarship. One of the many ironies of Jeffrey Williams' defense of the university star system is his argument for the self-origination of intellectuals whose claims to fame are the critique of identity, autonomy and origins. (Who were Judith Butler's mentors? Among several, she acknowledges[5] philosopher of science Evelyn Fox Keller, literary theorist Naomi Schor, historians Nancy Cott and Joan Wallach Scott, as well as the journal *differences*.) "People do not create alone," insists the Australian psychologist Judith Brett;

> they are members of groups or circles, they write for particular magazines, they paint for particular patrons or galleries, they share their boldest thoughts with one chosen other. Even when they may seem to be alone and solitary they will be working within particular traditions which involve dialogues with historical figures or long dead mentors and teachers. Here the expectation of being understood, or at least listened to attentively and sympathetically, is crucial. Many people only discover what they think when they are trying to explain themselves to a sympathetic other. We all know this. Yet to privilege competition as the spur to intellectual work is to assume that the main point of communication is to win the argument. (20)

Brett's very apt conclusion to these remarks was first published in 1997, in response to a decade of Australian higher education policy based on the belief that "increased competitive pressure will enhance the efficiency and productivity of the sector in various ways" (19). It is included here to remind readers of the ubiquity of higher education "reform," as well as the impossibility of anyone having the last word on this subject. I found her observations on the internet, which has served as an important resource for this inquiry and a salient indication that in a world full of people working through the same thorny questions, the injunction to be "world-leading" may be faintly absurd. For some mental workers (and not just the schizophrenics among us), that realisation might be experienced as a form of persecution. Conversely, it might yet encourage what has wrongly been dismissed as a doomed resistance to institutionalised competitiveness in the academy. The love-hate relations of our celebrity culture (one of the most paranoid structures of group psychology) might even give way to something less delusional. If the search engine really has become our suggestion-apparatus, our influencing machine, let it function to remind us that in mental work the hero is no one but ourselves.

NOTES

1. See Copjec, "Anxiety"; also Sobcheck.
2. See V. Bell et al.
3. Although the footnote quoted from *Totem and Taboo* (1912–13) suggests that the uncanny was being considered by Freud at that time, a letter to Ferenczi of May 12, 1919, indicates that he began revising an old paper on the subject that Spring. "The 'Uncanny'" was published in Autumn, 1919. (See the Introduction to Freud, "'Uncanny'" 336.)
4. Harold Bloom's eponymous study of 1973 examined Romantic poetry to argue that all literary texts are influenced by those that precede them.
5. In correspondence with the author, May 2011.

2 Mass Enjoyment and the Society of the Camp

The Revised Case of Dorian Gray

Josiane Paccaud-Huguet

In 2002 the British novelist Will Self published *Dorian: An Imitation,* which transposes Oscar Wilde's *The Picture of Dorian Gray* (1890) into a culture of shifting social bonds and vacillating identity models in the late twentieth century. Wilde's late-Victorian novel is a story of magic inversion based on a pact whereby the lovely portrait painted by Basil Hallward and locked in an attic for private contemplation will absorb the marks of physical and moral decay while Dorian's public features remain pristine, in *likeness* to his own image. It is therefore a drama of identifications for a Narcissus who likes his own likeness too much.

The incipit of *Dorian: An Imitation* underlines the similarities between the 1880s and the 1980s: "a Government at once regressive and progressive, a monarchy mired in its own immemorial succession crisis, an economic recession both sharp and bitter" (Self 3). Self's novel, however, outlines important differences: the collapse of the distinction public/private, the demise of old social codes and related ideals and, in the realm of art, the triumph of the commodity over the beautiful and the sublime—a situation which reflects the change of regime described by Walter Benjamin in his famous essay "The Work of Art in the Age of Mechanical Reproduction."[1] The emblem for these similarities and differences is the transformation of Basil's picture into a video installation significantly entitled *Cathode Narcissus*: no longer a beautiful semblance, but a virtual object accessible on a website by anyone from anywhere.

This essay will read the case of the late modern Dorian Gray in the light of the Lacanian analysis developed by Slavoj Žižek in *Welcome to the Desert of the Real!* (2002), a book focusing on the twentieth century's "passion for the Real," for the thing-in-itself beyond the veil of semblances:

> In contrast to the nineteenth century of utopian or "scientific" projects and ideals, plans for the future, the twentieth century aimed at delivering the thing itself—at directly realising the longed-for New Order. The ultimate and defining moment of the twentieth century was the direct experience of the Real as opposed to everyday social reality—the

Real in its extreme violence as the price to be paid for peeling off the deceptive layers of reality. (Žižek, *Welcome* 5–6)

Curiously enough, Žižek points out, the cult of the real thing easily reverses itself into the culture of semblances. This was already perceptible in the late nineteenth century, when the promotion of the body's sensations and perceptions by thinkers like Walter Pater was raised to the status of an aesthetic ideal—whose incarnation is the dandy, the man who turns himself into a beautiful image. With the longed-for New Order a century later, its logic of de-sublimation and immediate access to the real thing was dictated by a particular libidinal economy: the imperative to enjoy all aspects of one's life within a mass globalised culture of unrestrained expenditure. Interestingly it was in the 1950s that the word *hedonism* passed from the field of aesthetic philosophy to that of social economics.[2] Of course the advent of the televisual image as a mechanically produced semblance accelerated the phenomenon in the post-war period, offering new digitally-mediated forms of collective identification.[3]

Dorian: An Imitation illustrates particularly well how the artistic counter-culture of the 1980s was to become the "over-the-counter culture" (Self 91) dominated by the consumption of images, thriving less on visual pleasures than on scopic enjoyment.

ADDICTION TO "THE LOOKS THING"

In his reprising of Gustave Le Bon's work on the formation of human groups, Freud emphasised the importance of libidinal ties which determine social identifications in two ways: either vertically, through some leader figure, or horizontally, through features shared among the group by empathy.[4] Freud's observations may be re-formulated in the light of the Lacanian Real/Symbolic/Imaginary registers, and of the distinction between the big Other (the invisible agency that rules human lives and determines the symbolic coordinates in which we are woven) and the small other (my visible alter ego who shares my condition, who is more or less in my image and with whom I may share group interests and affects). In the case of vertical identification with some invisible/inaccessible figure of the Other, the subject aspires to an *ego ideal* which may inspire an ethical act or decision, the identifications being predominantly socio-symbolic—like the ready-to-wear ideals offered by the Church and the Army. If determined horizontally among the group, identifications are more a matter of mirror reflections and their related passions—for Lacan, love, hatred, ignorance: in other words, they are predominantly *imaginary*. To this should be added that in the age of economic hedonism and of the dominant passion for the real thing, the feature shared by a human group may be a mode of enjoyment focused on some object: drugs, alcohol or (why not?) the image of one's likeness sustaining narcissistic identifications to an *ideal ego*: to the looks thing mistaken for the real thing.

It will be useful to recall at this stage what the story of Narcissus is about. First of all it is a myth, that is, a fictional narrative enclosing a universal point of truth concerning the question of the gaze as object escaping the subject's grasp. When we look at ourselves in a mirror or a pool, there is always more than meets the eye, a point where we cannot meet our own gaze: an elusive blind spot out there, whose elision is the condition for setting up the coordinates of what we call reality—like the vanishing point for the construction of a classic perspective. In this sense, reality is a representation structured around a "sublime-mysterious point" (Žižek, *Looking* 110). The pictorial genre of the Vanity dramatises the gap between what belongs to the realm of "looks" and semblances, and the elusive gaze which "mortifies" the image by making it hopelessly incomplete. One of the most famous examples is Holbein's painting *The Ambassadors*; the uncanny spot in the foreground turns out to be, if we look awry, a hollow skull. The gaze without a subject looking at us from the picture makes us see that the image of knowledge and power embodied by the two ambassadors and the socio-symbolic reality they stand for is but a fragile semblance. Trouble begins when we are unable or unwilling to differentiate the actual body subjected to time and change from its ideal image projected onto the canvas/screen. When Narcissus looks at himself on the surface of the pool, he tries to reduce the gap and ultimately rejoins the elusive gaze "behind" the reflection; as his eye meets his eye, he becomes the inhuman gaze himself, and drowns in the liquid element, mired in his own mirror.

In *The Picture of Dorian Gray*, Oscar Wilde draws a link between the love of one's inverted mirror image and what was at the time called "sexual inversion." But this story of closeted homosexuality remains the drama of a single Narcissus, not of a whole culture. The topography of Wilde's London still reflects a dividing line between the individual's civilised life in the *chic* districts and the dark underside of aristocratic pleasures, the mere life of the masses in the sordid East End where Dorian leads his night life.[5] We recognise here the two forms of life, *bios* and *zoē* (civilised life and bare life) which, Giorgio Agamben argues in his seminal work on the *homo sacer* figure, lie at the foundation of political power. The inclusion-exclusion of bare life in the dark underside where the *homo sacer* figure is confined is not just a historical circumstance; it is inherent to social structure:

> *In the city, the banishment of sacred life is more internal than every interiority and more external than every extraneousness.* The banishment of sacred life is the sovereign *nomos* that conditions every rule, the originary spatialization that governs and makes possible every localization and every territorialization. (Agamben, *Homo* 111)

At the end of Wilde's novel, the socially symbolic fabric is reasserted with its clear-cut binary oppositions between inside and outside, up and down, rich and poor, the individual and the mass, fiction and reality. Both the phantasmagoria for Dorian, and the willing suspension of disbelief for the reader, come to an end. The late-Victorian order is restored; even the lovely image of Dorian Gray safely returns where it belongs, back to its frame hung on the wall of a bourgeois home: the marks of decay have been erased with the psychotic dissolution of Narcissus.

As if in response to Agamben's call for "a completely new politics—that is, a politics no longer founded on the *exceptio* of bare life" as an alternative to "the biopolitics of both modern totalitarianism and the society of mass hedonism and consumerism" (Agamben, *Homo* 11)—Will Self chooses to focus on the late 1980s, the decade "hung up on the looks thing" (Self 17). His aim is clearly not to stigmatise the gay culture; rather, his interest lies in its orientation as a group as symptomatic of a whole society's new mode of identification through addiction to virtual objects, including the de-realised televisual image whose medium is *Cathode Narcissus*. In our late global modernity, the market gives access to a whole range of virtual products deprived of their malignant properties—like caffeine-free coffee or fat-free butter: in other words, the virtual reality we bathe in is another case of the passion for the real thing having reversed itself into a passion for the semblance of the thing. As Žižek argues, it generalises

> this procedure of offering a product deprived of its substance: it provides reality itself deprived of its substance, of the hard resistant kernel of the Real . . . we begin to experience "real reality" itself as a virtual entity. (Žižek, *Welcome* 11)

The TV screen or video monitor is the chief instrument of this confusion: it has lost its function as screen, i.e. a resisting surface where the film of our fantasies can be projected. In our era of mass identifications where "everyone seeks to hang on to their childhood" (Self 220), the dividing line between fiction and reality has dangerously faded as digitalised special effects endlessly deliver the thrill of the real thing: voyeuristic reality *shows*, where people display on the public stage their innermost fantasies (like fashioning oneself into a Diana, a Dorian, or a Lolita) or, more gruesomely, catastrophe movies of crashing planes and colliding cars where everyone can safely enjoy the spectacle of another person's death.

Like narcissism, voyeurism is another case of the gaze being located in the viewer,[6] when the screen has lost its function of projection and protection—of distancing therefore. In Self's novel, Basil's artful installation of nine monitors ranged in a semicircle forces the spectator into the perverse position of involuntary voyeur. The first monitor shows the naked figure of a beautiful young man, posed like a classical Greek *kouros*:

> The sensation imparted as all nine monitors came to life was one of the most intense, carnivorous, predatory voyeurism. The youth was like a fleshy bonbon, or titillating titbit, wholly unaware of the ravening mouth of the camera. The ninth monitor displayed only his mobile pink mouth. (Self 12)

To the men *installed* in prime viewing position, the resistant surface of the monitor is abolished: the viewer's camera eye as it were penetrates the visual membrane of immaterial fluid—it goes through the film, closer to the pink flesh of the mouth. The men do not look at a virtual image; they *are* with their "cathode partners" immersed in a kind of suspended temporality and imaginary community. Dorian loses himself in night-clubs swaying in synchrony with his *alter egos* to the music of self-consciousness. He is also a sex addict, trespassing all possible bodily membranes, absorbing as much as possible of those who are not other people, but simply an "alternative me." If Basil Hallward's piece is most cunning in the way it blurs the distinction actual/virtual for the viewer, let it be noted however that for the artist himself no confusion is possible. Basil is not part of the group of addicts to the looks thing, and he makes Dorian angry when he reminds him of the transcendent nature of *Cathode Narcissus* where the swaying images are *not* the actual Dorian.

If this "portrait riff" has taken the resonance of a modern myth (Self 219), it is because the age of mechanical reproduction is too willing to forget the distinction between body and image, between the original and the copy: the reproducible image has become the equivalent of the real thing. The divine Dorian illustrates the social triumph of the *simulacrum* which is precisely a copy without an original, the very antithesis of the pictorial genre of the Vanity whose lesson is that one should not mistake the lovely fiction of one's fashioned image for the real, mortal body. Will Self's Narcissus is the perfect example of scopic addiction: looking at himself in a vanity mirror he snorts "vanity mixed with cocaine and heroin" (29), among other commodities. He revels in the imposture on the London scene with his best friend Diana, the "Princess of Bulimia"; for them, acting is much more real than reality and both are great friends with the politicians of the day. On the global stage, de-realised politics meets fashion which meets culture, all of them being subjected to the tyranny of visual enjoyment: "The late-twentieth century requires of us that all political statements be fashionable, just as all fashion statements must be political" (Self 144).

For Dorian and his groupies, any device to preserve one's beloved likeness will do, like making oneself a true image of the other sex. The nice young men spend days dressing up as dolls of Blanche Dubois, Barbra Streisand, etc. As to the bare "facts of life" like birth and death, they will be made into another spectral show, a performance of the Otherness of life, of course deprived of its actual Otherness. Henry Wotton recalls

> being at some avant-garde event and watching Leigh Bowery mimic a miscarriage on stage. It struck me then that it was Dorian who was truly orchestrating the mental couvade male homosexuals felt they were enacting in the late eighties. If Bowery was the mother, then Dorian was the mother of all mothers, showing us how to give birth to our own images. (Self 113)

In other words, to put it in Freudian-Lacanian terms, what happens here is two things. First, the fiction whose puppet-master is Dorian is mistaken for reality. Second, Imaginary relations (the looks thing) triumph over the Symbolic ties which regulate kinship through a cultural process known in postmodern theory as the paternal *metaphor*—a symbolic agency whose function is to provide a viable, temperate relation between the sexes or between generations through the filtering medium of language.

On Dorian's planet the paternal metaphor clearly derails and the symptom of this derailment is the proliferation of obscene father and mother figures of enjoyment. Dorian's Dickensian father, Johnny Gray, was a gambler and a drinker particularly vicious to his son. Henry Wotton, Dorian's mentor and the father of the primordial tribe, knows no law but the tyranny of unbridled enjoyment. While his mother insists on changing her name every time she changes her bed partner, his own father sexually abused him regularly during his childhood, so that he had to live apart from his body in order to bear this horror. All those disorders, it seems, are now regulated by socialised medicine which distributes Ritalin to disturbed, hyperactive children as if politics were now a question of administering and regulating the bare life of the citizen. The politics that meant to give you the real thing has turned into a mere semblance, a "politics without politics" in the place of the earlier modes of Symbolic regulation (Žižek, *Welcome* 10).

HOMO SACER, HOMO SUCKER

One of the striking features differentiating Will Self's novel from its nineteenth-century predecessor is its urban topology: New York, London and then the whole world seem to be part of the same immense suburb, as if the relationship of ban which in Oscar Wilde's London separated the "obscene" enjoyments of *zoē* from the "civilised" pleasures of *bios* in the chic downtown areas were a thing of the past.

We must at this point return to Giorgio Agamben and his *homo sacer* figure. For the ancient Romans, the distinction between the citizen enjoying full rights and *homo sacer* would be materialised by a strip of land, an area of banishment, a belt which could be as wide as a *lieue* (4 km): hence the name of *banlieue*, still used in modern French. The *homo sacer* of our medieval, early and late modern cities confined within such belts has often been identified from the dominant perspective as a figure given to all kinds of vices, enjoying the bare, indignant life of the body.[7] Let it be recalled that for the Romans, the life of *homo sacer* who can be killed with impunity is not even worthy of a ritual sacrifice.[8] Agamben's well-known thesis is that this area of "bare life" (*zoē*) paradoxically guarantees the consistency of civilised life (*bios*)[9] whose collective representations it also nurtures. Most of the time those radically excluded in the dwellings of shameful *zoē* have been left to live their own lives there, unsubjected to biopolitical considerations. At least it was so when Western bourgeois society clearly separated the body's private modes of *jouissance* hidden from the public gaze.

What if modern democracy itself promotes the right of each individual to enjoy their own bare life now transformed into a way of life, and made part of public life? What opposes modern to classical democracy, Agamben argues, is the fact that

> [it] presents itself from the beginning as a vindication and liberation of *zoē*, and that it is constantly trying to transform its own bare life into a way of life and to find, so to speak, the *bios* of *zoē*. Hence, too, modern democracy's specific aporia: it wants to put the freedom and happiness of men into play in the very place—"bare life"—that marked their subjection. (Agamben, *Homo* 9–10)

Hence the transformation of politics into what Michel Foucault has called biopolitics, the expert administration of life—including mental life—in the modern democratic state. Does it mean, then, that the relationship of ban is a thing of the past? Probably not, if we follow Agamben's argument that this relationship is inherent to social power. We must therefore "learn to recognize this structure of the ban in the political relations and public spaces in which we still live" (Agamben, *Homo* 111), just as we must learn to recognise the new manifestations of the *homo sacer* figure. And we are not at the end of our surprises.

The first place for the "scientific" administration of bare life at the service of a State apparatus was the concentration camp, a new dwelling for the *homo sacer* figure,

> the one who is deprived of his or her full humanity being taken care of in a very patronizing way . . . [C]oncentration camps and refugee camps for the delivery of humanitarian aid are two faces, "human" and "inhuman," of the same socio-logical formal matrix. (Žižek, *Welcome* 91–92)

The systematic destruction of the Jew, the Tzigan, the homosexual, the crippled, by the Nazi machine devoted to the likeness of an imaginary "race" was the first example of what the scientific administration of bare life may lead to. The rest of the century has shown that this was less an accident of history than the first sign of modern politics giving up its symbolic mandate. Žižek's point that the latest versions of *homo sacer* will be found in the humanitarian camp where the dividing line now falls between the citizen endowed with *legal* rights and the person who is barely entitled to vague *human* rights may be shocking, but it seems hardly deniable.[10] As suggested by the ambivalence of the French word *personne,* which means both *a person* and *nobody*, the dweller of the camp is not a citizen but a human being deprived of a symbolic body.

Here again the dividing line is uncertain and may shift according to circumstances: anyone who was the citizen of one country may suddenly become no citizen of any country. It then appears that the true problem is less the status of the excluded than the fact that we may all one day or other be excluded, whenever the fragile knotting together of the Real with the Symbolic and the Imaginary is threatened—for example when a human group is deprived of its own image and its symbolic identity by exceptional circumstances like a war or economic exile.[11] Or when the image of the body is mistaken for the real body which itself tends to be treated as a mere inert thing. In the eyes of the scientific administration of public health, we are less symbolic bodies than bare flesh to be operated upon, grafted upon, dissected—in other words, the potential objects of biopolitics. And it may well be that in today's "post-politics," the very democratic public space is a mask concealing the fact that, ultimately, we are all *homo sacer,* so that the distinction between the legal citizen and *homo sacer* is less the distinction between two groups than between two ways "of how *the same* people can be treated" (Žižek, *Welcome* 32)—according to the use being made of their bodies.

Dorian: An Imitation perfectly reflects the evolution of the *homo sacer* figure as a result of the liberation of *zoē* on the market-place governed by *the looks thing*, as a result of the reversal of the passion for the real into the passion for semblances. The image *is* the body which itself can be treated as mere substance in the process of maintaining and restoring the image. Dorian, the name given in the nineteenth century to the figure of the homosexual as a figure of exception, is now at the vanguard of "a mutton army dressed as denim lambs" (Self 220). The passage from the figure of the *lamb*, the archetypal symbol of sacrifice, to bare *mutton* meat beneath the fashionable denim is itself symptomatic. Indeed the twentieth-century Dorian represents a rather widespread form of subjectivity in modern democracy which has given up its symbolic mandate: the vindication of the body's bare life, and the inability to differentiate the seductive fiction of oneself on the screen from actual reality. It is the fragile binding and bonding between the Imaginary body (the image), the Real body (the flesh) and the Symbolic body (labelled by a name) that has gone loose.

The gay counter-culture, we are told, was first a rallying cry around the mythical figures of Rimbaud and Verlaine celebrating the triumph of a wildly romantic life, a sort of remote symbolic ideal. But in a context where the voyeuristic consumption of images has become a sort of universal right in itself, what happened was much less romantic as those young people got "absorbed, then packaged and retailed like everybody and everything else" (Self 91). We see the new topology of the camp appearing in those luxury camps like gay California or Bendor on the French riviera, a pseudo-place with "its utterly chichi falsity" (Self 102), where Dorian and his likes can enjoy the looks of the real thing. Besides, this century provides all sorts of means to vindicate the bare life as a lifestyle, to publicly enjoy the *bios* of *zoē*—including the spectacle of one's own death and reanimation. There is plenty among the new technologies—cryogeny, nanotechnology and so on—at the service of narcissistic-voyeuristic enjoyment. Dorian is a great fan of rituals like "cryonic suspension" at Dr Bloody Kildare's suburban theatre, where everyone can attend the operation of "de-animation" which consists in pumping the body's blood to replace it with glycerol in the hope of reanimation in some remote future. In other words we attend the globalisation of *homo sacer*, the latest commodity.

This reversal of the passion for the real thing into a passion for the simulacrum of the thing in itself, however, cannot last. There will always be something in excess, a little remainder, a "little bit of moisture" in the corpse's arteries making the miraculous reanimation impossible (Self 195). In other words, the Real will always return, insist and spoil the collective fantasy. We are told that during the first months of 1997, the *Cathode Narcissi* spread throughout the social metabolism like a digital virus. But Dorian the sadistic genius was also the transmitter of an actual virus that would in those same years kill legions of young men. We see him dealing the deadly heroin shot in a kind of perverse distortion of the symbolic ritual of blood-brotherhood. In a grim parody of John Donne's poem "The Flea," he shoots Basil up, "As t'were a flea / That sucked on you and now sucks on me," while Basil sees in his eyes the cold passion of a voyeur and a murderer (Self 159). As for their gay companions, some of them will be disposed of in plastic bags, like those fellows in a Chicago hospital where the first cases of Aids appeared. Do not those "squadrons of young men" with their "radiator-grille ribcages and concentration-camp eyes" (Self 78) manifest the modern fate of *homo sacer*, the metamorphosis into what Žižek ironically calls *homo sucker*,[12] anticipating Everyman's condition in the hands of modern science, allied with the bureaucratic administration of life?

THE IMAGE STRIKES BACK

Of course, no socially symbolic fiction is restored at the end of Self's novel; the late twentieth century cannot rewind the film. As for the novelist's act *qua* novelist, it is not to offer alternative models for collective identifications. Rather, it may consist in enabling us to see otherwise by clearly drawing the dividing line between virtual and actual reality. *Dorian: An Imitation* offers a rich reflection on the necessity to reassert the ethical status of fiction as true lies, indispensable for structuring our reality.

In his analysis of the 9/11 attacks, Žižek reminds us that the unthinkable which happened was after all but a real-life version of the stuff of fantasies commonly enjoyed in catastrophe movies: "in a way, America got what it fantasized about . . . It is not that reality entered our image: the image entered and shattered our reality (i.e. the symbolic coordinates which determine what we experience as reality)" (*Welcome* 16). The underlying question is this: why, in the midst of our well-being, should we derive an enigmatic satisfaction from such nightmarish scenarios? Psychoanalysis gives a possible answer by arguing that the structure of fantasy, a form of fiction, is Janus-faced: our fantasies are *both* pacifying, as they enable us to stand the abyss of the Other's desire within us—like watching people die on the screen—*and* inassimilable in our reality: their proper place is the dream, or the screenplay of fiction, whatever its shape (film, novel, work of art). What, then, if we mistake fiction for reality? The point about the 9/11 spectacular "show" is that it awakened us Westerners from our hypnotic consumption of such scenarios: the nightmare was that it was as if the image actually delivered the thing itself. One of the lessons to be drawn, Žižek observes, is that just as the passion for the Real ends up in the pure semblance of the spectacular effect of the Real, "in an exact inversion, the 'postmodern' passion for the semblance ends up in a violent return to the passion for the Real" (*Welcome* 10).

Dorian's experience of the death of his virtual sister Diana, a perfect fashion victim, is strangely reminiscent of the endlessly repeated shot of the planes approaching and hitting the WTC. As he sits down and watches the twenty-four hour news channel on the central monitor, he tries to "take in" what happens on the screen,

> still trying to take it in five hours later, when the same footage of ambulances speeding to the Salpêtrière had been shown over and over again, and the same onlookers interviewed, and the same crumpled-up Mercedes lovingly dwelt upon by the caressing camera. No, Dorian Gray couldn't take it in. Princess Diana. Dead. Impossible. (Self 275)

The "caressing camera" dwelling "lovingly" on the car betrays the voyeur's libidinal investment. But this time, the image on the screen breaks through Dorian's de-realised reality, this break-through marking the first step of his descent back to life. Because we are in the triumphant age of virtual reality, the people's infantile identification with the Princess, however, does not end here: the gathering in front of the gates of Buckingham Palace comes as another simulacrum, a fake symbolic gesture of mourning which keeps nurturing the film of the collective fantasy in which even the police with their downcast eyes seem to participate. Dorian watches "while the infantry of grief threw up a cellophane-wrapped rampart to protect themselves from the bombshell that had already fallen" (Self 276). The story of modern history hung up on *the looks thing* continues, and there is nothing the novelist can do about it; Diana the huntress "slain by the paper hounds of the press" is not an invented but an historical figure. Her death is a public event, confirming that "history is nothing more or less than the confused wet dream of a humanity yoked to its own adolescent erotic fantasies" (Self 274). But the novelist can invent whatever fate pleases him for his own invented characters.

Clearly, Self's satire is aimed at those *taking themselves* for Dorians or Dianas. Its moral is twofold, not only that we should not mistake reality for fiction, but that we should not overlook the blind spot of the Real in what we experience as fiction.[13] Basil Hallward vainly tries to warn Dorian that he should get real, but it is too late: Dorian now suffers from severe hallucinations. One day, he takes a walk in Hyde Park, accompanied by a spectral voice and figure dressed in a fashionable red jacket whom he mistakes for Henry Wotton—who is now dead. The image, however, strikes back as it turns out to be an actual person, Ginger, who has come to seek revenge for the death of a former lover caused by Dorian. Ginger wants to take a leak and drags Dorian inside the public toilets below, where he cuts his throat. Standing in "the piss-filled urinal," the place of *zoē* underneath the civilised grounds of the park, Dorian comes to terms with the fact that "the beautiful new tie Ginger had just given him with his knife was a warm, sticky, fluid thing, and hardly likely to remain fashionable for very long at all" (278). The red tie is no longer a fashion item but rather real blood that now leaks into the common urinal: the leak which makes a *stain* and a shapeless spot at last differentiates the mortal body from the image. The occurrence of the word *tie* at this strategic moment may not be accidental either. Ginger's slash in the lovely image is also a gift which ultimately ties Dorian back to his humanity as he loses his impossible immunity. Such a gesture is surely reminiscent of the contemporary self-inflicted practice of cutters, those young people who, immersed in our virtual environment of products deprived of their substance, seek in a desperate strategy to regain a hold, to "ground the ego firmly in bodily reality" (Žižek, *Welcome* 10) made at last palpable through blood. But here of course it is another fellow-being that grounds Dorian in reality exposed as no longer a pretty fiction.

The question for the novelist will also be to draw a dividing line enabling us to differentiate the realm of fiction and fantasy from actual life, still preserving the "*alibidinal*" dimension of his "true lies" enclosing a blind spot, a kernel of truth. It is not a question of either-or, but of a relation of conjunction-disjunction—as Jacques Lacan pointed out, we have no access to truth but through the veil of fiction. We have seen that what characterises the narcissistic and voyeuristic modes is that the gaze is "blocked" inside the viewer, the consequence being that the gap between the body and the image is abolished. The question is not to separate them totally, but to bind together the dimensions of the Real, the Imaginary and the Symbolic which constitute a human body. The trick for the novelist as forger of true lies which concern our common condition will be to rehabilitate the function of the screen by locating the gaze outside the viewer: by producing a blot, some leaking, vanishing point making the image incomplete—just as Ginger does in the story. Regarding the art of literary fiction, a reference to the dynamics of cinematic montage—the reverse of the paralysed gaze—will be useful here:

> [the] transformation of fragments of the real into cinematic reality produces, through a kind of structural necessity, a certain leftover, a surplus that is radically heterogeneous to cinematic reality but nonetheless implied by it, part of it. That this surplus of the real is, in the last resort, precisely the gaze *qua* object, is best exemplified by the work of Hitchcock. (Žižek, *Looking* 116)

In terms of novelistic montage, *Dorian: An Imitation* is both a stunning novel and, I would argue, a socially symbolic act.

Its double ending, a classical postmodernist topos in itself, produces a clash between different realities and a shift in symbolic places: a possible relief, in all the senses of the word. In the first ending, Dorian dies like his predecessor, after a long process of psychotic dissolution. Then comes an epilogue: after Henry Wotton's death, his widow gives a manuscript to Dorian who is actually not dead but enjoying the full status of a citizen, one of a new generation of gay men and lesbian women who for the first time openly assume positions of power. What the epilogue suggests, then, is the possibility of reconsidering symbolic law as a set of contingent social arrangements open to change, and not as global biopolitics. Our postmodern Dorian is no dumb image addict; he reads Wotton's fiction with critical distance and is fully aware of the stylistic distortion in the portraits of himself and his friends to the point of caricature, for the reader's enjoyment.

Within his own fictional tale, Will Self makes ample use of the same features. In its gesture against the "repressive de-sublimation" of our age, the novel is quilted with references to actual artists as a possible way of re-constructing the readership's artistically symbolic Other: Jerome Bosch, Marcel Duchamp, John Donne, Arthur Rimbaud—so many names and models for the reader possibly to identify as references, not to identify with. Self-conscious winks at styles and genres constantly betray the artefact, like this parody of a baroque *trompe-l'œil*:

> Over all this arched the empyrean, cold bright blue, curved like the ceiling of a Byzantine church. Through the oculus at its very apex could be seen the entrance to Heaven . . . and finally, surmounting everything, inconceivably high . . . God Himself, who . . . had assumed the form of Dorian Gray. (Self 199)

In an era all too eager to suspend all disbeliefs, it is certainly useful to revive the function of the willing suspension of disbelief. The use of the past perfect tense here ("God . . . had assumed") is crucial to re-introduce a perspective in time and space: Dorian Gray, then, was but a visual form temporarily suspended out there in the place of the Other—here the Holy Spirit, for whom there is precisely no image. His disappearance from the oculus leaves a blind spot around which the whole baroque picture is structured.

Ultimately, the very title of this truly baroque novel, *Dorian: An Imitation,* invites us to reconsider the sameness-difference dichotomy. Sameness is less a question of *imitation* or likeness than of what makes us *one among others*, a singular entity irreducible to others but bound to the group through symbolic ties, the gift of words received from the invisible Other out there.

NOTES

1. Commenting on the crisis brought about in the theatre by the development of the film, Benjamin concludes: "Nothing more strikingly shows that art has left the realm of the 'beautiful semblance' which, so far, had been taken to be the only sphere where art could thrive" (Benjamin 224).
2. According to *Dictionnaire Le Robert*, this new meaning of "hedonism" appeared in 1956 to designate a doctrine according to which the end and the aim of any economic activity is nothing but the pursuit of a maximum of satisfaction with as little effort as possible ("doctrine . . . selon laquelle la raison et la fin de toute activité économique n'est au fond que la poursuite du maximum de satisfactions avec le moindre effort") (*Le Robert* 137).
3. "The authentic twentieth-century passion for penetrating the Real Thing (ultimately, the destructive Void) through the cobweb of semblances which constitutes our reality thus culminates in the thrill of the Real as the ultimate 'effect', sought after from digitalized special effects, through reality TV and amateur pornography, up to snuff movies" (Žižek, *Welcome* 12).
4. See for example Chapter V of "Group Psychology," where Freud deals with the example of two artificial groups, the Church and the Army: "It is to be noticed that in these two artificial groups each individual is bound by libidinal ties on the one hand to the leader (Christ, the Commander-in-Chief) and on the other hand to the other members of the group" (Freud, "Group" 124–25).
5. In other words, what is at issue here is the distinction between on the one hand the acknowledged social pleasures to be reached on the scale of desire, and on the other hand something beyond the pleasure principle to which Lacan gave the name of *Autre jouissance*.
6. As Žižek explains, the perverse character of pornography lies in the fact that

   > the spectator is forced a priori to occupy a perverse position. Instead of being on the side of the viewed object, the gaze falls into ourselves, the spectators, which is why the image we see on the screen contains no spot, no sublime-mysterious point from which it gazes at us . . . it is the spectator himself who effectively occupies the position of the object. The real subjects are the actors on the screen trying to rouse us sexually, while we, the spectators, are reduced to a paralyzed object-gaze. (*Looking* 110)

7. Whether Jew, Arab or other; whether slave, servant or poor worker: the determinations will vary according to class divisions, continents and cultures.
8. " . . . those who, although they were human, were excluded from the human community, which is why one can kill them with impunity—*and, for that very reason, one cannot sacrifice them (because they are not a worthy sacrificial offering*)" (Žižek, *Welcome* 141).
9. "Sovereign violence is in truth founded not on a pact but on the exclusive inclusion of bare life in the state" (Agamben, *Homo* 107).
10. See the old distinction between human rights and the rights of a citizen: "rights of all members of humankind (to be respected also in the case of *Homo sacer*), and the more narrow rights of citizens (those whose status is legally regulated)" (Žižek, *Welcome* 95).
11. "What if the true problem is not the fragile status of the excluded but, rather, the fact that, on the most elementary level, we are *all* 'excluded' in the sense that our most elementary, 'zero' position is that of an object of biopolitics, and that possible politics of citizenship rights are given to us as a secondary gesture, in accordance with biopolitical strategic considerations?" (Žižek, *Welcome* 95).
12. "The predominant liberal mode of subjectivity today is *Homo sucker*: while he tries to exploit and manipulate others, he ends up being the ultimate sucker himself. When we think that we are making fun of the ruling ideology, we are merely strengthening its hold over us" (Žižek, *Welcome* 71).
13. "We should be able to discern, in what we experience as fiction, the hard kernel of the Real which we are able to sustain only if we fictionalize it. In short, we should discern which part of reality is 'transfunctionalized' through fantasy, so that, although it is part of reality, it is perceived in a fictional mode. Much more difficult than to denounce/unmask (what appears as) reality as fiction is to recognize the part of fiction in 'real' reality" (Žižek, *Welcome* 19).

3 Interview with Ernesto Laclau

Ruth Parkin-Gounelas

From the late 1970s, the work of Ernesto Laclau has continued to play a pivotal role in debates about collective formation and action, centering on his concept of "the people" as historical agent. Laclau's work heralds the arrival of what he sees as the new political era under global capitalism. The challenge today, as he and Chantal Mouffe described it in their groundbreaking book *Hegemony and Socialist Strategy* (1985), is to theorise the plurality of antagonistic demands emerging on a mass terrain in ways other than class. In this revisionist Marxist view, the subject is constituted not prior to revolutionary struggle but rather through the coincidence of historical circumstances which give birth to a popular force or collective will. Identity is not fixed but relational, just as "society" is not a founding totality or essence but rather a radical heterogeneity that can't be attached to any transcendental signified. Concepts like "the social" and "the individual" are expressions of a desire for fullness that is permanently deferred—which is not to say, however, that it is not constantly sought.

As the terms of this formulation indicate, Laclau's project is posited upon a psychoanalytic (Lacanian) framework, giving it a breadth attractive to cultural theorists from a range of disciplines. For Laclau, psychoanalysis is fundamental for a coherent theory of political subjectivity; the psychoanalytic discovery of the unconscious, he has written recently, "is one of [those] epoch-making events whose ontological dimensions we are only starting to glimpse" ("Glimpsing" 315). As important as the concept of the Real (that impossible fullness) from the Lacanian schema is that of the demand, articulated need which is always striving towards but never achieving fulfillment. The minimum unit of analysis is thus not the group, but the socio-political demand, in fact the heterogeneity of demands or articulations that constitute the so-called hegemonic link first outlined by Gramsci. Together, these articulations may unite to form a moment of revolt under a common signifier—such as "democracy" or "justice."

It is here that in addition to the psychoanalytic, the prominent linguistic dimension of Laclau's thought comes into play. Against Foucault's distinction between the discursive and the non-discursive, Laclau proposes a form of speech act theory whereby the name, performatively, becomes the ground of the thing. In a post-Saussurean move, following the Copenhagen and Prague schools, the social becomes synonymous with the discursive; just as the processes of combination and substitution are primary in linguistic analysis, so those of equivalence and difference are fundamental to an understanding of the struggle for representation in a popular movement. Through common signifiers, different groups may unite against a shared opponent, temporarily overcoming their differences in a moment of illusory unicity, and in this way bring about change. Subsequently, however, the removal of the opponent is likely to return the relations among the groups to a differential rather than an equivalential basis, with the reinstatement of old (or new) antagonisms. Just as the symbol's meanings are over-determined, always in excess of it, so the political and social demands will always exceed the unity of their expression. The hegemonic signifier unifying the group, therefore, is necessarily empty. If "the people" in Laclau's terms is that which resists power, it is also that which has ultimately no fixed referent. "Never succumb," he warns at the end of *On Populist Reason* (2005), "to the terrorism of words" (249), as in their tendency to become emotionally-charged fetishes ("Fascism," "the working class"), they may blind us to an understanding of their historically-specific relativity.

However it is words, after all, which hold popular movements together and give them form. Laclau pays (an unfashionable) tribute to Gustave Le Bon for his recognition that "The power of words is bound up with the images they evoke, and is quite independent of their real significance" (Le Bon, qtd. in Laclau, *Populist* 22). Groups are held together by symbolic representations which operate, however, not by some magic and deluding power, as Le Bon saw it, but rather as a temporary umbrella, the expression of a common goal which is always deferred. The truly innovative point that Laclau makes, via linguistics and psychoanalysis, is that particular demands which have taken on an equivalential relation are *strengthened* through their links along the signifying chain; an empty signifier can only play a central role if it is highly cathected. Some recent psychoanalytic theorists are wrong, Laclau explains in the interview that follows, to dichotomise affect and representation: "Neither of the two dimensions can be logically thought without the other." This highlighting of affect in psychoanalytic political theory has been instrumental in returning us to the contentious debates within crowd theory in the late nineteenth century in order to reformulate the terms for a contemporary age. It is in this context that Laclau denounces "the inanity of dismissing emotional populist attachments in the name of an uncontaminable rationality" (*Populist* 111).

So how are social and cultural identities constituted? When do particular claims become universal, mobilising crowds out onto the streets? Why, indeed, has the concept of universality come to occupy the attention of so many recent social and cultural theorists? And what is the role of historicism in these discussions? In addressing these questions, Laclau has been at the forefront of approaches to social and political phenomena specific to our time, characterised above all by a blurring of the line between state and civil society. As he puts it in a recent book co-authored with Judith Butler and Slavoj Žižek:

> The globalization of the economy, the reduction of the functions and powers of nation-states, the proliferation of international quasi-state organizations—everything points in the direction of complex processes of decision-making which could be approached in terms of hegemonic logics. (Butler, Laclau and Žižek 53)

The hegemonic politics of advanced capitalist societies in the last century and a half have witnessed a multiplication of democratic positions increasingly removed from the clear-cut positions of "the state versus the people." The modern period, in other words, has ushered in a new type of relation among social differences as well as an "irreconcilable plurality" of the social. Against the identity politics of multi-culturalism, a radical democracy calls for an understanding of the ways in which heterogeneities may group and re-group in their opposition to power. The important thing, in this praxiological model, is not the diversity itself but what you do with it.

INDIVIDUAL-COLLECTIVE, SINGULAR-HETEROGENEOUS

R. P.-G. Much of what you have written runs counter to postmodern conceptualisations of the subject such as those assumed in multicultural "identity politics." You have emphasised the way that identity is never complete, is always a failed attempt at self-determination—or, in Lacanian terms, that the subject is the gap in the structure, between the Real and the impossibility of its symbolisation. In opposition to the concept of "the individual" you postulate identity as a complexly-articulated collective will—one in which, however, concepts such as ethnic group or class are not fixed but rather transient points of stabilisation. In your repeated attack on "immanentism" and the unity of the collective will of classical Marxism, you theorise the category of non-dialectical negativity, a primary constitutive diversity which, following a Gramscian trajectory of dispersal or heterogeneity, describes a radical democratic practice as a "negotiated consensus among a plurality of social actors" (Butler, Laclau and Žižek 8). The theory of hegemony, however, postulates that no overall historical transformation is possible unless particular social struggles are superseded via political articulation and action, to form a wider collective will ("Can Immanence" 8). Although you have insisted that in your work you are interested not in groups as such but rather in the logic of their constitution and dissolution, would you be prepared to comment on the forms available for social bonding and/or transformation today under global capitalism?

E. L. Let us say, in the first place, that I am not exactly against multicultural identity politics. What I question in that type of approach is not pluralism or the dispersion of subject positions, but the assertion that political practice should simply remain at the level of such plurality. If that was the case—and it is, in several multicultural approaches—we would have a purely defensive politics, easily integrable into the status quo. We would have a situation similar to what Gramsci called a "corporative class"—as opposed to a "hegemonic" one—with the only difference that in this case we would be dealing not with classes but with ethnic, sexual, racial or other kinds of groups, but the logic of closure around a pre-given identity would be the same. It is for this reason that I have maintained that the really important point is not cultural and social diversity as such, but what you construct out of that diversity. In my view one has—although fully recognising the autonomy of the various demands—to concentrate on the logics that are able to articulate them in wider political identities. That is the reason why I have insisted on the specific logic of equivalence as one that allows us to start the construction of the "people" as a global subject confronting power.

As for the Lacanian notion of the subject as a gap in the structure, this is a central tenet of my argument, although the latter did not start from the Lacanian formulation. If we had a closed structure and a simple dispersion of subject positions within it, particularisms would be definable points within an underlying totality, and the autonomy that one intended to achieve with the multicultural approach would be impossible. If, however, the subject is seen as the subject of the lack, that is, a subject before subjectivation, identities have to be mediated by a process of identification. There is identification rather than mere identity, because the original lack which is at the root of subjectivity cannot be ultimately superseded. This presence of an original lack, which makes every identity a precarious and malleable one, is what makes possible movements between identities and, among other things, to equivalential logics and the emergence of the "people" as an historical actor.

And this leads me to the question of "heterogeneity" in global capitalism to which you refer. Classical Marxism had been a theory of the progressive homogenisation of society. The basic thesis had been that there is an increasing simplification of social structure under capitalism: capitalist endogenous tendencies were leading towards the disappearance of the peasantry and the middle classes and towards an increasing proletarianisation, which would make the last antagonistic confrontation of history a simple showdown between the bourgeoisie and the proletariat. What has happened, however, is exactly the opposite: we live in more and more heterogeneous societies and, although these societies are no less ridden by antagonisms and inequalities than in the past, the latter tend to be dispersed over the whole social body instead of being concentrated in a single point, such as the relations of production. That much had already been understood by Gramsci who, for that reason, insisted on the priority of political articulation over economic determinism. Things have, obviously, advanced a great deal more in that direction since the days of Gramsci, and it is in this connection that, in my view, we have to approach social struggles in our globalised world.

THE CROWD

R. P.-G. In *On Populist Reason*, you emphasise the importance of the way Freud deconstructed simplified assumptions about crowds (such as those of Le Bon), in particular the distinction between the rational individual and the irrational crowd. Within the Freudian model, attributes considered as belonging to the individual are transferred to the group, thus establishing the foundation on which modern social psychology is based. Although you have denied that your analysis of group functioning is strictly Freudian (*Populist* 63–64), would you accept that Freud's formulations of the function of the leader are relevant today? Freud's famous definition of the social bond, which you quote, is that of "a number of individuals who have put one and the same object [a leader or a cause] in the place of their ego ideal and have consequently identified themselves with one another in their ego' (qtd. in *Populist* 56). In view of the so-called crisis of the paternal function in the modern bourgeois nuclear family, often linked with a crisis in leadership, in what ways do you think group formations have been affected by shifts in the paternal function in today's (fragmented, global) social structures?

E. L. Freud's distinction between ego and ego ideal is crucial in order to understand the role of the leader in group formation. In "Group Psychology" he distinguishes three types of identification that he summarises in this way:

First, identification is the original form of emotional tie with an object; secondly, in a regressive way it becomes a substitute for a libidinal object-tie, as it were by means of introjection of the object into the ego; and thirdly, it may arise with any new perception of a common quality shared with some other person who is not an object of the sexual instinct. (Freud, "Group" 137)

It is obviously this last case which is most relevant for the discussion of group formation. The definition of the social bond that you quote, with its distance between the egos and the ego ideal, is directly linked to the third form of identification. As far as the dynamic of group formation is concerned, however, it is important to realise that the distance between egos and ego ideal is not for Freud rigidly determined because, as he mentions, it can vary considerably from group to group. After asserting that the "prodigy" of group formation lies in the fact "that the individual gives up his ego ideal and substitutes for it the group ideal as embodied in the leader," he makes what he calls a necessary correction because

[i]n many individuals the separation between the ego and the ego ideal is not very advanced; the two still coincide readily; the ego has often preserved its earlier narcissistic self-complacency. The selection of the leader is very much facilitated by this circumstance. He need often only possess the typical qualities of the individuals concerned in a particularly clearly marked and pure form, and need only give an impression of greater force and of more freedom of libido; and in that case the need for a strong chief will often meet him half-way and invest him with a predominance to which he would otherwise perhaps have had no claim. (Freud, "Group" 161–62)

This is important because, as I have tried to show in my book on populism, it involves that the leader should not be at an infinite distance from those that he leads, so that the father can be one of the brothers. This makes possible a far more democratic vision of the role of the leader.

As for your second question concerning the crisis of the paternal function in the bourgeois nuclear family, I would say the following. Firstly, even for Freud, the paternal function is not necessarily associated with the biological father. Any other figure—an uncle, for instance—can fulfill the paternal function. A teacher, anybody, can play that role. With lesbian couples we can perfectly well see one of the two women incarnating that function. So what I think is essential is to dissociate the notion of the paternal function from any kind of specific institutional arrangement, familial or otherwise. In that case, what is the root of the distance between the egos and the ego ideal? I think it is the impossibility of closing any communitarian space without constructing a unity by means of some symbols around which that unity crystallises, without some transcending point through which the community mirrors itself as a totality. This explains why, in those situations in which the distance between ego and ego ideal has not advanced too much, the need for a transcendent point of identification will diminish, and the leadership will necessarily be weak. Power, to put it in other terms, will be immanent in institutions. Conversely, in an organic crisis, this immanence will tend to dissolve, the importance of the external point of identification will increase, and as a result the gap between ego and ego ideal will widen and the role of the leader will become more central. A society can never reach such a perfect adjustment that an external image of itself is no longer necessary, so the distance between ego and ego ideal can never be closed. This means that the paternal function can never be eliminated, but it is no longer associated with any particular family structure and, indeed, not even with the family as its primary locus of constitution.

UNIVERSALITY-PARTICULARITY

R. P.-G. You have defined the hegemonic relation as one where "a certain particularity . . . assumes the role of an impossible universality" (*Populist* 115). Along with Judith Butler and Slavoj Žižek you have focused on universality as one of the most contested topics within recent social theory. Butler writes:

> Many have voiced the fear that constructivist and poststructuralist accounts of universality fail to offer a strong substantive or procedural account of what is common to all citizen-subjects within the domain of political representation. (Butler, Laclau and Žižek 14)

For his part, Žižek has suggested that it is time to move beyond Fredric Jameson's slogan "Always historicize!" (Butler, Laclau and Žižek 10),[1] recommending (as you yourself do) the notion of universality as both impossible and at the same time necessary. Could you elaborate further on your position in relation to the universalism-historicism debate?

E. L. I think the notion of historicism is ambiguous. It can mean the primacy of a radical contextualism, with which, of course, I am in disagreement, because it would mean that the context itself would be an absolute referent, which would not be itself historicised. If, however, the context is itself historicised, what could be the point of reference of that historicisation?: perhaps some kind of "universal history" which would remain as some kind of *fundamentum inconcussum*, giving its proper meaning to every context? However we look at the matter, we cannot avoid coming to the conclusion that "historicism" is a red herring which cannot stand without pointing to its very opposite as its condition or ground. But that opposite cannot do the trick either, because it cannot provide the notion of context with any clear or univocal meaning. So that we end in a no man's land: the ground is shaken by contextualisation, but contexts are not possible without appealing to that very ground that they are subverting.

The real question is whether we cannot make of that process of mutual subversion, in its undecidability, the very terrain within which the incompatible poles of universalism and particularism are constructed. An extreme universalist, like Habermas, would make of the universal a ground. But the notion of ground would be equally present in a particularist like Lyotard: if the social is constructed through a plurality of heterogeneous language games, what is the terrain making possible such heterogeneity? Even if we say—which is not exactly what Lyotard says—that there is not such a terrain as a positive underlying presence, but that those heterogeneous practices coexist one beside the other, one cannot fail to ask oneself what is to be heterogeneous and what is to coexist in a heterogeneous non-terrain.

You know the way in which I have tried to approach this question. Simplifying things a lot, the argument runs this way: the differential relationship between identities can never be consummated because the totality which would be the only terrain allowing the emergence of difference as such is unreachable. That is the reason why every differential identity is penetrated by an ultimate impossibility (the Real, in the Lacanian sense). In that case, however, how do differences achieve some kind of discursive identity? Only if one of them divides its own identity between its original particularity and its role of representing an (absent) totality which is incommensurable with its own particularity. This is the hegemonic or empty signifier, whose genesis and role I have tried to theorise in my work. This is the point where the moment of the universal emerges. But the universal, becoming so only through a cathexis of the particular (so without being at an absolute distance from the latter but being only an overinvestment in it), can only have a hegemonic universality. Putting it in other terms, the universal is not a ground but a horizon. Conversely, because the particular lacks a proper terrain to fully constitute itself as particular, it cannot reach a full constitution either. So the tension between particularity and universality is irresolvable, because neither of its two poles can be fully constituted and both exist only through the mutual subversion of each other. This undecidability is the abyss on which the social is constructed—the *Ab-grund*, as Heidegger calls it.

THE PARTIAL OBJECT AND THE DRIVE

R. P.-G. This leads us to the question of the partial object. Following the logic of Lacan's *objet a*, especially in its recent development by Joan Copjec, you define a partial object as not something that forms part of the whole, but rather a part which functions as a whole. One of the most fruitful aspects of your recent work, it seems to me, is the conjunction of this theory with your post-Saussurean theory of naming: that a name given (to, say, a particular political demand) functions in this very same way, as the signifier of an unachievable but necessary universality. Crucial to the formulation of this partially universalised particularity is Copjec's elaboration on the partial object of the drive. For Lacan, the drive aims not at the object itself, but at the satisfaction to be derived from it. Copjec insists, however, that this does not mean that the drive aims beyond the object, at the satisfaction beyond it. Rather, in her reading, "drive and object are soldered together" (Copjec, *Imagine* 39). In other words, the *objet a* and the external object, as objects of the drive, are a single object, one, however, which does not coincide with itself (Copjec 59–60). This formulation has important implications for your theory of signification, in that the name ("justice," "the people") is both object of satisfaction and that which is incapable of coinciding with itself—is, in other words, both full and empty. Is this what you have in mind when you call for "the opening of a new transcendental horizon within which the whole field of objectivity has to be thought again" (Butler, Laclau and Žižek 72)?

E. L. Yes, it is exactly that. The basis for that argument is what we have been discussing before. As I have argued in my work, the logic of the *object a* and the logic of hegemony are not simply homologous: they are identical. It is the same logic which has been detected, in one case in the field of psychoanalysis and in the other in the field of politics. The *object a* in Lacan is one which is overinvested in such a way that it comes to occupy the place of the (impossible) Freudian Thing. The Thing is an unreachable fullness which only exists as a retrospective illusion; this means that such illusion only exists if it is projected onto partial objects incarnating it. These objects are partial but such a partiality does not simply remain as such: it ceases to be so because it transforms its own (ontic) partiality in the means expressing the impossible totality. The logic of hegemony is exactly the same. As I have argued at length in my work, it is impossible for the moment of totalisation of a signifying field to express itself in a direct way. So we are left in a situation in which the totalising moment is necessary if there is going to be signification at all; but it is also impossible, because the closure which is the very condition of such a totalisation is unreachable. So we are confronted with an object which is at the same time necessary and impossible, as in the case of the Lacanian *object a*. In such a situation the (partial) closure of a signifying field is only achievable if a particular signifying element, without ceasing to be partial, assumes the representation of a totality overflowing it—in fact which is incommensurable with it. This is the hegemonic function of empty signifiers.

This signifier presents the two structural features that you have pointed out. Firstly, there is the question of the satisfaction that this partial object brings about. This satisfaction results from the overinvestment that the object has received. This dimension of investment is crucial because it means that once the investment has taken place in a particular object, there is some kind of fixation which cannot be easily altered. But it also means, on the other hand, that there is no necessary attachment of the investment to any particular object and, as a result, that the investment can migrate from one object to another. Secondly, there is the question of naming that you mention. The more an object is subjected to an overdetermination of meanings—that is, the more it becomes hegemonic—the less it will be able to be subsumed under a clear conceptual label. So the unity of all its signifying dimensions will be expressed through a name and not through a concept. In psychoanalysis the symptom, for instance, works in such a way; but the same is also true of what in politics concerns the nature of the hegemonic signifier.

RHETORIC

R. P.-G. Within this context you have often spoken in your work of a rhetorical ontology. What is meant by that, and in what way does it relate to the argument concerning empty signifiers which we have been speaking about?

E. L. The two arguments are intimately connected. In my work I have sustained that, although I agree with some philosophers, such as Alain Badiou, that at the primary ontological level there is no "unicity," I disagree that the only alternative is "multiplicity." What there is, for me, is "failed unicity." A failed unicity presupposes that there is no exact overlapping between the ontic and the ontological (as Hegel would have it), but that some ontic elements are invested, as we have seen, with the ontological function of representing a totality (unicity) which is both necessary and impossible. The side of impossibility is the one that leads us into the rhetorical dimension. Because if unicity is impossible, it means that no direct representation of it is going to be possible, and as it has, however—given its necessity—to have some access to the field of representation, this distorted representation will only be possible by deforming the literal meaning of an ontic content. This means—and here the rhetorical dimension comes to the fore—that such representation will be constitutively tropological. Even more: it will be catachrestical. We have catachresis whenever an object can only be named by a figural term to which no literal one corresponds (as when we speak of "the legs of a table" or "the wings of a building"). In actual fact, catachresis is not a particular figure, but an index of rhetoricity as such. Even when we use ordinary metaphors or metonymies, which could in principle be substituted by literal terms, the employment of figural ones adds dimensions that non-figurative language would be unable to transmit and, in that sense, there would be something essentially catachrestical in them. If we go back to the operations that we have approached in terms of "empty signifiers," we see that this catachrestical component is fully present. In the case of the *objet petit a*, the object does not name its own particularity but is a substitute for the Freudian Thing—i.e. an object without any content because it is a retrospective illusion and in the case of the hegemonic construction, a certain particularity assumes the representation of an impossible universality.

This rhetorical dimension is not an external addition to signification but is actually constitutive of signification as such. Saussure had already pointed out that the relationship between signifying elements can be of two types: relations of combination—the syntagmatic pole of language—and relations of substitution—the associative or paradigmatic pole. While the first pole is submitted to strict syntactic rules, the second pole is free from any such rules. Roman Jakobson extended this distinction to the rhetorical field: syntagmatic relations he associated to metonymy and paradigmatic ones to metaphor. We have here a basic opposition that we see reproduced, in a homologous way, on all levels of analysis of human reality. In linguistics, it is the opposition syntagm/paradigm; in rhetoric it is the one metonymy/metaphor; in psychoanalysis we speak of the duality displacement/condensation; in politics, finally, we have established the homologous distinction difference/equivalence.

AFFECT

R. P.-G. With reference to Freud's insight that the social link is always a libidinal link, you have placed emphasis in recent work on the mediating role of affect as a crucial dimension for the understanding of the political. For Freud, of course, affect is not a direct emotional expression but a trace or residue ("mnemic image," [Freud, "Project" 322]) triggered by repetition, a position developed by Lacan in his view of affect as "a function without a functionary" (*Écrits* 676) ("un service qui n'y a pas de titulaire" [*Écrits* (Fr) 799]), which appears in the (repetitive) insistence of the signifier. Affect, as you put it in *On Populist Reason*, "constitutes itself only through the differential cathexes of a signifying chain" (111).

Recent developments in neuro-psychoanalysis have been returning to Freud's early work (the "Project for a Scientific Psychology" and *Studies in Hysteria* in particular) with its insight that the "talking cure" implies an inextricable bond between affect and representation, a bond which can be studied in the way speech (in the transference) can be seen in brain scans to activate areas in the brain related to memory and affect. After the *Dreams* book, however, Freudian and Lacanian psychoanalysis took a turn towards representation and away from affect in the affect-representation conjunction. Am I correct in assuming that you would like to see this trend reversed, or rather a new balance restored?

E. L. You are right in saying that in the early work of Freud there is an inextricable link between representation and affect and that this duality is one that I have reaffirmed in my work, though I think that in both the later work of Freud and in Lacan there is much less of the exclusive emphasis on representation than you suggest. Anyway, I'll tell you how I see the matter by giving you a couple of examples. The first is the notion of the "empty signifier" we have already discussed. As I have said, an empty signifier is for me one which transforms its particular representational content in the means of expression of the totality of an equivalential series. This means that at the same time that its extensionality expands, its intensional content decreases. This reduced representational content, however, can only play that central role if it is highly cathected, and it is here that the affective dimension is crucial and becomes constitutive of signification. There is no signification without a quilting point, and there is no quilting point without cathexis—i.e. affect. That is the reason why for me there is no duality representation/affect, but an inextricable unity of the two dimensions, which can only be separated for analytic purposes.

But even that analysis leads only to the conclusion that neither of the two dimensions can be logically thought without the other. From this point of view I do not think that there is a decreasing role of affect in the later work of Freud or in Lacan; a Lacanian notion such as that of "master signifier" would be unthinkable without cathectic investments.

I go now to my second example, which is the notion of "antagonism." My central thesis is that social antagonisms are not objective relations but relations representing the limit, the breakdown of all objectivity. Antagonism is what prevents a society from constituting itself as an objective order, the latter being such that it would be susceptible of an unlimited representation. The possibility of this unlimited representation is the illusion of all rationalist conceptions, from Leibniz to Hegel. For them affect would be entirely external to signification/representation. What happens, however, if antagonism is conceived as the limit of all objectivity? Two things. First that the two poles of the antagonism cannot be inscribed as moments of an underlying substratum which would reabsorb them within a homogeneous space of representation. The chasm separating them could not itself be represented. But, second, in that case each of the two poles of the antagonism would make its own contents the pure expression of the fullness of society, reducing the contents of the other pole to the pure expression of negativity. In other terms, the impossibility of representing the moment of chasm between antagonistic forces will lead to a situation in which each force would endow its own ontic contents with the ontological function of expressing the fullness of society, whose impossibility of an ultimate achievement is given by the presence of the antagonistic force, whose ontic contents will thus be reduced to pure negativity. This overflowing of the ontic contents by this new ontological role means, first, that this role results from a breakdown in the process of representation and, second, that the role itself, to be possible, requires the cathexis—positive in one case, negative in the other—of determinate ontic contents. This cathexis is, obviously, nothing else than affective investments. So at the very moment in which ontic representation retreats, that space is occupied by differential cathectic investments in fewer signifying elements. This, of course, is nothing else than the process of overdetermination as established by psychoanalysis, and its correlate in the field of politics is the unevenness of the social inherent in hegemonic links.

It is for these reasons that in an exchange with Jason Glynos and Yannis Stavrakakis[2] I have insisted that one should not unduly separate signification from affect; signification requires affect as one of its constitutive dimensions, and affect can only exist as the differential and uneven investment in a signifying chain.

CONTINGENT UNIVERSALITY OR THE "NON-GROUNDING GROUND"

R. P.-G. Your work since *Politics and Ideology in Marxist Theory* (1977) has traversed a wide range of disciplines, from the political and philosophical to the linguistic and psychoanalytic. How would you locate your political analysis within the general framework of contemporary thought?

E. L. On several occasions I have asserted that I see the intellectual history of the twentieth century as starting with three illusions of immediacy, of immediate access to things themselves as a primary ontological terrain. These three illusions were the referent, the phenomenon and the sign, and out of them emerged the three main intellectual traditions of our time: analytic philosophy, phenomenology and structuralism. Now, the history of these three traditions shows a remarkable parallelism: at some point those illusions of immediacy dissolve and in all three cases we see a transition by which they end up attributing a primary ontological centrality to one form or another of discursive mediation. This is what happens in analytic philosophy with the Wittgenstein of *Philosophical Investigations* through the introduction of the notion of "language games," in phenomenology with Heidegger's existential analytic, and in structuralism with the post-structuralist critique of the sign, to be found with different nuances in the works of the late Barthes, in Derrida's deconstruction and in Lacan's logic of the signifier.

Let me refer to this last tradition, which is the one that has been most influential in my own work. The bedrock of Saussure's linguistics was the postulate of a complete isomophism between the order of the signifier and the order of the signified. To each sequence of sounds would correspond one and only one conceptual unit. This, however, presented an insurmountable difficulty: as, according to Saussure, it is also a basic structural principle that language is form and not substance, we have to forget that the signifier is phonic substance and the signified a conceptual one and just concentrate on the formal dimensions. But in that case, if there is a strict isomorphism between the two orders, both of them are identical, and the duality constitutive of the sign, which is the cornerstone of structural linguistics, collapses. Later structuralist schools—glossematics, especially—tried to supersede this obstacle by starting linguistic analysis from units smaller than the word, so that the problem of isomorphism was obviated. This led to an expansion of linguistic formalism and to a generalisation of linguistic analysis well beyond language as a regional socialsphere—a process which was going to culminate in a generalised semiology as postulated, especially in France, in the 1960s and 1970s.

The next step was accomplished once it was realised that there are intrinsic logical difficulties in achieving the self-enclosed structural totality that classical structuralism had postulated. Deconstructive approaches and the psychoanalytic logic of the signifier were attempts at providing responses to how limited closures were possible once it was perceived that there is no transcendental signified which could bring about a true foundational closure. My notion of the "empty signifier" about which we have been speaking is also an attempt at providing a logic for the operation of a weak or "non grounding" ground.

What is important, however, for political analysis, is that this very transition from the illusion of a ground conceived as a reachable ultimate immediacy, to a contingent ground which is discursively constructed, has also taken place in the historical terrain of Marxist discursivity. When we move from the strict essentialism of the Marxism of the Second International to Leninism and finally to Gramsci, we see a progressive and systematic debasement of the ontological ambitions of an "ultimate" ground. Earlier in this interview I have explained some of the reasons why this transition took place. The logic of hegemony is, like the logic of the *objet petit a* in Lacan, grounded in the contingent investment in a particular object, in bestowing on it a universality which is ultimately incommensurable with that particularity. The only universality available in the socio-political world is a hegemonic—i.e. contingent—universality. And this contingency contaminates all the other central categories of Gramscian analysis—historical bloc, war of position, intellectual and moral leadership, etc.

NOTES

1. Jameson's slogan appears in the Preface to *The Political Unconscious* (ix).
2. See Glynos and Stavrakakis; also Laclau, "Discourse" and Laclau, "Glimpsing."

Part II

What's in a Crowd?

4 Crowds, Agency and Passion

Reconsidering the Roots of the Social Bond

Stephen Reicher

THE SCOPE OF CROWD THEORY

In this chapter I will outline a model of crowd action. I will also argue that crowd action provides the basis for understanding much wider issues, both in social psychology and in the social sciences more generally. In particular, crowds give us insights into the fundamental nature of the social bond. How is it that people become so attached—so *passionately* attached—to each other and to the groups that they belong to? Why is it that, even after the most sophisticated political and economic analysis of opportunities and interests, people often act in the most unexpected ways? Why do we cling on to attachments that seem outdated, redundant and an impediment to change? What psychological inertia exists in the system and is necessary in order to understand the progress (or lack of it?) in our society?

These are questions which social thinkers have grappled with for well over a century. It is the question which Marx grapples with in his "Eighteenth Brumaire of Louis Bonaparte" when he asks why, with conditions well set for revolution, did the French people opt for a reactionary Monarchy after 1848? Marx famously declares that:

> Just when they seem engaged in revolutionizing themselves and things, in creating something that has never yet existed, precisely in such periods of revolutionary crisis they anxiously conjure up the spirits of the past to their service. (K. Marx 300)

To put it in more modern terms, Marx is seeking to understand the nature of *investment* in social categories. It is a critical area in which other social scientists have need of psychology and where contemporary psychology tends to let social science down. As a result, theorists resort to older bodies of work, notably the Freudian tradition, which certainly do address the question of investment. This might help explain the rather odd situation whereby the one psychological theorist who is widely used outside academic psychology is generally ignored inside academic psychology (the website for my department used to have a page showing a picture of Freud with a big cross through it accompanied by the legend "this is not psychology").

The key text where Freud develops his ideas on these matters is his 1921 monograph "Massenpsychologie und Ich-Analyse"—usually translated as "Group Psychology and the Analysis of the Ego." Freud's arguments develop out of observations concerning the nature of crowd psychology and, in recent years, this work has been revived and used by theorists such as Ernesto Laclau in order to reconsider the emergence of political identities.[1] At one level, this is to be welcomed. For a long time now, crowds have been treated as the "elephant man of the social sciences" (Reicher, "Psychology" 182): they are seen as a figure of fascination, as something exotic and exceptional. They don't tell us about society because they are the negation of the social, an eruption of atavism into the present. If they are of periodic interest it is only because they constitute an assault upon society. It is gratifying, therefore, to see some contemporary theorists such as Ernesto Laclau beginning to see a wider significance to the crowd, and seeing the study of crowds as a location in which to understand the fundamental nature of the social and political bond.

At the same time, I am bemused by the way in which this work treats Freud's crowd psychology as promising terrain in which to develop general theory. Even if some conceptual critique is allowed, the assumption is that the description of crowd phenomena is accurate. Indeed Laclau explicitly states that "we should distinguish the descriptive validity of the features of mass psychology enumerated by Le Bon from the normative judgements with which those features are associated in his discourse" (*Populist* 24). In this, Laclau echoes Freud, who himself states that, in order to describe the "specially striking and characteristic facts to which our inquiry can be attached" he can do no better than quote from Le Bon's "deservedly famous work *Psychologie des foules* [1895]" (Freud, "Group" 98)—and then proceeds to provide verbatim extracts over the next seventeen pages. Amongst other features, the crowd member is described as "irresponsible" (101), "no longer conscious of his acts" (102), "an automaton who has ceased to be guided by his will" (103), "impulsive, changeable and irritable" (104), "extraordinarily credulous" (104), having "no critical faculty" (104) and "entirely conservative" (106). Putting these together: "by the mere fact that he forms part of an organized group, a man descends several rungs in the ladder of civilization. Isolated, he may be a cultivated individual; in a crowd, he is a barbarian—that is, a creature acting by instinct" (Le Bon qtd. in Freud, "Group" 103–4).

It is worth noting that, in this depiction Le Bon drew heavily on Taine's writing on the French Revolution—to cite just one passage: "from the peasant, the labourer, and the bourgeois . . . we see all of a sudden spring forth the barbarian, and still worse, the primitive animal, the grinning wanton sanguinary baboon, who chuckles while he slays, and gambols over the ruin he has accomplished" (qtd. in Pick 56)—and that Freud too both read and was influenced by Taine's history. He noted that the book "suited him well" (qrd. in Van Ginneken 25). In short, Taine, Le Bon and Freud (and Laclau) all subscribe to a common description of crowd action, even if they adopt different normative stances.

There is just one difficulty with this. The problems with this work are not only normative, they are descriptive as well. To be blunt, the classic account of crowds is quite simply wrong. It is not rooted in close observation or systematic analysis of actual crowds. Rather, it reflects the fears and fantasies of external observers who looked on with horror as crowd members seemed to endanger all they held near and dear. I shall expand on this point in the next section. But, as a taster, consider this famous comment by Freud about the people of Paris:

> They are possessed of a thousand demons: instead of "Monsieur" and "Voila *l'Echo de Paris*," I hear them yelling "A la lanterne," and "A bas" this man and that . . . They are a people given to physical epidemics, historical mass convulsions, and they have not changed since Victor Hugo wrote Notre Dame. (Freud, *Letters* 187–88)

The comment, written in December 1885 to his future sister-in-law, Minna Bernays, may have been designed to amuse her but nonetheless reveals the external gaze through which he—like other early crowd theorists—constituted his understanding of crowds.

Not a science of fantasy, then, but a science based on a fantasy—and that is an altogether different matter. It meant that theorists asked questions, and sought to provide answers, about phenomena which were no more than chimera. And, as Thomas Pynchon pithily observed in his "proverbs for paranoids," if you get people to ask the wrong questions, you don't need to worry about their answers (Pynchon 251). To restate Pynchon's point in relation to the specific concerns of this chapter, a misdescription of crowds is not promising territory on which to base an understanding of the social bond. So, in subsequent sections, I shall seek to substitute a better-grounded analysis of crowd action, of the processes that shape such action, and of what this has to tell us more generally about human sociality. That is, can we use a new crowd psychology to develop an alternative account of the nature of investment? Or rather—since this is an insanely ambitious task in the limited space I have here—can we at least use a critical discussion of crowd psychology in order to raise different ways of thinking about the bases on which we invest in our groups and each other?

In order to create the space for this new crowd psychology, first a ground-clearing exercise is necessary. I need to spend some time addressing the origins and nature of the old psychology, how the two are interlinked and where the problems lie.

CLASSIC CROWD PSYCHOLOGY: LOSING ONESELF IN THE MASS

If you want to find examples of elitist disdain towards the masses, especially the masses assembled in crowds, you will be spoilt for choice. Starting with the father of recorded history, Herodotus (who proclaimed "I hate the blind mass"), virtually every thinker has had something acerbic to say on the matter. My favourite has always been Kierkegaard, who advised that if you want to know what to do, look at the crowd—and then do the opposite.[2] However, crowd psychology only emerged as a field of study in the late nineteenth century, primarily (though not exclusively) in France—that is, at a time and place where the masses had not only entered history but appeared poised to take it over.

Over the course of the nineteenth century, industrialisation created a mass society.[3] Whereas, at the start of the century, the subordinate classes generally lived in small communities under the everyday surveillance of their masters, by the end they were characteristically living in cities, congregated in factories, dwelling in separate neighbourhoods. They were separated both physically and (increasingly) ideologically from their masters. They not only became other, they became an *unknown* other. Venturing into a working-class neighbourhood was, for a gentleman adventurer, almost as exotic and fearful as venturing into darkest Africa. For the elite, each city had its very own heart of darkness.[4] I use this image with Edward Said's comment about the European ruling classes in mind:

> what they saw, disablingly and disparagingly, as a non-European "darkness" was in fact a non-European world resisting imperialism so as one day to regain sovereignty and independence, and not, as Conrad reductively says, to reestablish the darkness. (Said, *Culture* 33)

In exactly the same way, Western elites represented their domestic masses as attacking the very possibility of society rather than contesting an unequal status quo. Issues of domination and exploitation were turned into an issue of social order. The core question became how, in the absence of direct control, the masses could be kept in check. If the mass was an imminent threat to order, the crowd—the mass in action—was that threat made manifest. As a consequence, the crowd became a dense symbol that regrouped just about every other fear of the patriarchal elite. Independent women threaten to destroy the family and society? Well then, the crowd is both metaphorically feminine and the worst crowds, such as the petroleuses of the Paris Commune (more on the Commune soon), are composed of women. Drink is a menace to social discipline? Well, again, crowds are both metaphorically drunk and the worst crowds are inevitably intoxicated.[5] The crowd, then, was the moment the masses would rise up and smash society; it was all one's worst nightmares come true.

All this was true, to some extent, across Western Europe. However, in France the threat of the masses loomed especially large. In France, the mass uprising was not just a possibility, it had happened. The Paris Commune, albeit repressed in the bloodiest manner, had revealed the vulnerability of the French State. The elite had glimpsed the future and they did not like it. Taine and Le Bon were amongst those who had experienced events first hand (Le Bon as chief of ambulance services) and were deeply marked by the experience. Taine saw the uprising as pathological and, accordingly, he initiated a tradition of using a medical discourse of pathology to explain crowd action. Taine bemoaned the vulnerability of the French to collective madness. And he concluded from this that universal suffrage could only be disastrous. These were the concerns that led him to write his histories of France (Van Ginneken 26–33; Nye 23–24).

The Third Republic, which grew on the ashes of the Commune, remained weak, vulnerable and beset on all sides by collective movements: clericalist agitation, the populism of General Boulanger, and, above all, the seemingly ceaseless rise of working-class action. This was the context which spawned "crowd science." These were the phenomena which preoccupied crowd psychologists. Their simple over-riding concern was to counter the collective threat. And if Le Bon came to predominate over all the other contenders—Fournial, Sighele, Tarde, amongst others—it was not so much that he was the most original theorist (he largely synthesised existing ideas) but more that he was the most effective activist (Nye 159–66). His book was brief and punchy, aimed as a primer at right-wing politicians who wished to use crowds against the left. He courted, wined and dined the most prominent reactionaries of his day. In return he received many plaudits. Mussolini claimed to have built the Italian state on the principles of Monsieur Le Bon and the ever-modest Goebbels claimed that, after himself, Le Bon was the man who best understood the crowd mind.[6]

Le Bon proposed that crowd psychology derives from one fundamental negative transformation. When people become an anonymous part of the mass, they lose their individual sense of self. Because of this they likewise lose the norms and values which normally constrain their behaviour. They become incapable of evaluating the various influences that impinge upon them and so they helplessly follow any passing idea or emotion. This is akin to a hypnotic state, a state of extreme suggestibility. These suggestions may come from many places but in particular they derive from the "racial unconscious"—an atavistic residue that lurks beneath our civilised surface. It is because the racial unconscious is primitive, passionate and violent that crowd behaviour is necessarily marked by these characteristics.

As we have already seen, Freud entirely endorses this picture "so impressively described in Le Bon" ("Group" 148). Crowd members, he agrees, do regress to an emotional, suggestible, extreme hypnotic state. His only query lies in locating the source of hypnotic influence: "We cannot avoid being struck with a sense of deficiency when we notice that one of the chief elements of the comparison, namely the person who is to replace the hypnotist in the case of the group, is not mentioned in Le Bon's exposition" (103). In other words, Le Bon fails to place sufficient emphasis on leadership. This, for Freud, is the key to understanding crowds, to understanding the ties that bind members to each other and to the group. It is the key to understanding *investment*. Crowd members, he suggests, have all put a single father-like figure of the leader in the place of their ego ideal. As a consequence they all revere the leader and it is the identical nature of this reverence which links them together. In other words, the vertical and hierarchical subordination to the leader assures the horizontal and egalitarian relationship amongst people in the group. It is certainly true that Freud does temper this view and acknowledges that he might have overplayed the dominance of leaders. But, having acknowledged that things may be somewhat more nuanced, Freud quickly reasserts that, still, dominance is at the root of things: “Many equals, who can identify themselves with one another, and a single person superior to them all—that is the situation that we find realized in groups which are capable of subsisting” (153).

I shall return to this issue of leadership towards the end of the chapter (although along the way I shall point to evidence that casts questions upon the empirical claim that groups need leaders to survive). For now, I want to comment on the validity of the Le Bonian/Freudian depiction of the crowd. The over-riding theme, as we have seen, is one of loss and absence—above all a loss of agency. In crowds, people have lost identity, they have lost control, together they have lost their civilisation. And it is this loss which puts them under the spell of leaders and their words. From Le Bon’s perspective, this is their one saving grace. The canny orator can use the ferocity and power of crowds as an instrument against, rather than for, those forces which challenge the state. The fact that crowds are an empty vessel into which any political substance can be poured thereby becomes an opportunity and not only a crisis—this stance (in practice almost more than in theory) is what differentiated Le Bon from his peers, constituting his genius and producing his success. But, analytically it says no more than that the crowd can be “our” mindless beast rather than “theirs.” It is not to question but rather to underscore the inherent mindlessness, the inherent beastliness, the inherent descent of “man” in the crowd. There is another more foundational absence. Indeed, perhaps the most striking thing about Le Bon’s whole account is more what is not there that what is. Remember that Le Bon was writing about the class struggles of late nineteenth-century France. The events that concerned him were those such as the great miners’ strike at Decazeville in 1886 (Barrows 20–22).

These arose out of *inter*group struggles between workers, owners and the state. More immediately they involved confrontations between company officials, police and (occasionally) militia. However none of this appears in the pages of crowd theory. The crowd appears alone, as if it were fighting nothing, just fighting because its nature is to fight. The patterns of anger one finds in the crowd make no sense at all since one cannot see how they relate to the actions of the other—repressive laws, wage cuts, police charges. Pattern thereby turns into spasm. The crowd is transformed from a social actor into a psychopathic jack-in-the-box which suddenly leaps forth, goes through its violent gyrations and equally suddenly disappears.

Hence classic crowd psychology repeats the same ideological operation as its parent body, mass society theory. By removing the "establishment" from view (and hence from scrutiny), it represents the pursuit of an alternative to an unfair and unjust society as both anti-social and asocial action. It represents action which violates dominant limits on acceptability and civility as action which is purely irrational and unlimited. It represents the behaviours of those who act in terms of a politicised subject position (as miners, as workers, as citizens) as the behaviours of those who have lost all subjectivity.

At a political level, this delivers a substantial pay-off. First, it denies voice to the crowd: the critiques and demands of the masses can be dismissed as no more than the babblings of a mad creature. Second, it denies responsibility for conflict: violence inheres in the very nature of the crowd, it doesn't derive from the intransigence of the elite or the brutality of their forces. Third, it legitimates repression: if the crowd is inherently violent it cannot be reasoned with, it can only be cowed through force.[7]

At a theoretical level, however, there is a substantial cost. The political act of desocialising the crowd context leads to a desocialised description of crowd action underpinned by a desocialised conception of the psychological subject. The only basis of controlled action is the isolated individual with an individual identity. Put the individual in the crowd, you take away this identity. Take away this identity and you take away control. You are left with a psychological void and with social chaos. Now, of course there is space to develop the notion of the "racial unconscious"—or the "unconscious" more generally—in order to try and re-establish links between people and constraints upon their behaviour. However all this work is consequent upon subscribing to the notion of original loss and chaos. Dispense with this idea—a profoundly ideological notion that involves a profoundly misleading view of how people are in crowds—and all the work done repairing the damage becomes redundant. In other words, if you are looking to get to a comprehension of the social bond, don't start from Le Bon. If you want to analyse human sociality, don't begin with a fundamentally desocialised account of our outer and inner worlds. If you aim to understand the political subject, don't be led by a politics which denies subjectivity to those you study. Let us start instead by actually looking at crowds.

ON THE PATTERN OF CROWD ACTION

There is a strong case to be made that, of all the crowds in history, the single most significant event was the St. Bartholemew Day's massacre of 1572—the culmination of a long series of religious conflicts. This is the event that generated the great expulsion of Protestants from France, that founded the modern French nation, and that generated the revolution and was thereby critical to the foundation of modernity itself.[8] Perphaps that may be taking things to extremes, but it certainly was a very bloody event and, at first glance, an event that seems to confirm Le Bonian prejudices about crowds.[9] Catholics murdered Protestants. They ripped open the dead bodies and pulled out the entrails; they hacked off the heads and the genitalia; corpses were burned, thrown into the river, thrown to the dogs. Protestants also murdered Catholics and they also committed outrages beyond murder. They used holy oil from Catholic churches to clean their boots; they smeared excrement on holy vestments; they fouled the holy water.

These are brutal acts. But they are not random acts. There is a clear patterning to what took place. The pattern was different for Catholics and Protestants. What is more, in each case, the pattern makes sense when viewed from the perspective of the respective groups. To repeat, these were religious riots, riots about proper practice and about heresy. For Catholics, heresy lay in the body of the Protestants and so the body itself was desecrated. For Protestants, heresy was centred more on the rites of Catholicism—the "demonic mass." So, in their case, the objects of ritual became targets for desecration. In each case, albeit in the most horrific way, we see collective beliefs enacted and inscribed on the designated target. To cite Barbara Diefendorf, who herself is drawing on Natalie Davis's seminal analysis of this ritualised violence:

> the "rites of violence" enacted here did not spring up from the collective unconscious, where they had been buried since the dawn of time, but rather "were drawn from a store of punitive or purificatory traditions current in sixteenth century France." (Diefendorf 103; Davis)

Taking even the most extreme, bloody and apparently Le Bonian of events, then, one soon finds a very different picture once one looks more closely. Time and time again, different historians studying different events come up with the same conclusion. Crowd events are not inchoate explosions. What seems like meaningless or random action viewed from the outside becomes comprehensible when analysed from the perspective of participants.

This is true even of the most visceral and basic of events—those where one might think simple biology would trump ideology. I refer to food riots. Surely people just get hungry, get desperate, get angry and seize what grain or bread that they can from the stores? But no. E. P. Thompson has analysed the approximately 700 food riots that occurred in England between 1750 and 1820. He shows, first, that they didn't happen at times of greatest dearth but characteristically when grain supplies were increasing. Second, they were generally initiated by specific events, notably the transport of grain out of the locality. Third, the "riots" were far from inchoate: grain was seized, sold at a "popular" price, the money and often the grain sacks were handed back to the merchants. Thompson shows that the riots were based on the clash between two "moral economies": a traditional view of rights and obligations based on the locality where there was a requirement to meet local needs when resources were available versus an emergent market morality where goods are taken to wherever they can command the best price. These two conceptions came into conflict at the moment when grain was transported. Hence, both the onset and the unfolding sequence of crowd actions were governed by long-standing shared social beliefs. In Thompson's own words: "What is remarkable about these 'insurrections' is, first, their discipline, and second, the fact that they exhibit a pattern of behaviour for whose origin we must look back several hundreds of years" ("Moral Economy" 108). William Reddy, another student of food riots, in France this time, also found discipline, pattern and collective belief all intertwined. His conclusion can stand as a conclusion about riots in general: "the targets of these crowds thus glitter in the eye of history as signs of the labourers' conception of the nature of society" (Reddy 84)—just omit the word "these" and substitute "participants" for "labourers."

There is one more point to be made from these historical studies, and a key point at that. It relates to the issue of leadership. In both religious riots and food riots—indeed almost whenever a riot occurs—it is regularly argued that agitators are to blame. Either overtly, or as a "hidden hand" someone is guiding events. Sometimes, indeed, crowds do have leaders. But not always. And the supposition that they must is more a reflection of political prejudices than of historical evidence. It flows from the assumption that crowds are mindless. Hence, on the one hand, they attract agitators like bees to honey. On the other, any evidence of directed action must be traceable to a director.[10] Thompson insists that food riots did not need and did not have leaders because they knew how to act together. Occasionally crowd members did kidnap a magistrate or some other dignitary in order to give their acts a greater semblance of legitimacy, but here the apparent leaders were more puppets than puppeteers. Again, Reddy reinforces Thompson's message. He recounts how, following one particular event, "The interrogator (as always) was seeking leaders, searching for a structure, a cabal that could be identified and punished; but there was none" (83). The woman under interrogation, however, would have none of it: people assembled, they acted, no-one told them to come or what to do: "It was the *lack* of organization that she chose to throw in the face of her social betters. What could be more threatening? Surely only a just grievance could bring so many together without planning?" (83).

All this raises an intriguing set of questions—but they are questions that are diametrically opposed to those which framed the old crowd psychology. Far from trying to explain why behaviour is mindless and emotional, impulsive and credulous, primitive and irresponsible, our task is to understand how people can act together in ways that are patterned and culturally meaningful, and how they can do so even in the absence of any organisation or formal leadership. That is, our task is to understand the *spontaneous sociality* (not the desocialisation) of crowd action. It is precisely because of this sociality—rather than its absence—that crowds are such a promising site for understanding the social bond. But, in order to get a handle on these issues, these new questions demand a new crowd psychology.

A SOCIAL IDENTITY MODEL OF CROWDS: BECOMING THE SUBJECTS OF HISTORY

There is an issue I have been tip-toeing around for a while. It is time to address it explicitly. In all this talk of crowds, what exactly do we mean by a crowd? The classic crowd psychologists never really confront this question. But, implicitly at least, Le Bon and his contemporaries seem to have something physical in mind. The entry into crowd psychology is the experience of becoming a small and anonymous element submerged in a substantial whole. Hence the psychological and physical aspects of the mass are conflated. A crowd is a gathering of people that is big enough for people to become submerged—even if "big enough" is hard to pin down to an exact number.

But this conflation is problematic—and to illustrate the problem consider an experience that will be painfully familiar to British readers and, hopefully, comprehensible to others. You are in a densely packed compartment on a train. You are certainly part of a physical mass of people. But, psychologically, you remain separate from everyone else. You turn away from them. You avoid eye contact. You may be reading the same paper as everyone else but you would neither look at theirs nor countenance anyone looking at yours. And sensuous contact—if someone presses into you or even brushes against you—is experienced with a shudder. Then the train stops. It stays stopped. After a seemingly interminable delay a voice comes over the loudspeaker and makes some unconvincing excuse. Leaves on the line. The wrong type of snow. That sort of thing. Now things change. People start to turn towards each other. They start to talk. They start to smile and laugh. They might even (and remember, they are British) consider sharing their sandwiches. Because now, a mental shift has occurred. Nothing has changed physically, but psychologically, people stop thinking of themselves as distinct individuals and start to think of themselves in terms of what they have in common—as commuters in contrast to the train company.

As the example suggests, a physical gathering is not the same as a psychological crowd. A gathering may contain no psychological crowds, it may constitute a psychological crowd or even several psychological crowds (if, say, fans of different football teams were travelling in the carriage). The example also points to the transformations that occur when people form part of a crowd. There are three such transformations which I shall consider in turn.

1. *A cognitive transformation*: The key transformation that takes place when people become crowd members is that they shift from thinking of themselves in terms of *personal identity* to thinking of themselves in terms of *social identity*. This distinction is central to the social identity tradition

which, over the last quarter century, has become the dominant approach to group phenomena in social psychology.[11] According to this view, the self is not unitary, it is a complex system defined at different levels of abstraction and at different times, in different places, different elements of the system may be salient. Sometimes we define ourselves in terms of what makes us unique compared to other individuals ("I" vs. "you"). This is personal identity. At other times we define ourselves in terms of what makes a group membership unique compared to other group memberships ("we" vs. "they"). This is social identity. Moreover, we all have various social identities (I am simultaneously a man, an academic, British, a socialist, a Tottenham Hotspurs fan—and that's probably enough revelations for now) which themselves become salient in different contexts.

Now, just as crowd membership entails a shift in identity rather than a loss of identity, so it also leads to a shift in the bases of behavioural control rather than a loss of behavioural control. Insofar as people define themselves on the collective level, the things that matter to them are likewise to be defined on the group level in at least two senses. On the one hand, the well-being of the group becomes their well-being, the fate of the group their fate. Accordingly events are evaluated and responded to on the basis of what they mean for the group. A good for the group is a good for the (collective) self and embraced as such, just as harm to the group is harm to the self and rejected as such. On the other hand, the definition of good and bad is a function of collective values, norms and priorities. These determine the goals we pursue and the outcomes we seek to avoid. One implication of this is that for different crowds—and even the same person in different crowd contexts—different things matter. As an academic, writing or lecturing, I strive to be seen as reasoned, as a dispassionate seeker of truth, as rooting arguments in evidence. As a football fan, I strive to be passionate, loyal and committed. I am most unlikely, as a Tottenham fan, watching a game against our old rivals Arsenal, to declare "well, to be fair Arsenal are better than us and the referee was quite right to turn down our penalty appeal."

All this can be summarised by saying that, in the crowd, the "self'" of "self-interest" changes. People become neither more nor less rational—indeed rationality isn't the issue. Rather, the issue concerns the grounds of interested action. These are transformed to the collective level. As a consequence behaviour becomes more socially meaningful because it reflects a social meaning system—social identity. That explains the patterning that I have noted in historical studies of crowds. Our own contemporary studies of crowds—urban uprisings, student demonstrations, football crowds, environmental protests, amongst others—allow us to go a step further and show: (a) how people construe themselves and their social relations in terms of social identities, (b) how their behaviour has clear limits and shape, and (c) how that shape is intelligible in relation to the ways that participants define their collective selves. Certainly each crowd has a different social identity with a set of understandings and meanings. Certainly each crowd behaves differently with different limits to what they will do. But equally certainly, there is a consistent relationship between these two across the range of crowd events.[12]

2. *A relational transformation*: When people form a psychological crowd, when they redefine themselves such that common category members stop being "other" and become part of one's collective self, then there is a fundamental shift towards intimacy and solidarity in our social relations. There are two aspects to this. First, those who share a common identity expect to agree with each other, they seek out agreement with each other, they trust and respect each other.[13] All in all, they share a common perspective on the world and see their experience as shared by others. In short, their views are validated by others. This is particularly powerful for those immersed in the middle of a crowd. They are surrounded by others who chant the chants they chant, carry banners and slogans that are their slogans, even look, dress and smell like they do. Their sensuous universe is one that affirms their take on social reality.

Moving on to the second aspect of relational transformations in the crowd, consider the following experimental study.[14] Manchester United football fans are recruited for an experiment. On arriving they are told that the study concerns their club support and they are asked to walk to another building where the research will take place. On the way, they see someone run along, fall over and clutch their leg in pain. This person is either wearing a Manchester United shirt, a Liverpool shirt (Liverpool are the big rival team) or a plain red t-shirt. In the first case people help. In the other two cases they don't. Then we do the study again. All is identical except for one thing. We don't tell the Manchester United fans that we are studying them as *club* fans but as *football* fans. In this case they help someone when he is wearing either the Manchester United or the Liverpool shirt, but not when he is wearing the plain t-shirt. The study shows that people are more likely to help people when they are ingroup members and that the more inclusive the category, the more people they will help.

The study might seem a rather flimsy foundation for such a weighty conclusion about the categorical basis of social solidarity. So now consider two rather more significant examples. In his pamphlet "The ABC of National Socialism," Goebbels asks the question "what is the first commandment of every national socialist?" He replies: "Love Germany above all else and your ethnic comrade [Volksgenosse] as yourself" (qtd. in Koonz 7). Solidarity within the group, then, but the group is defined in ethnic terms such that this solidarity does not extend to "outsiders" such as Jews and Gypsies. We know their fate under the Nazis. However the fate of the Jews was not the same in all areas under Nazi influence. The most remarkable instance comes from Bulgaria. Twice the Nazis tried to deport the Jewish population. Twice they were thwarted by popular mobilisations. In the end, not a single Jew from the lands of old Bulgaria was deported to the death camps. When we examine the arguments used to mobilise solidarity,[15] we find that the word "Jew" is rarely used—the issue is about defending a national minority. Or, if "Jews" are referred to, it is to make an explicit case for their ingroup status. To cite Todor Polyakov, speaking to the National Assembly in December 1940:

> Bulgaria's Jews . . . speak and think in Bulgarian, have fashioned their style of thinking and their feelings after Botev, Vazov, Pencho, Slaveikov, Yavorov [Bulgarian cultural icons] etc. They sing Bulgarian songs and tell Bulgarian stories. Their private selves are modelled on ours—in the street, on our playing fields, at school, in the barracks, in workshops and factories, in the mountains and the fields, our sufferings are their sufferings, our joys their joys too. (qtd. in Todorov 65–66)

Here, the categories are more inclusive; Jews form part of the national ingroup and hence are the deserving recipients of national solidarity.

As with processes of validation, there is evidence that such mutual support operates especially strongly in crowds. People routinely help each other in a thousand small acts of civility: not pushing and shoving, sharing food and drink, giving precedence to those who need it. But they can also put themselves at serious risk to help others—often strangers—whom they see as ingroup members. For instance on several occasions we have found instances where people wrestle with the police to stop fellow protestors from getting arrested—thereby putting themselves in danger of arrest. When asked, they had no personal connection to those they helped. And though, in retrospect and on reflection, they found their own actions surprising, it seemed self-evidently the right thing to do during the event.[16]

Putting all this together, the transformation of social relations in the crowd creates the conditions for effective coordinated action. People, both metaphorically and literally, align themselves and aim their efforts in the same direction. Their actions begin to complement and supplement each other rather than work against each other and cancel each other out. Rather than feeling isolated under the surveillance of the police and other authorities, they feel united in relation to these authorities. To revise Foucault's famous image of the panopticon as the paradigm of power in our society—authority in the centre gazing on a population round the circumference, each separated from the other—it is as if the barriers between people are broken down so that they gaze on (and recognise the commonality of) others. Instead of all having an individualised experience of one on one with authority, they have a collective experience of fifty or a hundred or a thousand on one. They therefore feel empowered to enact *their* collective values and beliefs irrespective of the resistance they might experience from the guardians of the status quo. Crowd members feel empowered to act on their own terms (Drury and Reicher, "Intergroup").

3. *An affective transformation*: In a partial sense, Taine, Le Bon and Freud were clearly right. Crowds are indeed passionate affairs. People

express strong emotions in crowds, whether of joy, of anger, of hate. Watch fans when a critical goal is scored. Watch the images of waiting crowds when a paedophile is taken into court. Watch the brutality with which anti-capitalist demonstrators assault the police (and vice versa) at a G8 summit. I have no quarrel with the classic emphasis on the affective dimension of crowd events. Where my quarrel lies is in the way that heightened emotion is taken as a token of diminished reason and as a sign that both identity and control has been lost.

My argument is that the three transformations of crowd psychology are integrally interlinked. First, social identity provides crowd members with a perspective on how the world is and how the world should be. Second, a sense of *shared* social identity produces (a) a validation of this perspective and (b) the solidarity (and hence the social power) to implement their perspective. Each of these outcomes is crucial, so let us dwell on them a little longer in order to understand how and why they might make people passionate about their groups.

To understand the importance of validation it is important to understand that both the human advantage and the human predicament flow from the fact that we stand in a mediated relationship with social reality.[17] That is, we do not react directly to stimuli. Rather, we interpret the meaning of events by reference to representational models of reality and we consider the implications of different courses of action upon social reality. The great advantage of being thus disembedded from the present is that we can plan how to create our future—how to create a social world that fits us rather than we fitting it. Yet simultaneously, our predicament is that the way we see the world is necessarily uncertain. We live in a state of chronic contingency. In our everyday lives our perspective is constantly open to challenge and disconfirmation by others. Our views, if expressed, are liable to meet with the disagreement or even the disapproval of our peers. But in the crowd this contingency is removed by certainty. As I have already intimated, we can shout slogans, show rage or express joy, confident that others will understand us and join in with us. Critically, then, our understanding of the social world and our position in it is confirmed. For a while, at least, our social being is beyond doubt.

Add to this solidarity and social power, and people don't just have a clear perspective on the world. They are able to implement that perspective. They are able, collectively, to make their own social worlds. This is a point that the great historian of the French Revolution, Georges Lefebvre made long ago. Perhaps it is only in the crowd, he said, that people cast off their petty day-to-day concerns and become the subjects of history (Lefebvre 271–87). *So, far from people losing agency in the crowd, the crowd is one of the few occasions where people gain agency.* Validation and solidarity: social being and agency. It is the connection between these two pairs of factors which makes crowds such passionate affairs and which makes people become so attached to the groups that these crowds represent.[18]

Take one small illustration of this. A while ago I had members of a class I was teaching participate in some crowd event and then come back and talk about it. Many of them attended the massive "Make Poverty History" demonstration which coincided with the G8 summit held in Scotland in July 2007. They came back exhilarated. When I asked them what was exhilarating they said for the first time in their lives they were telling Governments how things should be rather than the reverse. They were not only speaking truth to power, they were instructing power on the truth. Or at least they felt they were. And while the belief that one is involved in making history is exhilarating in itself, another aspect of this phenomenon is the actual experience, within the collective event itself, of creating a social reality that implements core collective values and beliefs. John Drury and I term this "collective self-objectification" and we show how it is associated not only with immediate joy but also with more enduring well-being.[19]

All in all, the emotionality of crowds derives from rather than negates the socially meaningful nature of crowd action. Emotion and reason are not locked into a zero-sum game. Rather, the more meaningful the action and the more cohesive the crowd, the more powerful the emotions, whether they be joy at implementing the collective vision or anger at those who thwart such implementation. But that is another story for another time.[20] For now, it is time to draw the threads of my argument together and to make some preliminary conclusions concerning what we can learn from crowd psychology to help us understand the nature of psychic investment in general.

CONCLUSIONS: ROOTING INVESTMENT IN SOCIAL BEING

At the start of this chapter, I expressed some dismay at the attempt to root an understanding of collective investment in classic models of crowd psychology. By now, the reason for my concern is, hopefully, self-evident. These models all start from the assumption that conscious social being and agency are obliterated at the moment of entry into a crowd. It follows that one must look elsewhere—notably to the unconscious processes that fill the gap—in order to understand crowd behaviour and relationships amongst crowd members. Yet the starting assumption is wrong. Classic investigations of crowd sociality rule out the most powerful and promising lines of enquiry right from the start. In arguing that the transformations of crowd psychology consolidate rather than obliterate social being and agency, I am thereby reintroducing them as candidates for the explanation of our attachments in the crowd and to the crowd.

My argument, building on the social identity tradition in social psychology, can be encapsulated as follows. The social bond derives from the cognitive act of social identification (Turner)—of defining oneself in terms of a social category membership. By this act, fellow group members cease being other and become part of one's collective self. The bond, then, is not a matter of connecting different selves but rather of including others within the self. Or, to put it differently, the support and care deriving from the bond is not a matter of self-abnegation but rather of self-extension. This extension applies not only to the self *per se* but also to every "self" related term: self esteem relates to the standing of the group not the individual and hence the achievements of other members become one's own achievements, a matter of pride rather than jealousy; self-efficacy equally relates to the effectiveness of the group; most importantly self-interest, and calculations of self-interest, have to do with whether the group thrives in terms of achieving group goals and realising group values.

This approach differs from the Freudian account in three critical ways. First, identification is a conscious commitment. People are aware of the act of identification and of what it entails in terms of a commitment to particular norms, values and beliefs. Second, the link to others is primarily horizontal. As in any "imagined community," to use Benedict Anderson's term, we are all equal in terms of our membership of the group. This is not to say that hierarchy may not emerge in the group (I will deal with that shortly) but rather that it has to be actively built and legitimated against a default position of equality. Third, passion is not located in the nature of the bond *per se* but rather derives from the consequences of this bond in terms of the achievement of agency and social being.

One way of illustrating this difference is to return, as promised, to the issue of leadership which, for Freud, is the key to crowd psychology. I have already provided historical evidence that crowds do not necessarily need leaders. The social identity approach also provides an explanation of why this need not be the case: crowds can cohere perfectly well without formal leadership insofar as they share a common understanding of who they are, the nature of their world, and what they are about. However, this is not to say that leadership is unimportant. It can be extremely important and indeed social identity researchers have devoted much attention to the matter in recent years.[21] Unlike much traditional research in the area, leadership in this model is seen as a social relationship between leaders and followers rather than simply a set of qualities that inhere in particular chosen individuals—this is much like Freud. However, in contradistinction to Freud, social identity researchers view leadership as a relationship between leaders and followers *within* a social category. Or, to quote S. Alexander Haslam, leadership

> is a process of mutual influence that revolves around a partnership in a social self-categorical relationship. It is about the creation, co-ordination and control of a shared sense of "us." Within this relationship neither the individual nor the group is static. What "us" means is negotiable, and so too is the contribution that leaders and followers make to any particular definition of us-ness. (Haslam 85)

Leaders, then, need to be seen as representing the norms and values of the group—in the language of the social identity tradition, they must be prototypical of the groups they seek to influence. Moreover, even then, they cannot get people to do what they like. They are constrained by the fact that their messages must, likewise, be seen to encapsulate the group perspective. That is, it must be consonant with the norms, beliefs priorities of the relevant social identity. This idea is encapsulated in the well-known dictum, attributed to everyone from Ledru-Rollin to Gandhi: "I am their leader, I must follow them."

Many years ago—in 1986 when I was only just becoming interested in the study of leadership—these ideas were vividly illustrated to me. I was in Trafalgar Square at the culmination of an Anti-Apartheid demonstration. The struggle in South Africa was re-igniting and the numbers were far higher than expected. So people were squeezed into the Square, many pushing up against police lines outside the South African Embassy on the west side. Scuffles began. It looked like widespread fighting was about to begin. On the stage Jesse Jackson, the leading black civil rights activist of the day, was speaking. He quickly departed from his prepared text and told the crowd that those involved in conflict were acting as agents of Apartheid. They would silence the message of the demonstration and ensure that the next day's headlines would only talk of violence. He appealed to crowd members to hold hands and chant the slogan of the movement, "Free Nelson Mandela." Jackson was entirely successful in redefining peaceful action as appropriate for the ingroup (and violent action as an asset to the outgroup). But, as he tried to move back to his text, he was silenced as waves of chanting—"Free Mandela," "Free Mandela"—echoed back through the crowd and smothered his words. The voice of the collective ultimately took precedence over that of any individual speaker, however prominent, however eloquent, however prototypical.

Leaders, then, can be seen as "entrepreneurs of identity" (Reicher and Hopkins 49). They are effective to the extent that they are seen as telling the crowd, not what they believe, but rather the implications of what crowd members believe for what they should do. This is, of course, an interpretative and creative activity, which is why the skilful leader has considerable autonomy in representing his or her own policies and proposals as the realisation of collective identities. But, as I have already argued, it is generally an activity in which the group audience are equally involved in interpreting the relationship between proposals and identities. Leadership is a mutual conversation.

Nonetheless there are times when this leadership can be skewed or even totally distorted. In extreme cases, the leader is no longer an interpreter of identity; rather, he or she becomes positioned as the actual living embodiment of the category: a God more than a prophet or a simple spokesperson. At that point the voice of the leader is by definition the voice of the group and anyone who even questions the leader *ipso facto* is attacking the group.

At that point a primarily horizontal relationship becomes a strictly vertical relationship. That was the position achieved by Stalin and by Hitler.[22] But the important thing to note is that this is a rare extreme that results from a long and intensive process of ideological construction and political repression. As Goebbels once boasted, the Hitler myth was his finest achievement (Kershaw 4). To ignore what is involved, to see these atypical extremes as the virgin state of leadership, is therefore to misunderstand both leadership itself, the bonds from which it arises and the constraint under which it operates.

To conclude, then, let me reprise a quotation which I used earlier to criticise Freud, but now, at a different level, I want to use in his favour. If you get people asking the wrong questions, you don't need to worry about the answers. As a corollary, however, if you get people asking the *right* questions, you provide an invaluable service irrespective of your answers. And, in raising the question of investment in groups—of the passionate attachment that people feel to those categories through which they define themselves—Freud provided just such a service. No wonder that so many in the humanities and the social sciences turn to Freud when they see no-one else really addressing this issue in the world of academic psychology. However distorted, his, after all, is the only voice in town. In response, it is not enough for academic psychologists to bemoan Freud's popularity and carp at his failings. Rather, it is incumbent upon us to produce an alternative and more satisfying explanation of group investment. As it was said during the French Revolution (or at least so I once heard from a speaker defending his theory from attack—and the phrase has amused me ever since), don't tear things down unless you have something better to build in their place.[23]

To sum up: Freud asks the right questions about investment in groups but gives the wrong answer. His error derives from an erroneous account of crowd action. Therefore a more satisfactory account of crowd psychology is the obvious place in which to produce a more satisfactory account of investment and the nature of social bonds. Such an account involves turning round the classic assumption that crowd members lose identity and become automatons. In crowds people gain social identity and this allows them to gain social agency. My contention is that our passion for the group is not to be understood through the prism of the unconscious, of libido and of *individual* being, but rather through the triad of social identity, collective practice and *social* being.

NOTES

1. See, for instance, Laclau, *Populist* and "Populism."
2. For a compilation of such comments, see Riewald.
3. See Giner; also Stedman Jones.
4. See Emler and Reicher; also Chevalier.
5. For a wonderful analysis of late nineteenth-century visions of the crowd see Barrows.

6. Nye 178; Moscovici 92–95; Frankfurt Institute 77.
7. For a powerful expression of these views, see Trotter. For a more extended critique, see Reicher and Potter.
8. Anthony Marx also suggests that "it is the day in which the infant nation of France was born, bound in blood" (A. Marx 89).
9. Indeed many accounts of the massacre do use Le Bonian terms to describe and explain it. See, for instance, Garrisson.
10. See Reicher and Potter; also Reicher, "St. Pauls."
11. For social identity, see Tajfel or Tajfel and Turner. For self-categorisation theory, see Turner, Hogg, Oakes, Reicher, et al. For a recent summary of work in both areas, see Reicher, Spears, and Haslam.
12. For urban uprisings, see Reicher, "St. Pauls"; for student demonstrations, see Reicher, "Battle"; for football crowds, see Stott and Reicher; for environmental protests, see Drury and Reicher, "Collective Action."
13. For a review of this evidence, see Reicher and Haslam.
14. See Levine, Prosser, Evans, and Reicher.
15. For the texts, see Todorov. For an analysis of these texts, see Reicher, Cassidy, Wolpert, et al.
16. See, for instance, Reicher, "Battle," or Stott and Drury.
17. For a more extended outline of this argument see Reicher, "Making."
18. These are key factors, but perhaps not the only factors involved. See Prayag Magh Mela Research Group.
19. See Drury and Reicher, "Intergroup," and Drury and Reicher, "Collective Psychological." See also Reicher and Haslam, and Reicher, Spears, and Haslam.
20. For some thoughts on these matters, however, see Reicher, Haslam, and Rath.
21. See, for instance, Haslam, Reicher, and Platow. See also Reicher, Haslam, and Hopkins.
22. See, for instance, Overy.
23. Note that, in this paper, my aim is to address not Freud's more general account of psychic investment, but rather the dangers of a simple extrapolation from his individual psychology to a social psychology and the use of such a reductionistic social psychology by other social scientists.

5 "A Swinish Multitude" versus "A Crowd of Golden Daffodils"

Jina Politi

GENESIS OF THE BEAST

The inaugural moment which fissures the cohesive representation of the social, by introducing into the dramatic structure the oppositions public/private, individual/mass, is marked by Euripides' *Orestes*. Here, for the first time in Greek tragedy, the heavy gates of the palace open to admit the spectators into the privacy of its interior spaces—"εν δόμοις"—where they see Orestes crouched in bed undergoing his paranoid fits, Electra sitting by him tending him tenderly. The image of a tightly knit community, whereby protagonists and Chorus shared in common the unfolding of the tragic events in the public space before the palace, seems to be a thing of the past.[1] The universality of the mythical narrative is here being reduced to a personal matter. Now, beside the Chorus, a large, noisy multitude has assembled offstage and is being urged by the mob orators of the Argive council to decide on the future punishment of the mother-killers. Euripides, as C. W. Willink notes, is the first to introduce into drama the theme of "the bad demagogue" who tries to seduce by wily words the irrational multitude (Willink 231).

Thus, Talthybius, who is a mere instrument of those in power, adopts a "trimming tone" and proposes death. The crowd assents, yet when prince Diomedes "makes harangue" proposing exile, the crowd stands divided: "some murmur their assent . . . others disapprove." Next, a fellow "with a pleasant trick of speech but of unsound principles," "one whose impudence [was] his strength," following the directions of Tyndareus, father of Clytemnestra, urges that the guilty should be stoned to death. When an honest yeoman moves that Orestes should instead be crowned for avenging the murder of his father, "only the better sort are convinced by his words." Finally, the villain who spoke in favour of stoning Orestes and Electra gains his point "by appealing to the mob" (Euripides, *Orestes* 139–41).

In contrast to the Chorus, the main psychological characteristics which distinguish the multitude are: lack of judgment, manipulation by the rhetoric of and identification with the wily demagogue, adoption of contradictory positions, unruly passion and a misdirected sense of power. Unknowingly, the "mass" functions as an instrument to further the interests of those in power.

This prototypical representation of the multitude, which persisted throughout the centuries and up to our own times, seems to have marked indelibly the social imaginary. For, by not taking into account social transformations, it erroneously conceived "the fundamental psychical forces as destined to remain essentially unchangeable in all epochs . . . in an unhistorical manner, like other natural forces." The fact that "the psychical and physical elements that determine the constitution of human nature are an integral part of historical reality" was totally ignored (Horkheimer 36–38).[2] Hence, the question was seldom raised as to whether these representations of the multitude reflected the dominant ideology, whether the dramatist himself assumed the discourse of the demagogue and tried, from his position of power, to manipulate the affect of his audience, as well as whether these very representations were based on passional rather than on rational grounds. This persisted even when the "mass" became, in the late nineteenth century, a theoretical object of sociological and psychological investigation.

Yet, in contrast to this unhistorical position perpetuated by social and political theory, literature in its discursive representations was the first to take into consideration the fact that "masses" were products of specific historical moments marked by social transformations. Shakespeare, in *Coriolanus*, redefined the "mass" as a political collectivity united by common interests as against those who held rule. The play is said to have been written around 1608–9. As Philip Brockbank observes, "many points of contact have been alleged between the political concerns of the play, and events and attitudes in the first decade of the century." For,

> although the corn riots were taken by Shakespeare from Plutarch . . . food shortages in the towns and peasant discontents in the country were commonplace both in Elizabeth's reign and James's, owing to the displacement of tillage by pasture and to the widespread enclosure of common land. Among the several insurrections, particular attention has been drawn to the . . . Midlands disturbances of 1607–8. (Brockbank 26)

Here, it is interesting to compare the degree of "veracity" characterising the literary and the historical text. In referring to the Midlands Revolt, the historian J. P. Kenyon, in *Stuart England*, simply observes: "when the lower classes were helpless victims of the least climatic fluctuation . . . they cannot be blamed for absorbing the chiliastic ideas put forward by unlicensed, independent preachers" (16).

Thus, though Shakespeare's play is set in Roman times, it seems to parallel the political situation and the political actors of the time.[3] Significantly, in addressing the crowd, one of the Roman citizens voices a seditious speech reminiscent of Shakespeare's times: "They ne'er cared for us yet. Suffer us to famish, and their storehouses crammed with grain; make edicts for usury, to support usurers; repeal daily any wholesome act established against the rich, and provide more piercing statutes daily, to chain up and restrain the poor" (Shakespeare, *Coriolanus* 100). It was to counter such seditious discourses that Thomas Lodge, in his *Wits Miserie, and the Worlds Madnesse* (1596), refers to the agitator as the one who in the country "storms and railes, against inclosures, telling the husbandmen that the pleasure of their Lords, eates away the fat from their fingers; and these rackt rents . . . are the utter ruin of the yeomanrie of England: the conclusion of his talke always is insurrection, and commotion" (K. Muir 107).

In contrast to the situation in *Orestes*, here the dramatic conflict directly arises between the mass and the ego of an individual in power: Coriolanus. Yet this "individual," as the other of the "mass," does not conform to the rational image which was to be constructed in the centuries to come. For, Coriolanus' actions and reactions spring from the same unruly, elemental passions of soul as those of the mass. Consequently, the dramatic confrontation between the two agents of the opposition is not *agonistic* but fiercely *antagonistic*. What should be noted is that the abusive representations of "the many headed multitude" (180) materialise in the play mainly through Coriolanus' gaze.

One could perhaps hazard the observation that Shakespeare's Roman plays seem to herald the civil war that was to break out forty years later. One thing, however, is certain: that the *we* and the *they*, as emerging political identities in struggle, have marked literature and history ever since.

BEASTLY PASSIONS/NOBLE SENTIMENTS

The traumatic moment marking the repression of the revolutionary passion known as "enthusiasm," which had turned the world upside down in the 1640s in England, was already under way during Cromwell's sway, and was fully repressed when the monarchy was restored again in 1660. For over a century, what followed this repression was a fascinating ideological process of discursive sublimations aiming to transform the elemental passions of the soul into the higher, soft sentiments proper to a civilised society. For "the progress of society" and the grand narrative attendant on its ascending stages entailed a significant revision in the taxonomy of human passions, which now came to reflect the vertical order of class and race distinctions: the elemental, uncivilised passions were found to lodge in the collective body known as "the mass" and the inferior races, the soft, rational, civilised, sentiments in the individual members of the genteel classes of the western world. As the OED informs us, it was in 1713 that the "mass" came to be defined as "an aggregate in which individuality is lost" (*Shorter Oxford English Dictionary* II, 1285).

In his *Theory of Moral Sentiments* (1759), Adam Smith wrote: "The amiable virtue of humanity requires surely a sensibility much beyond what is possessed by the rude vulgar of mankind . . . and a self-command which astonishes by its amazing superiority over the most ungovernable passions of human nature" (28). Thus, the rise of capitalism also announced the birth of the sensible, restrained "individual." Yet, as William Godwin observed in his *Enquiry Concerning Political Justice* (1793): "Philosophers to this hour dispute whether human beings in their most virtuous exertions are under the power of disinterested benevolence, or merely of an enlightened self-interest" (124). Albert Hirschman, in *The Passions and the Interests* (1977), pointed the way towards the end of this dispute by entitling the First Part of his seminal study: "How interests were called in to neutralise the passions." The construction of the sociopolitical opposition *rational individual/irrational mass* has dominated western thought ever since.

Meanwhile, the repressed passion of collective "enthusiasm" lay in wait. The hegemonic defence mechanism was destined to collapse and the regressive symptoms to erupt once more towards the end of the eighteenth century: the outbreak of the French Revolution clamorously announced the return of the repressed. Edmund Burke, in his famous *Reflections on the Revolution in France* (1790), hastened to declare: "a perfect democracy . . . is the most shameless thing in the world. As it is the most shameless, it is also the most fearless." For the multitude now requires of state officials an "abject submission to their occasional will," while it gives itself up as prey "to the servile ambition of popular sycophants" (191).

According to Burke, the "multitude" violates the physical and moral disposition of things, to which man must be obedient by consent or force. The multitude, by turning necessity into an object of choice, breaks the law, disobeys nature and is "exiled from this world of reason and order and peace and virtue, and fruitful penitence, into the antagonist world of madness, discord, vice, confusion and unavailing sorrow" (195). Alas, the return of the repressed, in the guise of Jacobinism, was now leading England to the loss of the old fundamental principles, and "learning along with its natural protectors and guardians," the aristocracy and the clergy, was being "cast into the mire and trodden down under the hoofs of *a swinish multitude*" (173).

The "swinish multitude" was quick to respond. The Jacobin Thomas Spence entitled his penny weeklies "Pig's meat or Lessons for the Swinish Multitude," while Daniel Isaac Eaton published his "Politics for the People, or Hog's Wash." Burke's affect of *disgust* for the "swinish multitude," along with the ironic feeling of *contempt* with which the multitude countered it, are significant emotive reactions as they imply the beginning of a radical restructuring of class relations in England at the time.[4]

In his seminal study *The Anatomy of Disgust*, William Ian Miller observes that though "disgust" is a psychological, emotive reaction, it is nevertheless related to ideology for it turns out to be "one of our more aggressive culture-creating passions" (xii). "Disgust," together with "contempt," as defensive, reactive passions, "motivate and sustain the low ranking of things, people and actions deemed disgusting and contemptible" (xiv). They constitute, therefore, key emotions in the maintenance of rank and hierarchy. Thus the adjective "swinish" attached to the "multitude," and the repulsive sensations which this metaphor arouses, rather than referring to objective qualities pertaining to the multitude, reveals the feelings of anxiety, hatred and insecurity which the upper classes were beginning to feel at the time. For, with "the emergence of the self-disciplined patterns of the new working class movement" (Thompson, *Making* 81) "contempt," which signified the social superiority of the upper classes in England, ceased to be their privilege, and was now fearlessly expressed by the "rabble" for the masters.

William Godwin countered many of Edmund Burke's reactionary positions in his *Enquiry Concerning Political Justice*. "All the arguments that have been employed to prove the insufficiency of democracy," he writes, "grow out of this one root, the supposed necessity of deception and prejudice for restraining the turbulence of human passions" (493). "Democracy is a system of government according to which every member of society is considered as a man and nothing more. So far as positive regulation is concerned, every man is regarded as equal" (486).

Yet when it comes to "political associations," Godwin shares the fears of his class: "among the disadvantages of political association," he observes, "is its tendency to disorder and tumult . . . There is nothing more barbarous, blood-thirsty and unfeeling than the triumph of a mob" (288). Godwin's model of "political association" seems to foreshadow that of Habermas. The promotion of "the best interests of mankind," he maintains, "depends upon the freedom of social communication." Conversation "accustoms us to hear a variety of sentiments, obliges us to exercise patience and attention, and gives freedom and elasticity to our disquisitions" (289). Thus interaction, mediated by language, will tend towards "intercomprehension," for "every man will be eager to tell, to hear, what the interests of all require them to know." The advantages of political disquisition, "undebauched by political enmity and vehemence" and free of professorial sophistication, will be rendered "common property" and will be brought to daily use with consequences "of inestimable value" (290). Towards this goal, rule-governed language is seen as a more powerful weapon than the misrule of passionate praxis. I venture to suggest that a careful re-reading of Godwin's *Enquiry* will prove many of our contemporary social and political thinkers who opt for deliberative democracy to be "neo-Godwinians."

What seems to be of significance here is the new metaphors which attach to the representation of the mass and the messages of fear and loathing which they communicate to the collective imaginary: the mass is "monstrous" and "blood-thirsty," an unbridled barbarous force threatening to destroy public security and order. The spectacle of the "many headed multitude" now seems to arouse in the beholder the feeling of terror once reserved for the mighty forms of the *natural sublime*.

THE BEAST AND THE MAIDEN

In his youthful days, William Wordsworth was fervently on the side of the "swinish multitude." When he visited France in the early 1790s, he was deeply inspired by the revolutionary ideals; witness his autobiographical *The Prelude*, where he describes "France standing on the top of golden hours / And human nature seeming born again" (67). Soon, however, his Jacobin sentiments and republican principles underwent a severe crisis and he found himself "now believing / Now disbelieving; endlessly perplexed" (75). As Graham Hough observes, Wordsworth underwent a severe moral crisis: "The revolutionary fervour and the doctrines of the age of reason had played their part in forming his mind, but they could carry him little further" and after a long and painful interval "it became apparent that new life and new hope were flowing in upon him from entirely different sources" (39). His dilemma was resolved when revolutionary passion gave way to tranquil contemplation, and collective being "to a saving intercourse / With my true self " (Wordsworth, *Prelude* 76).

In 1804 Wordsworth wrote the famous poem "I wandered lonely as a cloud," which encapsulates his escape from the confusion of the world of revolutionary action into the privacy of the sovereign self and the serenity of natural religion. I quote selectively:

> I wander'd lonely as a cloud
> That floats on high o'er vales and hills,
> When all at once I saw a crowd,
> A host of golden daffodils
> . . . . . .
> Ten thousand saw I at a glance
> Tossing their heads in sprightly dance.
> . . . . .
> I gazed—and gazed—but little thought
> What wealth the show to me had brought;
> For oft, when on my couch I lie
> In vacant or in pensive mood,
> They flash upon that inward eye
> Which is the bliss of solitude;
> And then my heart with pleasure fills,
> And dances with the daffodils. (Wordsworth, "I wandered lonely" II. 63)

To dance in a world of natural beauty with "a crowd of ten thousand golden daffodils" is clearly a much merrier activity than to join in step with ten thousand of the "swinish multitude." Wordsworth's later Toryism is well known. He accepted "the patronage of Lord Lonsdale and Sir George Beaumont, and ultimately, a Crown sinecure" (Hough 92). Graham Hough quotes the following lines from a poem by Browning which refer to Wordsworth's abnegation of republican ideals: "just for a handful of silver he left us/Just for a riband to stick in his coat" (92).

In contrast, Percy Shelley, the only romantic poet who remained faithful to radical ideals, in "The Masque of Anarchy: Written on the Occasion of the Massacre at Manchester," where, on the 16th of August 1819, a massive peaceful demonstration of workers with their families was attacked by the Cavalry and the streets of the town filled with the innocent blood of the "swinish multitude." In this poem, Shelley urged the workers of England to

> Rise like Lions after slumber
> In unvanquishable number,
> Shake your chains to earth like dew,
> Which in sleep had fallen on you—
> Ye are many—they are few. (40)

According to Shelley, England had become a nation where "Rulers . . . neither see, nor feel, nor know, / But leech-like to their fainting country cling," and prophesied that the Army, Religion and Senate "Are graves from which a glorious phantom may / Burst, to illumine our tempestuous days" (51–52). Thirty years later, Marx in the *Communist Manifesto* announced the phantom's threatening emergence.

Among various discursive practices, fiction was also called in to help exorcise the spectre which was haunting Europe. The new genre, known as the Industrial Novel, organised its narrative and plot structure on the antagonistic relations between working class and capital. Here, the ideological mechanism for the production of hegemonic representations was mobilised to reproduce the age-old *topos* of earnest, sensible individuals turned, against their better interests, into an agitated "multitude" by the inflaming words of demagogic leaders. The following "portrait" of the union leader in Dickens' *Hard Times* is revealing:

> Judging him by Nature's evidence, he was above the mass in very little but the stage on which he stood. In many great respects, he was essentially below them. He was not so honest, he was not so manly, he was not so good-humoured; he substituted cunning for their simplicity, and passion for their safe solid sense. An ill-made high-shouldered man, with lowering brows, and his features crushed into an habitually sour expression, he contrasted most unfavourably, even in his mongrel dress, with the great body of his hearers in their plain working clothes . . . it was particularly strange, and it was even particularly affecting, to see this crowd of earnest faces, whose honesty in the main no competent observer free from bias could doubt, so agitated by such a leader. (170)

Fiction surely does the job much better than politicians. For what is the narrator's discourse here but disguised demagogy? From his position of authority, he at the same time flatters and admonishes the workers not to fall victims to the seducing words of the villainous union leader but to preserve their native dignity and, though victims of an inhuman, unchristian system, humbly to continue doing the work destined for them by the divine scheme of things. The "class struggle," the Industrial Novel urged, could only be resolved by the "religion of humanity" which would enable society to transcend its bitter class divisions. The reformative gospel of love would resolve the antagonism between worker and capitalist and all would live happily ever after, with the system left intact.

APOCALYPSE

By the end of the nineteenth century, the labour movement had become a powerful political opponent in its confrontation with capital and the state. Conservative politicians and intellectuals infused public opinion with the fear of an imminent catastrophe, claiming that institutions were in a state of accelerative decadence and society in danger of falling into "the waste Wide Anarchie of *Chaos*" (Milton 323). In 1895, the French social psychologist Gustave Le Bon published *La psychologie des foules* (*The Crowd: A Study of the Popular Mind*), which soon achieved great popularity. The book was hailed as a study which submitted this disturbing social phenomenon to an analysis proper to a scientific object of investigation, as it revealed the immutable psychological structure which determined the behaviour of "masses," whether these were religious, racial, national, military, political, ancient or modern. In the Introduction to his book Le Bon noted:

> On the ruins of so many ideas formerly considered beyond discussion, and today decayed or decaying, of so many sources of authority that successive revolutions have destroyed, this power, which alone has arisen in their stead, seems soon destined to absorb the others. While all our ancient beliefs are tottering and disappearing, while the old pillars of society are giving way one by one, the power of the crowd is the only force that nothing menaces, and of which the prestige is continually on the increase. The age we are about to enter will in truth be the ERA OF CROWDS . . . The divine right of the masses is about to replace the divine right of kings. (Le Bon, *Crowd* 4–5)

The articulation of this sweeping *political* generalization, based on the rhetoric of fear, surely leads the critical reader to question the "objectivity" of Le Bon's analysis. For, rather than a disinterested description of the phenomenon, the aim of his analysis seems to be on the one hand to direct public opinion against the "multitude" and on the other, as he himself explicitly states, to provide the authorities with a "handbook" for confronting and manipulating this social menace. These aims become more than apparent in his book *La psychologie politique et la défense sociale* (*Political Psychology and Social Defence*), written in 1910,[5] where he remarks that though the rules which he set down in *The Crowd*

> are in daily use by army officers and regularly taught in the School of War, they have not won as yet the attention of politicians. In fact, these do not cease to praise the wisdom, the judgment and the good sense of the masses, qualities of which they were always deprived. French legislators, having a very inexact idea of popular mentality . . . continue to pile up useless or dangerous laws, uniquely destined to please the multitude. Not in the least suspecting the intense *contempt* felt by the masses for their weakness, they fail to understand that their perpetual concessions before the menaces gradually denude them of all *prestige*. (125–26, italics mine)

Echoing Burke, Le Bon sees an antagonism "which is getting fiercer and fiercer every day separating the multitude from the elite" (122).

Le Bon's model of description is constructed on the antithetical pair *individual/mass*. On the basis of this opposition, he reaches the conclusion that the psychological mechanism of the "collective psyche" differs radically from that of the "individual psyche" in its manner of reasoning, in the expression of its feelings, in the form of its interests and in its ways of acting. For, "so far as the majority of their acts are considered, crowds display a singularly inferior mentality" (*Crowd* 2). In contrast to the individual, the masses are: irrational, passionate, irresponsible, savage, victims of repetition and possessed by a misplaced sense of power and pride. Yet the violence which guides their passionate behaviour is at the same time accompanied by the contradictory traits of submissiveness and obedience. Being credulous and prone to manipulation, masses easily become a plaything in the hands of a prestigious leader. Consequently, when one knows how to guide them, their docility and credulity resembles that of children and primitive races.

According to Le Bon, popular belief and opinion are established by identification, seduction and persuasion. His "grammar of persuasion" is composed of four principles: the *prestige* which the leader suggests and imposes, the *affirmation without proof* which issues from his discourse, *repetition*, which leads to accepting certain things which have been affirmed, and *mental contagion*. Thus, the true manipulator of men exercises a hypnotic, discursive seduction and the seduced have but one opinion, one will: that of the seducer. Le Bon notes that psychologists must delve into this obscure region, the "subconscious," in order to explain the "mysterious mechanism" which regulates the psyches of both the seducer and the seduced (*Psychologie politique* 136–39). Freud was soon to try and fill in this gap.

Clearly, Le Bon's representational model of the mass is founded on the old rhetorical trope encountered in literature. Yet there seems to be a significant difference as far as the other term of the opposition is concerned: *the individual.* Le Bon's model seems to be grounded on the ideology of *progress*, since the "individual" is seen as being situated in historical time and as having gradually progressed from lower to higher states of civilization. "Masses," however, are shown to be permanently situated in what precedes the body politic, that original, savage state of nature, a repressed state which invariably threatens to return and lead civil society back in a catastrophic and lawless regression:

> Crowds are only powerful for destruction. Their rule is always tantamount to a barbarian phase. A civilisation involves fixed rules, discipline, a passing from the instinctive to the rational state . . . crowds act like those microbes which hasten the dissolution of enfeebled or dead bodies. When the structure of a civilisation is rotten, it is always the masses that bring about its downfall . . . is the same fate in store for our civilization? There is ground to fear that this is the case. (*Crowd* 5–6)

What is of special interest in this descriptive model is not the opposition *per se* but the fact that for an aggregate of individuals to be constituted into a "mass," the intervention and presence of a charismatic leader is deemed necessary. Here the question arises as to why an individual, whose "psyche" is by definition graced with all the opposite characteristics which distinguish it from the mass, should undertake to play the role of a "leader" in the constitution of a destructive multitude. Inevitably, the question of social responsibility arises: is it the irrational, savage mass which is responsible for menacing the order of society, or the rational, culturally elevated individual who seduces it? Would there be "masses" if there were no charismatic leaders, or are these a necessary consequence of his hypnotic, discursive power? An ethical problem seems to be involved here, as far as the "civilized," "rational" psyche of the individual is concerned. For no matter what the motive for arousing the masses is, whether it be "noble" or "wicked," the leader is in full knowledge of the fact that he is manipulating and inflaming the crowd to act in accordance either with his own personal interest, or with the vested interests of a power group to which he belongs. In other words, by choosing to function as an instrument of propaganda, the individual bears full responsibility for the constitution of the mass and for inspiring it either to act disinterestedly, in the service of what have been culturally established as "noble" causes (like engaging in war against an external enemy for the sake of the fatherland) or destructively, in the service of "ignoble" causes (as in the class struggle when the multitude turns against an "internal" enemy).

As is well known, the notion of the "charismatic leader" relates to a form of historiography which cannot admit of the fact that people may act of their own free will as *a collective subject* with rational aims in mind whose realization, however, may entail, precisely as in the case of a national or a religious war, recourse to modes of *violence* which antagonise those practised by legal and other institutions or by the repressive state apparatuses. Perhaps this is what Le Bon's descriptive model endeavours to conceal under the axiom of a "psychological determinism" operating in masses.

In his later work, Le Bon was to qualify this unhistorical, general conception of the masses by introducing, however, other "deterministic" criteria. Thus, in *Le déséquilibre du monde* (*The Disequilibrium of the World*) written in 1923, he observes that certain "masses" were able to transcend their archaic limitations and to exhibit those "individual" traits relating them to social progress. This psychic progress of the mass towards "individuation" was vitally related to and determined now by that larger, inclusive "psyche" of the nation or of the race to which the multitude belonged:

> The psychological characteristics the totality of which constitute the soul of a people, differing greatly from one country to another, cause the various peoples to feel, reason, and act in dissimilar ways in identical situations . . . All the individuals of an inferior race share between them a very great resemblance. In contrast, where superior races are concerned, they are differentiated from one another more and more as civilization progresses. It is not therefore towards equality that civilized men are marching, but towards an ever increasing inequality. Equality is the communism of the first ages, differentiation is progress. (174)

In the final analysis, what Le Bon's reactionary, racist narrative betrays is the anxiety of the hegemonic classes of the West about their loss of *prestige* and the new distribution of power in the national and international spheres. It comes as no surprise, therefore, when he maintains that the new popular dictatorships like Communism, besides basing their principal force on mystical elements, have as their unique support "very material appetites since what seems to count is to plunder one class for the benefit of another" (Le Bon, *Le déséquilibre* 83). This astounding definition of the class struggle is not dissimilar to the way in which Dickens' industrialist Mr Bounderby conceives of it in *Hard Times*: "I see traces of the turtle soup, and venison, and gold spoon in this, Yes, I do!" (114). Italian fascists, on the other hand, are to be praised, since their aim is to restrain the Communist torrent "which threatens to submerge the industrial life of their country, and against which the government proves impotent" (Le Bon, *Le déséquilibre* 88). Le Bon entitles one of the last chapters of this book "The Creation of Moral Habits by the Army" and advises: "All modern peoples, the Latin ones especially, are in need of a moral education which will provide them with a solid mental capital. Only the army, I repeat, could enable them to acquire it" (253).

In "Group Psychology and the Analysis of the Ego," Freud devotes a whole section to Le Bon's *La psychologie des foules.*[6] Freud's fundamental departure from Le Bon's narrative is located in his critique of the binary opposition *individual/mass.* According to Freud, the "individual" cannot be thought of as a unitary abstraction, given the fact that one always already exists within a network of relations, knowing oneself *ab intitio* as a member of a group: "In the individual's mental life someone else is invariably involved, as a model, as an object, as a helper, as an opponent; and so from the very first individual psychology . . . is at the same time social psychology as well" ("Group" 95). It is, therefore, within the space of familial relations and the emotions generated therein that the explanatory model of the group psyche should be sought.

In contrast to Le Bon, what interests Freud is not the alterations observed in the behaviour and feelings of a rational individual upon its insertion into a crowd, or the emergence from the individual's unconscious of the hereditary impressions stamped upon it by the inclusive "psyche" of the nation or of the race (though the "archaic heritage" does play its part in his analysis). Rather, it is the unconscious mechanism of "bonding," which transforms the heterogeneity of disparate individuals into a homogeneity, which holds the group together. Thus, Freud's narrative derives not from an antithesis based on the ideology of progress, but from a unitary nucleus: the *libido*:

> We call by that name the energy . . . of those instincts which have to do with all that may be comprised under the word "love." The nucleus of what we mean by love naturally consists . . . in sexual love with sexual union as its aim. But we do not separate from this—what in any case has a share in the name "love"—on the one hand, self love, and on the other, love for parents and children, friendship and love for humanity in general, and also devotion to concrete objects and to abstract ideas. (119)

Eros, therefore, being the power "which holds together everything in the world," constitutes "the essence of the group mind" (120) and accounts for the individual's giving up his "distinctiveness" for the sake of a harmonious bonding with the other members of the group.

What is of especial interest in Freud's analysis of the group mind is his observation that the cohesion of the group is insured by a projection of the negative, antagonistic feelings towards an external object: the "outsider." For, the evidence of psychoanalysis shows that "almost any intimate emotional relation contains a sediment of feelings of aversion and hostility. This escapes perception because of repression" (130). Thus, even Christianity, which calls itself "a religion of love, must be hard and unloving to those who do not belong to it" (128). The formation and cohesion of a group, therefore, necessarily entails the *friend/enemy* opposition. Significantly, Freud evades a further elaboration of this opposition, one which would open up the space of the *political*.

Freud's main incentive in the study of the group psyche seems to have been to meet the challenge and provide a psychoanalytic interpretation of what Le Bon designated as the "subconscious mysterious mechanism" which regulates the psyches of the seducer and the seduced—in short, the discovery of those psychic operations which ensured the dependence and subjection of the crowd to the will of the leader. Freud is perceptive enough to introduce the distinction between groups which have a leader and leaderless groups: "We should consider," he notes, "whether groups with leaders may not be the more primitive and complete, whether in the others an idea, an abstraction may not take the place of the leader . . . and whether a common tendency, a wish in which a number of people can have a share, may not in the same way serve as a substitute" (129).

Nevertheless, in spite of the fact that he observes that as far as "leaderless groups" are concerned, "the question would also arise whether a leader is really indispensable to the essence of a group—and other such questions besides" (130), he lets the matter rest at that and focuses his analysis exclusively on those groups which are under the spell of a leader. For, were he to focus on "leaderless groups," this would in all probability entail a departure from the "familial" libidinal model and an entry into that other area which, historically, came to be known as the *public space*. This was an area which would require of him an examination of discursive practices other than those employed by the *seducer*, namely, the discursive activity of groups themselves which, from the seventeenth century onwards, created "a new kind of urban political culture" (Withington 1018). To approach this historical discursive formation through the notion of libidinal "substitution" and the "ego ideal" would in my opinion be reductive.

It is not within the scope of this chapter to examine in detail Freud's psychoanalytic narrative concerning group psychology and the adventures of the ego. What is of special interest to our topic is that as far as the representational model of the mass is concerned, Freud also reproduces the hallucinatory one that had gripped the bourgeois imaginary at the dawn of the industrial revolution: the mass is irrational, led by unbridled passions, childish, primitive, prey to brutal, destructive instincts and to the seductive wiles of prestigious leaders. What is more, it collectively exhibits the psychopathology of neurotics.

Again, it is to be wondered why in sociological and psychological studies of the "mass" which appeared at the end of the nineteenth and the beginning of the twentieth centuries, the "leader" was to assume such a seminal position, as if the analysts, as was previously mentioned, unconsciously reproduced the defunct historiographic model of "hero worship" and applied it either directly or indirectly to all "groups." For, it is an undeniable fact that in the history of the working class movement we encounter a "swinish multitude" without a "swineherd," a self-constituted, self-organised mass with specific, rational aims in mind. Such, precisely, must have been the "masses" of demonstrators and strikers which Le Bon and Freud encountered in their daily experience. The "monstrosity" of their representations, therefore, besides the affect of hatred, which is engendered by the psychic mechanism of "exclusion," betrays an imaginary, unconscious subtraction: they confront society *minus* class, mass *minus* the relations of labour. Thus, by a kind of automatism, theory continued to reproduce the "barbaric" representations of the mass—a mode of unconscious defence, perhaps, to project outward onto the world the "object" which was inwardly experienced as a threat to the bourgeois ego. This projection onto the world of the uncanny "other" indirectly sanctioned as well the brutal force exercised upon the multitudes by the repressive state apparatuses.

Another historical factor which should seriously be taken into account is that both Le Bon's later work and Freud's "Group Psychology" were written after the world-shaking event of the Russian Revolution. In his study, Freud's only reference to the political field concerns his remark that "the undeniable weakening of religious feelings and the libidinal ties which depend upon them" account for the fact that "to-day . . . intolerance no longer shows itself so violent and cruel as in former centuries" ("Group" 128). This, however, should not be viewed as "a softening in human manners." For, "if another group tie takes the place of the religious one—and the socialistic tie seems to be succeeding in doing so—then there will be the same intolerance towards outsiders as in the age of the Wars of Religion" (128). The equation of socialism with a religious creed was to be long lasting.

The trope of the "savage mass" and the reduction of socialism to a mystical religion went on being reproduced way into the twentieth century. Jules Monnerot, whose political allegiance shifted through the years from the communist left to the extreme right, in his famous *Sociology and Psychology of Communism* (1949) observed that the appearance of the masses upon the stage of history in the nineteenth century meant that "the primitive will play a more important part both in history and in the actual behavior of collectivities . . . the new society in process of formation was more *primitive* and *barbarous* than the old." What is more, this meant "the appearance of 'crowd situations' propitious to the growth of myths" (148). In the nineteenth century, "there was a vast resurgence of mythical thinking" (149).

The first chapter of Monnerot's book is entitled "The Twentieth Century Islam." According to the author, what is happening in the West is that "a religion is propagating itself in terms of political economy . . . The communist campaign could not exist if it were not religious" (21). As a secular, messianic religion, Marxism "socializes obsessions and delusions and cultivates paranoiac projections which are lived and exteriorized *communally*"

(142). Monnerot's theoretical vocabulary elaborates in greater detail, and with specific references to historical events, persons, ideas and strategies, what had been employed by Le Bon and Freud in their analyses of crowd formation and collective praxis: *individual* regulated emotions *versus collective* delusional passion, *suggestion*, *identification*, *projection*, *introjection* and the cult of the great *leader*, "a man with an exceptional power of infecting others with his own obsessions" (145) and the seductive power of his words:

> Is there a more powerful drug today than certain words administered in regular doses? They are administered according to the most efficacious magic ritual of our time, by men who well know their effects. In massive doses, following well-tried prescriptions and a carefully perfected technique, these words . . . can turn whole crowds of men into lions or into sheep. These are our modern vampires. (141)

I believe that the above suffices to show that the archetypal, representational model of the "swinish multitude" has been permanently stamped onto the Western social imaginary. The scientific vocabularies of sociology and psychology, by investing the analysis of the mass "psyche" with the aura of "objectivity," nevertheless fail to conceal the biased viewpoint of the theoreticians, which reflects the anxiety, fear, insecurity and hatred felt by the "civilised" individuals of the hegemonic classes towards the savage "proletariat."

RISE LIKE LIONS

In our super-capitalist, supra-national days, a death and a rebirth have been announced: "classes" are defunct, "individualism" has been resurrected. How the ideology of "individualism" which is propagated in our neo-liberal times can stand on its feet without the support of "class" is difficult to understand. As Volosinov observed in *Marxism and the Philosophy of Language*:

> What mostly complicates our problem of delimiting psyche and ideology is the concept of "individuality." The "social" is usually thought of in binary opposition with the "individual" and hence we have the notion that the psyche is individual while ideology is social. Notions of that sort are fundamentally false. The correlate of the social is the "natural" and thus "individual" is not meant in the sense of a person, but "individual" as natural, biological specimen. The individual as possessor of the contents of his own consciousness, as author of his own thoughts, as the personality responsible for his own thoughts and feelings, such an individual is a purely socioideological phenomenon. (34)

According to Volosinov, the "we-experience" of the mass "is not by any means a nebulous herd experience" (88). What is more, "individualism is a special ideological form of the 'we-experience' of the bourgeois class . . . The structure of the conscious, individual personality is just as social a structure as is the collective type of experience" (89). Here, one could say that Volosinov was in agreement with Freud, were it not for the *origin* of this sociality. For, where Freud sees the *libido*, Volosinov detects "a particular kind of interpretation, projected into the individual soul, of a complex and sustained socioeconomic situation" (89).

Now, as the "we-experience" always entails the "they-experience," the "swinish multitude" has once more hoofed its way onto the bleak, late-capitalist scene, where the voices of T. S. Eliot's "Unemployed" (in the Chorus from "The Rock") go unheard: "*No man has hired us / With pocketed hands / And lowered faces / We stand about in open places / And shiver in unlit rooms*" (Eliot 160).

Both in theory and in practice, the word "multitude" is being reinvested in our days with meaning and passion. The genre of the Manifesto, which as Martin Puchner observes in *The Poetry of the Revolution* attempts to "turn words into actions and demands into reality" (12), is with us again, creating "a vocabulary of the deed" (15), "a poetry of the future" (1). "Another world is possible": Seattle, Genova, Thessaloniki, Athens.[7] Leaderless, self-constituted multitudes have reappeared on the historical scene, in the words of Shelley's Demogorgon in *Prometheus Unbound*:

> To defy Power, which seems omnipotent;
> To love, and bear; to hope till Hope creates
> From its own wreck the thing it contemplates. (Shelley 387)

NOTES

1. The function of the Chorus in Euripides has problematised classical scholars. Though according to Aristotle, the Chorus should participate in the action, as H. D. F. Kitto notes, "it was when tragedy turned from public to private themes, like . . . the frenzied behaviour of Euripides' Orestes, that the chorus becomes a nuisance" (160). In opposition to Aeschylus and Sophocles, Euripides tends to make of the Chorus "a body of ideal spectators." Kitto wonders why "when . . . desperate deeds are afoot" Euripides has the Chorus engage in "a pleasant little essay" (194). He maintains that Euripides was "fundamentally detached" from his protagonists and unlike Sophocles could "retire for a moment and invite us to think of something else" (195). I believe that this dramatic "detachment" reflects the social rift which was at the time marking the imaginary unity of the polis.
2. Translation mine.
3. The "Roman" setting in Shakespeare's plays can be viewed as a dramatic strategy to evade the Censors and to communicate to his audiences subversive political messages. See Politi, *Shakespeare*; also Politi, "Re-Reading" and Politi, "Gibbet-Maker."

4. For a fuller exposition of this argument see Politi, "New Species."
5. All quotations that follow from Le Bon's books are translated by me.
6. Freud's detailed exposition and elaboration of some of the key concepts of Le Bon, and at the same time his curt dismissal of his predecessor, lead one to think that the familial structure and the theory of emotions upon which he based his own theory of the group mind were unconsciously projected onto the group "psyche" of the scientific community as well. He writes:

   > Le Bon's opinions, those touching upon the collective inhibition of intellectual functioning and the heightening of affectivity in groups, had been formulated shortly before by Sighele. At bottom, all that is left over as being peculiar to Le Bon are the two notions of the unconscious and of the comparison with the mental life of primitive people, and even these had naturally often been alluded to before him. ("Group" 110)

7. When I began working on this chapter, the murder of 16-year-old Alexis Gregoropoulos by a police guard roused the school students in Greece spontaneously to organise themselves into protesting "multitudes." These agonistic demonstrations have been seen as the first massive reaction to the economic crisis brought about by the global capitalist system, which ruthlessly deprives the young of hope for a viable future. Now, as this volume is going into press, the public squares of Greece and of other European countries are full of "indignant" multitudes.

6 The Masses as a "Vanishing Mediator"

Class and Politics in Dušan Kovačević's *The Professional*

Sean Homer

> [B]efore World War II, Soviet and American filmmakers believed that the "masses" represented in films were factual, not fictional categories, while postwar political cinema lost faith that a proletariat or any other collective entity really existed.
>
> Sasa Vojkovic (Vojkovic 41)

On the 11th of March 1981 student protests broke out in Priština, capital of the then Autonomous Province of Kosovo of the Socialist Federal Republic of Yugoslavia. The students' demands were initially restricted to the living conditions in the hostels at Priština University but, as meetings with the University administration got under way, a wide range of grievances were articulated including high unemployment, poverty, backwardness and social differences.[1] The meetings concluded with the students' demand for republican status within the federal state for the province of Kosovo. Fearing further demonstrations at the celebration of Tito's official birthday on the 23rd of March, just one year after his death, the authorities in Priština began to arrest the student leaders and other potential "troublemakers." The consequences were the exact opposite to those intended and on the 23rd of March, not only the students but also thousands of citizens of Priština came out onto the streets. By the 2nd of April massive demonstrations demanding republican status had spread across the province in a huge outpouring of popular anger. On the 3rd of April the Yugoslav People's Army entered the province and declared martial law, the first time this had happened since 1945 and the founding of the Federal Republic. The beginning of the long, slow and painful disintegration of Yugoslavia had begun.

In the decade that followed before the final demise of the former Yugoslavia,[2] strikes escalated, hunger strikes were staged, a general strike was called, peace movements were formed and hundreds of thousands of students and workers across the republics came out on the streets.[3] Today these mass protests have largely been forgotten, or written out of the story of the disintegration of the former Yugoslavia, as we have come to regard the conflict as essentially a Manichean struggle between the forces of democratisation and totalitarianism. In the historical record that has now been drawn up, there is a widespread understanding of the conflict as a straightforward struggle between neo-liberal reformers and democrats on the one side and hard-line communists and Greater Serb nationalists on the other.[4] The problem with this account is that most of the actors involved did not fit into this reductive opposition.[5] Milošević, for instance, was both an economic reformer and a Greater Serb nationalist, while the Slovenian liberals and Croats were no less ethnic nationalists.[6] What has been eclipsed in this polarisation of forces into two opposing camps is the voice of democratic socialists calling for democratisation, not within national sovereign states but within a Federal Republic. In other words, the mass protests that began this process of transformation in Kosovo in the early 1980s, one that would end in disintegration but would fit neither of these designations (neo-liberal reformers or hard-line communists), have been eclipsed by the very historical forces that they set in motion. In this chapter I want to consider the conspicuous absence of any representation of these mass movements in the extraordinarily creative cinematic output that was stimulated by the breakup of the former Yugoslavia.[7] I will do so by way of a film that is notable for its attempt to represent these protests, Dušan Kovačević's *The Professional* (2003). Through Slavoj Žižek's utilisation of Fredric Jameson's concept of the "vanishing mediator" I will attempt to account for the fate of political dissidents in the former Yugoslavia. Finally, I shall draw upon Alain Badiou's notion of the "particularity of the masses" and the impossibility of representing their "pure multiplicity" in order to account for the inherent limitations of these protests.

THE VANISHING MEDIATOR

Jameson developed the concept of the vanishing mediator in an early essay on Max Weber, specifically in order to account for the function of Protestantism in the transition from feudalism to modern capitalism. For Jameson, the vanishing mediator performs the function of a "catalytic agent that permits an exchange of energies between two otherwise mutually exclusive terms . . . and can be dismantled and removed when its usefulness is over" ("Vanishing" 25). In this sense, Protestantism, for Weber, performed the function of rationalising not only the social world but also our inner world. Once this task had been accomplished, writes Jameson, it had "no further reason for being and disappear[ed] from the historical scene" (25).[8] More recently Slavoj Žižek has used this concept to account for the fate of political dissidents in the former Eastern Europe (Žižek, *Tarrying*).

In the mid 1990s Žižek observed that the reform communists, the political agents who facilitated the transition from "actually existing socialism" to capitalism, fully deserved the designation "tragic" for the way they "lived up to their promise to make possible the peaceful, non-violent transition into pluralist democracy" but were then swept away by the very process they had set in motion (*Tarrying* 226). Once multi-party elections took place in Slovenia and Croatia, the reform communists not only lost power but became the enemy within and were accused of unprincipled and opportunistic behaviour in holding the elections in the first place. For Žižek, we can describe the logic of this shift—from an "open" condition prior to the elections, when a new social pact was generated, to its "closure," when that pact was firmly established, and its origins erased—in terms of Jameson's notion of vanishing mediators:

> [T]hose who triggered the process of democratization and fought its heaviest battles are not those who today enjoy its rewards—not because of any usurpation or deception on the part of the present winners, but because of a deeper historical logic. Once the process of democratization had reached its peak, it buried its detonators. (228)

In this specific passage Žižek is referring not to the reform communists but to the New Social Movements, Punks and New Left, those political dissidents such as *New Forum* (*Neues Forum*) in East Germany, who sincerely opposed "actually existing socialism" in the name of "true socialism" but only served to unleash the forces of their own destruction. Furthermore, once these movements were overrun by history, those who were now in power and had largely remained silent during the communist period accused the social movements and dissidents of being crypto-communists.

Here I want to extend Žižek's analysis of Eastern Europe's vanishing mediators to take account of the mass protests that swept across Yugoslavia in the 1980s and early '90s. What we can see in Kovačević's *The Professional* is that, while the dissidents believed themselves to be leading and directing the struggle against Milošević's regime, their fate was being determined by forces beyond their control. Indeed, from Kovačević's perspective the dissidents and political opposition of the 1980s and 1990s were not so much swept away by the forces of history as co-opted by them to become part of the new ruling elite. I will come back to this in my conclusion, as it directly takes us to the issue of Kovačević's own politics. Let me now turn to the film itself.

REPRESENTING THE MASSES

I suggested previously that there is a notable absence of representation of mass protests in films of the Yugoslav conflict; this is not to say, however, that such representations are completely absent. For example, in Srđjn Dragojević's *Pretty Village, Pretty Flame* (1996) we see both nationalist crowds cheering Serbian paramilitary forces as they go off to fight and (towards the end of the film) peace protestors outside the hospital where the wounded paramilitaries have been taken. In these scenes the crowd is satirised; in the former we see Skinheads mindlessly head-butting road signs to Zagreb, while in the latter a rather thin crowd of middle-aged figures light candles and sing "Give Peace a Chance" while the wounded fighters laugh hysterically and throw things from the hospital windows. In Dragojević's subsequent film, *The Wounds* (1999), the film is book-ended by scenes of crowds celebrating as part of the "100 Days" or "Egg" protests in Belgrade between 1996 and '97.[9] These scenes, however, are presented as much more of a carnival than a mass protest, with students dancing in the streets to the pounding rhythm of drums and wearing death masks.[10] As Ivana Kronja writes, with its focus on the "warrior chic" of Serbia's violent and criminal underworld of the 1990s, the film implies "that the demonstrators do not come close to the big truths, the thrills and challenges—the real rules of the game, which our anti-heroes learn during their short but exciting lives" (27). Kovačević's *The Professional* is unusual, then, at least as far as the films that have received international distribution are concerned, in that its narrative is inter-cut with scenes of mass street protests, scenes which are crucial to the motivation of the narrative itself.[11]

The Professional is adapted from Kovačević's play of the same name, originally performed in 1990. For the film Kovačević up-dated the script to set it in the autumn of 2001 and include the mass protests of the 1990s and Milošević's fall from power in October 2000. The film retains much of its theatricality, as the narrative is structured around a conversation between two characters in a single room: Teodor ("Teja") Kraj (Branislav Lecic), a former professor of literature and political dissident, who is now the managing director of a publishing company, and Luka Laban (Bora Tedorovic), a former colonel in the secret police, who now works as a taxi driver to supplement his meagre pension. *The Professional* shares certain similarities with Florian Henckel von Donnersmarck's *The Lives of Others* (2006), especially insofar as the film explores the intimate relationship that forms between Captain Gerd Wiesler (Ulrich Mühe), a surveillance officer for the Ministry of State Security (Stasi), and Georg Dreyman (Sebastian Koch), a dissident playwright. Kovačević's film, however, embeds this relationship much more overtly in a social and political context, in the sense that it is the fortunes of the opposition movement and specific mass actions that provoke the changes in Teja and Luka's relationship. In other words, the primary narrative of *The Professional* takes place against, and intersects with, two further diegetic threads: the history of the opposition movement in the 1990s and a strike fomenting in the factory as they meet. The narrative gradually unravels through a series of flashbacks, as Teja and Luka discuss the preceding decade of dissent and Teja's involvement. In one sense, then, we could perhaps suggest that Teja and Luka represent the two mutually exclusive terms of this conflict, the opposition and the State. The catalytic element here, the masses, is not directly presented but, as I will discuss, provides the necessary conditions of possibility for these two forces to come together and is then eclipsed in the process. *The Professional* complicates this reading, however, by suggesting that the opposition and the regime were not quite as exclusive as one might imagine. I will return to this issue later; first let me consider how the protests are at once present in and absent from the film.

IMAGES OF A BYGONE AGE

The narrative of *The Professional* is inter-cut with actual documentary footage of mass protests in Serbia in the 1990s, beginning with the October revolution in 2000, when hundreds of thousands of people poured onto the streets of Belgrade on the 5th of October.[12] Under pressure from this mass protest Milošević finally resigned on the 7th of October. The film also contains footage of the 9 March 1991 protests, when the opposition challenged Milošević, which turned into four days of conflict, resulting in two deaths and numerous injuries. Finally, we see footage of the "100 Days" protests of 1996–97, when students led protests against the electoral fraud of the Milošević government in the local government elections of 1996. These protests began in November 1996 and ran through to March 1997. At the peak of the protests, 250,000 people were on the streets of Belgrade and the opposition thought they had finally won. Although this material was shot in the 1990s, it is always shown in sepia, as if these are images from the turn of the century and the early days of cinema rather than of the very immediate past. It is as if the protests were relics of a bygone age. Moreover, when the scenes shift from a sepia tone to full colour there is an instant cut and we see the documentary footage not directly on the screen but now mediated by a bank of screens in the offices of the secret police. Furthermore, when the image changes from sepia to full colour, the content also undergoes a significant transformation. We no longer see mass mobilisations of people coming into Belgrade, violent confrontations with the security police and army or the occupation of government buildings, but two young women at a celebratory rock concert.[13] The potential violence of the protests is domesticated and the film formally instantiates a separation between its primary narrative, the relationship between Teja and Luka, and the historical events that are its conditions of possibility. It would appear as if these images cannot be directly represented on the screen and must be distanced from the spectator in some way. The narrative does contain one scene that depicts a mass rally organised by Teja and his companions, a protest against the treatment of the refugees from the Krajina region. Teja anticipates that thousands will turn out for this rally; approximately thirty turn up, half of whom are Luka's men from the internal security police. It would seem then that the film cannot directly present the mass protests, that they operate as a traumatic point in the narrative that cannot be integrated into its overall symbolic network. In other words, the mass protests function as *the representative of the representation*, that little bit of the Real that is the unrepresentable kernel of representation (Lacan, *Seminar VII* 43–70). They are a catalyst within the narrative that recedes into the distance as new forces crystallise: the hard-line communists transformed into neo-nationalists (Luka) and the dissident opposition transformed into neo-liberal democratic reformers (Teja). The masses permit, as Jameson puts it, the exchange of energies between these otherwise exclusive terms, but once that function has been performed they have no further reason to exist and disappear from the historical scene. I suggested previously, however, that the opposition and the State might not be quite as exclusive as we might expect, and it is now time to consider this issue a little more closely.

STRATEGIES OF CONTAINMENT

The narrative unravels through a series of flashbacks; as with many of the films of this period, it appears to be impossible to represent this particular historical period through a straightforward linear narrative and single privileged point of view. The narrative is fragmented, moving backwards and forwards in time, presenting often contradictory perspectives on the same situation.[14] The conflicting interpretations of this very recent past and the instability of individual memory are established at the outset of the film. Luka walks into Teja's office and immediately recounts one of Teja's own short stories entitled "My Friend from the Army,"[15] to which Teja responds "An interesting story, but unfortunately it's not mine." "Yes, yes it's yours," says Luka, "you've just forgotten it." Indeed, as Luka places on the desk four large manuscripts of Teja's own speeches and writings from the previous decade, it becomes apparent that Teja has forgotten just about everything he said or did. This is hardly surprising, as the film rather disparagingly depicts the dissidents as having spent most of the previous decade drunk, attempting to sing the government out of power from bars and taverns around Belgrade.[16] Indeed, even though Kovačević was a supporter of the opposition movement and spoke from the platform during the "100 Days" protests (Thomas 296), the image of the dissidents presented here is extremely ambivalent. How might we account for this?

Luka was assigned to follow Teja during his days of political activism and has recorded and documented everything he said and did from 1991 to 2000. As the narrative develops, however, it becomes apparent that Luka was not merely a passive observer and transcriber of Teja's life but increasingly an active agent in the course of Teja's career.[17] At one point he tries to kill Teja by running him down; this puts Teja in hospital for months and effectively ends his political aspirations. Luka also gets Teja sacked from his position as a Professor at the University by reporting his relationship with a female student to the Dean. He then sends photographs of them together to Teja's wife, destroying what remains of their marriage. The student in question is Luka's own daughter, Ana (Dana Todorovic), and when she discovers that her father has her lover under surveillance, he is forced to switch from attempting to kill Teja to keeping him alive. Paradoxically, it would seem, the internal security police, the force most loyal to the regime itself, can be seen to both persecute the opposition and at the same time sustain the opposition in order to *sustain itself.*

Writers on Serbian politics in the 1990s have reflected on one of the great paradoxes of Milošević's regime: given that his government was distinguished by its utter failure and lack of support, how did he manage to remain in power for so long?[18] I suggested at the outset of this chapter that the initial mass protests of the 1980s attempted to articulate a Federal and non-nationalist solution to the economic and political crisis facing the former Yugoslavia. By the mid 1990s, however, the discourse of nationalism had increasingly come to dominate the political landscape. As Milošević's Socialist Party of Serbia (SPS) was the successor of the former League of Communists and its socialist heritage, the opposition movement differentiated itself not through the discourse of the left but through its nationalist and royalist credentials. In short, they attempted to challenge the regime on the discursive field that it had already claimed for itself. It was because the opposition and the government fought to restructure the social space on the same terms that even when the regime conceded power (as it did after the "100 Days" protests in March 1997), it was able to continue by other means. Eric Gordy describes Milošević's strategy as the "destruction of alternatives," which then fostered a situation of "habituation, resignation and apathy" (7).[19] V. P. Gagnon Jr. calls this strategy "demobilisation," that is to say, the use of ethno-nationalist discourse to silence, marginalise and exclude previously politicised non-nationalist voices (xviii). Utilising images of ethnic violence against Serbs and threats to the State, Milošević was able to marginalise non-nationalist voices and co-opt the more nationalist elements of the opposition to his own government. Indeed, there was something of a symbiotic relationship between the regime and sections of the opposition, in particular the extreme right and nationalist wings of the movement (Thomas 136–42), which enabled it to remain in power long beyond its natural life.

THE "PARTICULARITY" OF THE MASSES

We can help to clarify how this process works, I think, by turning to Alain Badiou's discussion of the masses as a signifier. For Badiou, the "masses" designate one of the two essential parameters of the first cycle of modern emancipatory politics, the other being the "party."[20] The term "the masses" is not central in Badiou's more recent work, especially the work that an

English-speaking readership is most familiar with, from *Being and Event* (2005) onwards. But as Peter Hallward observes, in Badiou's first major work, *Theory of the Subject* (1982), "the masses figure as the dynamic, inventive and 'vanishing' term of history, an evanescent causality that comes to 'consist' insofar as a suitably organised Marxist-Leninist party is able to purify and sustain the revolutionary force of its eruption" ("Order and Event" 100). The masses function, that is, as the materialisation of inconsistency. Badiou's *Theory of the Subject* was written mainly in the late 1970s. Faced with the "historical wreckage of actually-existing Maoism" in the 1980s, Badiou shifted his frame of reference from history to ontology, from the masses to the "unpresentable being of all that is presented" (Hallward ,"Order and Event" 100). In other words "inconsistency" is now understood as the very being of being—on condition that strictly *nothing* can be presented or conceived of such being (101). Put otherwise, inconsistency, the truth of any given situation, shifts from the masses to the void. I will come back to this in a moment.

In his short essay "Politics Unbound" (2006), Badiou notes that the "masses" is usually a pejorative term today. The problem, he suggests, is not with the term itself, or with politics as such, but with the forgetting of politics and the re-articulation of its key signifiers through the figure of the bond. Any form of social bond, for Badiou, be it the bonds of solidarity of a mass movement or the administrative bureaucracy of the State, only serves to totalise, and thus bind, the particularity of the political event.[21] The social bond, he argues, depoliticises these signifiers by re-articulating them not in terms of their own being, that is to say their inconsistency, but in terms of their submission to the "supreme being" of the State (70). We may then be led to the conclusion that any form of mass politics gives rise to submission to a bureaucratic and authoritarian State. For Badiou, this is not inevitable, however, if we refuse the logic of the primordial bond:

> The way in which the theme of the bond enters into the consolidation of the "masses" is through the substitution of this term for another, quite different one, which is the "mass movement." The imaginary attributes of gathering, cruelty, folly, and so on, are ascribed to the masses insofar as they rise up, join forces, riot. It is solely from the movement of the masses that we infer that mass politics exists through the totalisable figure of the bond. (71)

Insofar as a mass movement binds the disruptive force of the masses in new imaginary relations, we must reject the notion of the mass movement in favour of the unbinding of the masses. For Badiou, it was Sartre who provided us with "an exemplary glorification of this figure of identificatory transparency," the mass movement, through what he called the "group-in-fusion" (71). According to Sartre, we exist in a state of serial dispersal and isolation, only occasionally, in periods of revolutionary or social transformation, fusing together as unified groups. As the life of the group extends, however, and the sense of urgency that provided its original impetus weakens, the group ossifies and mutates into a bureaucratic structure, as its members correspondingly slide back into their individual lives of serial dispersal as part of the masses.[22] Whereas Sartre valorised these fleeting moments of group fusion as authentic political experiences, Badiou argues that it is the other way round, that it is the very inconsistency of masses that is political. A "mass movement," in Badiou's sense, is an historical phenomenon that *may be* an event for politics but is not, strictly speaking, political in-itself.[23] Politics, as the possibility of a moment of rupture with what exists, is rearticulated by the mass movement through the signifiers of the existing order, ultimately reinforcing the existing social bond.

THE MASSES AS A SIGNIFIER

The mass movement, according to Badiou, exists on the edge of a void, is the inconsistency at the core of all consistency—or to put it another way, the unpresentable at the heart of historical presentation; the Lacanian term for this void would be the Real. The void is unrepresentable, but we know that it exists through the movement that circulates around its rim. The void thus testifies to the dysfunction of the primordial bond, the inherent flaw in the structure and the uncovering of new possibilities.[24] Politics, therefore, is not about the creation of a new social bond but about an unbinding; the masses are the materialialisation of "extreme particularity, of the non-bond" (Badiou, "Politics Unbound" 73). The masses, in this sense, present a moment of unbinding; within capitalism the masses are precisely what counts for nothing, the void at the core of all that is representable. The eruption of the masses is a moment of openness that undermines the illusion of the social bond, whatever form that may take (parliamentary, nationalist or "actually existing" socialism), but as such it cannot be represented.[25] It is here that Badiou's notion of the masses can be differentiated from Ernesto Laclau's recent formulation of the "people" as an empty signifier (*On Populist Reason*). For Laclau, the identification with an empty signifier is "the *sine qua non* for the emergence of a 'people.' But the empty signifier can operate as a point of identification only because it *represents* an equivalential chain" (162). Representation, then, is the key. We can only maintain the fragile identities we have insofar as there is representation in the first place and (following Žižek's line of argumentation in *The Sublime Object of Ideology*) it is the signifier, the name, which retrospectively confers unity on the object.[26] Clearly we are on similar territory to Badiou's conception of the masses here, so what is it that separates the two positions?

I argued previously that from the perspective of Badiou's *Theory of the Subject* (1982) it is the very inconsistency of the masses that signifies its potential as a rupture with the existing socio-symbolic order. As a pure multiple, the masses can only appear as *no-thing*, a void, or what Badiou subsequently calls an *Event*. An Event emerges *ex nihilo* and, as Žižek puts it, is the Truth of a situation that makes visible what the official discourse has had to repress (*Ticklish* 130). The Event, in other words, is the void separating one closure from another and we must distinguish between the Event itself and its naming. The difference, writes Žižek, between an Event and its naming is that an Event is the traumatic encounter with the Real, while its naming is the inscription of the Event into language. The process of naming resignifies the Event and establishes the new order, the new readability of the situation (144). As the inconsistency of the masses coalesces into a new social bond and is named "the party" or "the mass movement," its intensive energy and potential is dissipated, as it is rearticulated through the emblems and signifiers of the existing social order. Furthermore, to the extent that its energies are rechanneled in this direction, the mass movement no longer functions as the site of potential rupture but only serves to reaffirm that order. For Laclau, on the other hand, the identity and unity of the object results from the operation of naming (*Populist* 104); thus the *name* becomes the ground for the object and cannot be subordinated to any preceding designation (such as the Real in Žižek). If the Real preceded the symbolic, writes Laclau, then we would have a situation of continuous fullness without differentation. Thus, he argues, "the Real is *within* the Symbolic" (118) and what he calls an "empty signifier" functions in the same way as the *objet a* in Lacan (127). Indeed, for Laclau, the logic of hegemony is "simply identical" with the logic of Lacan's *objet petit a* (116). Laclau is, of course, fully aware of the "extimate" nature of the Real, what Lacan calls its "intimate exteriority" (*Seminar VII* 139), as can be observed from his frequent discussions of the Thing. In order to stress, however, the predominant role of representation in the constitution of political identities, he plays down its exteriority to the symbolic, that sense in which, for early Lacan, the Real is indeed "without fissure" (*Seminar II* 97) and "resists symbolisation absolutely" (Lacan, *Seminar I* 66) and for later Lacan, the Real is associated with the impossible encounter and the beyond of the Symbolic, that is, with the *unassimilable* kernel of trauma (*Four Fundamenal* 55). Indeed, for Laclau, this aspect of the Real as the void is always *within* signification (105) and not outside of it, as Žižek and Badiou propose. This chapter, as should already be clear, follows Žižek and Badiou in accepting the Real as the absolute limit of signification and as that which is radically unassimilable into our socio-symbolic order.

Badiou's notion of the masses as an extreme particularity helps to clarify, I believe, how the masses function as a vanishing mediator, that is to say, how they can function as a catalyst in moments of transition but are then to be eclipsed by the very forces they have unleashed. The masses unbound will give rise to new possibilities which will cohere around new political insignia and imaginary emblems of identification, the mass movement. This movement will then in turn subsume the disruptive energy of the masses in a new social bond. As Hallward writes, "Badiou admits that we can only ever experience or *know* what is presented to us as consistent or unified, but it can sometimes happen, in the wake of an ephemeral and exceptional event, that we have an opportunity to *think*, and hold true to, the inconsistency of what there is" ("Order and Event" 99–100). There is an inevitability to the formation of a new social bond, or of a binding of the inconsistency of the masses into the consistency of a political party or movement; maintaining fidelity to the Truth of the Event is the role, at least for Badiou, of the political militant (Žižek, *Ticklish* 127–70). In this instance, the mass protests in favour of a peaceful and federal resolution to the economic and constitutional crisis of the former Yugoslavia have been eclipsed and rearticulated by virulent forms of exclusivist nationalism and neo-liberal "democratic" reformism—although, as I argued previously, these are simply two sides of the same coin.

Let me give one final example from the "100 Days" protests. By the mid 1990s the flags and emblems of the old Serbian royal family became increasingly evident at opposition rallies. In order not to be out-manoeuvred by Milošević, the opposition "became more royal than the King," adopting ever more extreme forms of nationalist rhetoric in order to oust the nationalist government (Woodward 357). Through adopting the emblems and signifiers of the old monarchy, the opposition no longer signified a rupture with the existing order but its continuation by other means. We can also see this tendency in the carnivalisation of the "100 Days" protests of 1996–97. Drawing on the work of Michel Chion, Pavle Levi observes that the protestors challenged the blatant acts of media manipulation through the production of brute noise. In short, the silence of the media concerning the electoral fraud was confronted through the production of noise by the demonstrators. While in the short run these carnivalesque demonstrations appeared to result in the victory of the opposition, "in the longer run it also became clear that in some sense they actually helped extend the rule of the established political order" (Levi 137; Chion).[27] The carnival acted as a safety-valve, allowing the protests to run their course while the regime slowly reasserted its control. In other words, the carnival is an act of sanctioned transgression that can be easily contained within and reconciled to the existing power structure. Despite the serious acts of resistance, notes Levi, "the protests largely remained within the confines of ethnic collectivism and national patriotism" (138). The "sonorous haze" of noise production served to mask the genuinely anti-nationalist voices and thus "concealed everything that had to remain unspoken, or at least muted, so that the consistency of the ethnocollectivist ideational framework could be maintained even during the period of social unrest" (139). In conclusion I will consider Kovačević's own politics, as they can be discerned from the film.

MIRACLES DO HAPPEN!

As with other Kovačević scripts there is a certain postmodern irony and self-referentiality to *The Professional*. In the opening scene of the protests of

October 2000, as the camera pulls back and cuts to the bank of screens, we see the silhouettes of Luka and his men watching these scenes on the screens in front of them, accompanied by a voiceover: "Roger! Hawk! Hawk [Luka Laban's code name], Come in! Over! Is there anyone alive? What shall we do, people? Over! This is the end, folks!" The film has thus opened with the end, before cutting to an aerial shot, one year later, of a taxi and the sound of a woman's laughter, as Luka listens in on his taxi radio to Teja's flirting with his secretary in his office. The film will also conclude with a reprise of the beginning. As Luka is about to leave the office, he mentions a play that Teja has written; "now there you are wrong," responds Teja, "I have never written a play." At that point Luka takes a small tape recorder from his pocket; he has recorded the whole of their meeting and all Teja now has to do is transcribe it into a script. We now hear the voiceover from the opening scene, as Luka walks back to his taxi, before it cuts to an image of the security police spying on Teja's office. There is, in short, circularity to the film's narrative and behind this to history itself, and here we can see the conservatism of Kovačević's politics.[28] History is repetition and there appears to be no way out—as we can see from the third narrative strand running through the film.[29] The meeting between Luka and Teja takes place against a backdrop of renewed militancy from the factory workers, who are protesting against the management's decision to privatise the firm. In his complete disregard and contempt for the work force, Teja, formerly of the democratic opposition, appears to be no better than the hardliners he has replaced. Indeed, throughout the film the opposition have been presented as nothing but buffoons and drunks. The political slogan of Teja's companion, the poet Mr Cast (so known because he keeps getting beaten up and having his limbs set in plaster cast) is simply "Don't blame Slobo, we are all shit," hardly one of the most rousing of revolutionary slogans. The former dissidents do not disappear from the scene from Kovačević's perspective but willingly accept their position in the new social bond. Similarly, the former hard-line communists remain in place. The internal security police might have undergone a name change and retired a few of the old guard, like Luka, but as we see in the final image, continue business as usual.

So where are the masses in this equation? Does the renewed militancy of the factory workers offer hope for an alternative to more of the same? It appears not. While Teja is in his meeting with Luka, the leader of the strike committee, Jovan (Miodrag Krstovic), is pressing for a meeting to discuss their grievances, which Teja keeps delaying. At one point Jovan bursts into the office to demand an immediate meeting and recognises Luka, who takes him to one side and asks him to postpone the strike and take the workers off the streets and back to the shop floor, which he does. It appears not only that Jovan is currently an informer for the secret police, but also that he was one under the previous regime. Moreover this strike is being orchestrated by the secret police. In Kovačević's rather pessimistic view, an "unbinding" in Badiou's sense is simply not possible and the film concludes on this ultimately conservative and fatalistic note. Contrary to such postmodern resignation, as Žižek observes, for Badiou "*miracles do happen*" (*Ticklish* 135). While an Event offers us no ontological guarantee and we can't predetermine which way things will go, it does open up possibilities of radical change through an absolute break with the existing order of representation. The masses have that potential insofar as they can impose themselves on the situation and create *ex nihilo* new possibilities of restructuring the symbolic field. In order to do this, however, they must break not only with the symbols of the present but also with the emblems of the past.

NOTES

1. This account of the Kosovo demonstrations follows Branka Magaš's account in "Kosovo between Yugoslavia and Albania" (1983), rpt. in *The Destruction of Yugoslavia* (1993), Ch. 1. For Magaš, these demonstrations marked the beginning of the end of Yugoslavia. My reason for mentioning these protests in a chapter which focuses on mass movements in Serbia in the 1990s is precisely that they were non-nationalist in character and therefore suggest the possibility of alternative scenarios to the final disintegration of the former Yugoslavia. It is this aspect of the protests that has subsequently been ignored, as fatalistic interpretations of Balkan history have come to dominate our understanding of the conflicts.
2. The definitive end of the Federal Republic came almost exactly ten years after the Priština student protests when Slovenia declared independence and the YPA entered the country in June 1991. Kosovo finally declared itself an independent sovereign state on the 17th of February 2008.
3. For a brief account of the peace movement in the former Yugoslavia, see Jeffs. For further accounts of the opposition and struggles against the Milośević regime, see Cohen, Gordy, Lazić and Thomas.
4. Magaš herself concludes that the wars of succession were neither a civil nor an ethnic conflict but a traditional war of territorial conquest by an aggressor state, Serbia (*Destruction* 327). Susan Woodward, however, points to the fact that the Federal Government was acting under pressure from the IMF to change the 1974 constitution and reassert central bank control over the economies of these two provinces (82).
5. On the silencing or ignoring of non-nationalist voices, see Ch. 7 of Dina Iordanova, *Cinema of Flames*, which describes the dilemmas facing those refusing to "take sides." Pavle Levi also notes that the recognition of the three ethnonational parties as the sole representatives of the Bosnian people after the 1990 elections effectively negated the existence of a fourth faction, "the significant and certainly not all too easily dismissable segment of the population consisting of all those who refused to be labeled exclusively in ethnic terms" (2). Susan Woodward repeatedly notes that there was never a country-wide referendum or election on the fate of the Federal Republc.
6. See Woodward, Ch. 4, on the rise of nationalism in both Serbia and Slovenia; also Gagnon on nationalism in Serbia and Croatia.
7. Writing in 2000 Dina Iordanova estimates that there have been over 250 feature films and documentaries made about the breakup, "making the Yugoslav break-up the event that inspired the most active cinematic output in post-Communist times" ("Introduction" 6).

8. Jameson obviously does not mean to say that Protestantism *per se* disappears from the historical scene but rather that its role as a catalytic agent disappears. In this sense, I would want to argue that the role of the masses, once eclipsed by historical forces, does not completely disappear but remains open to acts of retrieval and reactivation (see Alain Badiou ["Communist"] on the possibility of the reactivation of "The Communist Hypothesis" today). I would like to thank Ian Parker for reminding me of this point.
9. The protests were so named as a consequence of their duration and the protestors' habit of throwing eggs at government buildings.
10. I will come back to these protests, as they are represented in *The Professional*, but it is worth noting here that the scenes serve a rather different purpose for Dragojević than the argument I am developing here. The death masks are part of the symbolic network of the film, involving images of crucifixes, wounding and religious iconography (see Krstić 99–100). The carnivalesque atmosphere of the protests also serves to highlight the estrangement and alienation of the two teenage killers, as they are caught in the middle of protests but remain sealed in their self-enclosed airconditioned BMW (see Kronja 27–28). For a detailed analysis of these protests, see Lazić; also Levi, Ch. 5.
11. Goran Marković's *Cordon* (2002) is the only other film I have seen that deals directly with the mass protests of 1996–97. Unfortunately I had not seen this film before writing the current chapter and hope to be able to write about it at a future date.
12. The use of archival and documetnary footage is a common feature of many post-Yugoslav productions, most notoriously in Kusturica's *Underground* (1995) but also in Dragojević's *Pretty Village, Pretty Flame* (1996) and Danis Tanović's *No Man's Land* (2001). A fuller analysis than can be developed here would need to relate this back to the practice of montage in Yugoslav "New Film" of the 1960s. See Levi, Ch. 1, for an excellent discussion of montage and Goulding, Ch. 3, for an account of Yugoslav "New Film."
13. On the centrality of Rock music and culture to the protests, see Gordy 103–64 and Steinberg.
14. See Halligan. Films from this period that involve fragmented narratives and/or flashbacks would include: Manchevski's *Before the Rain* (1994), Kusturica's *Underground* (1995), Angelopoulos' *Ulysses' Gaze* (1995), Dragojević's *Pretty Village, Pretty Flame* (1996) and *The Wounds* (1998), Paskaljević's *Caberet Balkan* (1998) and Brešan's *Witnesses* (2004).
15. The story is itself an account of failed recognition and memory:

    A man comes up to you on the street and hugs you. He says, "Do you see some of the boys?" You were confused, as you are now, and asked him, "what boys?" He responds "Well the boys from the Army." You felt better; at last you had some information. So you said to him, "of course I do." He then asks "And who do you see most frequently?" You said, "I often see Marko Sedler." The man looked at you, lowered his eyes and said, "I am Marko Sedler."
16. About the most radical act we see in this film is Teja and his two drunken companions insisting that the band plays "The Government Will Fall," while everyone in the tavern sings along.
17. Again, we can see similarities with von Donnersmarck's *The Lives of Others* here.
18. "By most measures of predicting the success or failure of regimes in political power, it ought not to have survived as long as it [did]. Since legitimising its power as the successor of Serbia's League of Communists in December 1990, it has engaged in three losing military conflicts, produced over 500,000

refugees whose interests it had come to power promising to protect, presided over the hugest hyperinflation in modern times, and turned back on its original dangerous and defining promise to see 'all Serbs in one state.' Aside from its long list of failures, the party in power [has] not once received a majority of votes in an election, and each election after 1990 has seen its support declining further" (Gordy 1).

19. Gordy explores the destruction of alternatives in four fields: politics, the media, popular culture and everday life.
20. This first cycle, for Badiou, is the emacipatory politics we associate with the names Marx, Lenin and Mao.
21. Badiou makes a crucial distinction here between a "singularlity"—a novelty that appears intensely but has few consequences—and an "event"—a singularity whose consequences come to appear as intensely and powerfully as possible and thus have duration (Hallward, "Order and Event" 106). The eruption of the masses in the social order is an event in this sense.
22. For an excellent discussion of Sartre's theory of the group, see Fredric Jameson, *Marxism and Form* 244–74.
23. For Badiou, politics is a truth procedure that is at once singular and universal. The essence of politics, he writes, "is the prescription of a possibility in rupture with what exists" (*Metapolitics* 24)—or, as he has put it more recently, politics is "collective action, organised by certain principles, that aims to unfold the consequences of a new possibility which is currently repressed by the dominant order" ("Communist" 31).
24. As Hallward points out, "The concept of one single, universal, all embracing totality is mathematically incoherent" ("Ethics" 28). Being is multiple and all forms of unity and identity are secondary in relation to the multiplicity and inconsistency of being.
25. "A genuinely political organisation, or a collective system of conditions for bringing politics into being, is the least bound place of all. Everyone on the ground is essentially alone in the immediate solution of problems" (Badiou, "Politics Unbound" 76). We should keep in mind here that singularity is not opposed to universality, so that a truth procedure such as politics is at once singular and universal. As Peter Hallward has pointed out in his review of "The Communist Hypothesis," however, if the masses do not reconfigure into some kind of mass movement, it is not clear what kind of politics can emerge from Badiou's position. Badiou's own example of this new non-party politics is the *Organisation Politique*, of which he is a founding militant.
26. As Laclau writes, "representation is the absolutely primary level in the constitution of objectivity" (*Populist* 115).
27. It is also noteworthy here that Luka's transition from attempting to murder Taja to keeping him alive takes place during the New Year celebrations in 1996–97.
28. Kovačević is a royalist and member of the Crown Council of Aleksandar Karađorđević.
29. On the conservatism of Kovačević's script for Kusturica's *Underground*, see Slavoj Žižek, "Multiculturalism," as well as Levi, Ch. 3. While acknowledging the conservativism of such fatalistic and circular views of Balkan history, I have tried to argue against the grain of these readings. See Homer,"Nationalism" and "Retrieving."

Part III

Global Networks and Mass Identifications

7 Globality, the Totalitarian Mass and National Belonging

Effie Yiannopoulou

The last couple of decades have witnessed a revived interest in the work of Hannah Arendt which has spilled over the boundaries of political philosophy into fields of thought as diverse as psychoanalysis and cultural and African studies.[1] Most commentators agree that what energises this return to her thought is both the current revival of interest in the idea of totalitarianism (Canovan 25) but, also crucially, a reappraisal of the powerful critique that she levelled at Western intellectual and political traditions in the aftermath of World War II, starting with the publication of *The Origins of Totalitarianism* in 1951. For a generation of thinkers engaged in the critique of Western metaphysics, her mid-century association of European imperialism and early-modern raciology with totalitarian terror, her attack on nationalism, her desire for supra-national forms of citizenship and her belief in the (civic) community as the space in which both individual and collective identities are accorded meaning come across as having been ahead of their time and well suited to addressing highly mobile and unstable global relations of the present moment. My own concern in this chapter will be with the emergence of racialised ethnicity in a global context, focusing particularly on the emergence of global Englishness in the late 1940s, later to develop into what is today contemporary British multiculture. My aim will be to trace points of contact between this hybridised space's often absolutist claims to national identity and the fascist identity structures against which Englishness has historically defined itself in the last fifty years. To this end I will be invoking Hannah Arendt's analysis of the totalitarian mass, which I believe lays out the problems inhering in forms of mass collectivity that are premised on the fixity of the (racial, national, cultural) bond and the unitary, self-present subject.

My argument pays special attention to the question of mobility that implicates Arendt's understanding of "radical evil" in the construction of mass mentality. According to Arendt, radical evil, as a synonym and effect of the massification of the civic domain, becomes wedded to a politics of discursive transparency and subjective immobility that was used in totalitarian regimes to ward off what were perceived as unruly and uncontainable forms of movement, be they of identities, ideas or peoples. In a 1951 letter to Karl Jaspers, Arendt wrote:

> What radical evil is I don't know, but it seems to me it somehow has to do with the following phenomenon: making human beings as human beings superfluous. This happens as soon as all unpredictability—which, in human beings, is the equivalent of spontaneity—is eliminated. (qtd. in Birmingham, "Holes" 84)

Here, as elsewhere in her philosophical writings, Arendt posits unpredictability as the basic premise in her political vision. Although uncertain as to its essential meaning, she still postulates radical evil as what cancels out the contingency of political action, aligning it with the desire for complete comprehensibility, uniformity of opinion and a fundamental commonality that is devoid of the plurality and regenerative estrangement that are foundational to truly progressive politics.

It is this idea of the totalitarian mass as a space of arrested discursive and subjective mobility that I find useful in thinking, in the first part of this chapter, about the highly racialised notions of national belonging—what Giorgio Agamben calls "The Camp as the 'Nomos' of the Modern" (*Homo* 166)—that have emerged within the mobile structures of globalisation since the Second World War. Following Paul Gilroy's engagement with the impact of fascism on contemporary British multiculture, I argue that these hybridised networks continue to harbour traces of fascist biopolitical raciology, not least in asserting unbridgeable racial difference as the common bond that glues together not only militaristic groups of the far right or genocidal armies but, equally, the most legitimate of political collectives such as the British multicultural nation. The second part of the chapter presents Arendt's ideas of the totalitarian mass in more detail, while the third part returns to the beginnings of Britain's multicultural experiment in the 1940s when English national identity is articulated in global terms for the first time as a result of an increased transcultural, cross-over mobility bringing masses of immigrants to Britain from its crumbling colonial periphery. The defensive closing off of the nation's space to the presence of other cultures on its own territory is followed through in a reading of Rebecca West's famous treatise on treason, *The Meaning of Treason* (1949; 1965). Hers is, as I argue, the case of a feminist intellectual whose antifascist discourse carries the insignia of fascism in promoting a pattern of belonging to England that is organised around a form of collective solidarity reminiscent of the totalitarian mass. For where Arendt postulates the association of evil with fixity, West's writings are motivated by a deep anxiety over the mobility and the multi-locationality of evil, causing her to respond to the post-war climate of fluid transnational exchange with the desire to fix the position of the enemy and that of the national self.

GLOBAL MOBILITY, RACIALISED MULTICULTURE AND (THE EVIL OF) FASCISM

For Paul Gilroy, appeals to a pre-given, internal identity such as West's aim to restore certainty and stave off doubt and anxiety and are by now routine responses to the "turbulent waters of de-industrialization and the large-scale patterns of planetary reconstruction that are hesitantly called 'globalization'." The growth of nationalisms and other absolutist religious and ethnic identities or the accentuation of regional divisions function as forms of sanctuary that confer "certainty about who one is and where one fits, about the claims of community and the limits of social obligation" (*Against Race* 107). Probing into the psychic and affective subtext underwriting cultural identity formations today, Gilroy warns against the ongoing racialisation of the world that these proliferating exclusive identities speak of. Part of his strategy in thinking the modern category of race out of early twenty-first century cultural and political life, a project central in both his books *Against Race* and *After Empire*, is to link "encamped" thinking and community models of the present with the biopolitical racial paradigms dominant in both totalitarian and imperialist systems. Using Arendt's, and crucially other black thinkers',[2] emphasis on the existence of an intellectual continuity between the genocidal brutalities of European colonialisms and the later totalitarian genocide in Europe, Gilroy goes a step further to seek out the residual traces of fascist raciologies in the multicultural present.

Gilroy's engagement with fascism can perhaps be described as a justifiably anxious response to the pervasive, self-gratifying feeling shared by apparently difference-loving communities in the West that the brutalities attendant on racialiased difference have been superseded, thanks either to governmental intervention or to greater citizen sensitivity. His claim that there is such a thing as multicultural racism, which we need to comprehend as part of a web of discourses and histories that must be excavated (*Empire* 163), is backed by his desire to trace the changing meanings of fascism and to call for our re-education in recognising its many faces. As he observes, we must update ourselves as to what fascisms look, sound and feel like and redeem the concept from mystification and a certain trivialisation that attends its use as a general term of abuse to express a "sense of evil" that is frustratingly abstract (*Against Race* 145). Unlike commentators who identify totalitarianism's legacy in present-day large-scale events such as the genocides in Rwanda or Bosnia (Canovan 39), Gilroy alerts us to the structural invisibility of fascist race hierarchies in patterns of everyday thinking and perfectly legitimate codes of cultural and political conduct. In his own words,

> Emphasis on the genocidal processes in which fascisms have culminated should not diminish our sensitivity to the proto-fascist potentials secreted inside familiar everyday patterns of government, justice,

> thought, and action. The notions of absolute ethnicity that have created a sense of culture as something organic that can be grown or husbanded by the state and owned as a form of property by individual subjects are an interesting example of this possibility. They suggest that members of the dominant social group in a racialised social hierarchy do not have to imagine themselves to be superior; they need only assert unbridgeable difference to awaken the possibility of a fascist solidarity. (*Against Race* 229)

Considering fascism outside its original historical context, Gilroy nonetheless recognises the legacy of its claims in the most unlikely political spaces where essentialist bonding is invoked: in popular culture, in forms of democratic governmentality, both Right and Left, in alternative countercultures and black resistance politics (as is, for example, the case of the Nation of Islam) and, importantly, in notions of absolute racialised ethnicity at work even in the most liberal of multicultural democracies.

To be sure, Gilroy is an active supporter of British multiculture, defending its vision of tolerant, transcultural coexistence, and the race-free cosmopolitan economy it gestures towards, against attempts to compromise or dismiss it. He speaks, however, for many critics of multicultural projects when he uncovers racialised national feeling as an organising principle in its mechanisms. Only in February 2011, the British Prime Minister David Cameron launched an attack on British state multiculturalism on the grounds that it had failed its objectives by encouraging "different cultures to live separate lives" and not providing its citizens with "a clear sense of a shared national identity, open to everyone" (Wright and Taylor). Implicit in his aggressively integrationist rhetoric is the assumption that the failure pointed to is attendant on the multicultural nation's inability to establish itself as commonality. As Sara Ahmed has usefully argued, the multicultural nation is a historically specific negotiation of "the nation" and strives to construct a coherent "we" not by abolishing cultural differences but by emerging through them (Ahmed 101). Following a twisted logic that identifies cultural segregation, the result of racist discrimination and the *cause* of multiculturalism's failure, as the *effect* of multicultural policies, David Cameron alerts us to what has been all along British multiculture's essential desire to subsume the cultural differences it apparently celebrates to the interests of a coherent national culture. That this hybrid ethnic core is encoded in terms of dominant white, hence race-bound, values becomes all too obvious when, as soon as it is threatened by the "unassimilable" differences of new immigrants or asylum seekers, its "cosmopolitan, creolised history" goes out the window. "Instead," as Gilroy points out, "we are transported into the frozen realm of mythic time" (*Empire* 161), a past in which the idea of the "common" exists *prior* to that of the national community as a "being-in-common," a contradictory and self-doubting articulation which comes about as a result of inserting the "common" into historically specific relations of sociality (Nancy, *Inoperative* xxxvii). For Gilroy, this "frozen" multicultural nation, whose registers effectively neutralise the mobile play of cultural differences by conceiving of the cultures on its territory as self-identical categories that have been assigned a static meaning before the cultural encounter (Ahmed 104), harks back to the principles structuring the imperial nation and its companion categories, the slave plantation and the concentration camp (*Against Race* 60, 68). All of them emerged as specific forms of political administration and population control that relied for coherence on the discursive predictability that Arendt attributes to the totalitarian masses. In what follows, I will briefly examine the affinities between Arendt's understanding of the "mass" and the loss of individual and collective heterogeneity allied with radical evil, before turning my attention to West's clinical dissection of home-grown fascist evils and the model of globalised Englishness it construes.

HANNAH ARENDT AND THE TOTALITARIAN MASSES

For Arendt, Nazi and Stalinist forms of totalitarian rule emerge out of political systems that have no precedent in human history. What effectively contributes to their uniqueness is their call, for the first time in human history, "for the extinction of man as an individual" (Lang 149). Arendt is in no doubt that, more than a route to political, racial or military dominance in the struggle for domination within or among nation-states, totalitarian ideologies aim at "the transformation of human nature itself" (*Origins* 623). As she writes, "Difficult as it is to conceive of an absolute evil even in the face of its factual existence, it seems to be closely connected with the invention of a system in which all men are equally superfluous" (624). This is perhaps the closest one can get to a definition of radical evil in Arendt's work. Conceptualised in the negative as that which cannot be comprehended or explained through recourse to rationally-coded motives (self-interest, greed, or lust for power, for example), and for this reason never punished or forgiven, radical evil manifests itself in every attempt to convert human beings into "holes of oblivion" (624), and thus register them as superfluous and expendable. This "lack of being" that Arendt recognises as underpinning the superfluousness of human beings in fascist ideologies consists not only in the physical elimination of the individual in totalitarian death camps but, primarily, in the erasure of all signs of subjective plurality, self-contradiction and impermanence in favour of "a completeness, an integrity promised in submitting to a fantasy of omnipotence" (Birmingham, "Lying" 35). Indeed, when Arendt identifies "superfluousness" as the condition of non-belonging to the world, of not "being recognised and guaranteed by others" (612), she allies it not only with the victims of Nazi and Stalinist horror—the Jews or the Soviet dissidents that were subjected to systemic exclusion and persecution—but, equally, with a more general state of ideological and political uprootedness responsible for organising economically and socially superfluous individuals into totalitarian masses. Berel Lang speaks for many Arendt commentators when he observes that, for Arendt,

> in totalitarianism, as in many other systems of evil, the perpetrator himself also was affected, if not in the same *terms*, equally fundamentally. At its extreme, totalitarianism obliterates individual freedom and reason on both sides: the superfluity of man, in other words, becomes a general principle, encompassing the system as a whole and everyone caught up by it. (150)

The "superfluity of man" in totalitarian systems underscores the loneliness that Arendt posits as a key structural principle in the "collectivism" of the masses (*Origins* 456). Even though they invoke, and effectively rely for their existence on, large numbers of people, the masses, in Arendt's understanding, are a space of loneliness, atomisation and loss of self. Historically, they emerge following the breakdown of the class system in European nation-states in the twentieth century, when masses of "dissatisfied and desperate men" feed on a climate of "social atomization and extreme individualization" (421) to join together in the name of political apathy and failed citizenry.[3] In Arendt's words, "Masses are not held together by a consciousness of common interest and they lack that specific class articulateness which is expressed in determined, limited, and obtainable goals" (414). Bereft of party affiliation or common social and economic bonds, what the "mass men" share is a feeling of "selflessness" that is less an expression of "individual idealism" (419) than a sign of ideological homelessness, a radical loss of self-interest that renders them vulnerable to propagandistic rhetoric and accentuates their expendable status within the totalitarian system. A chaos of individual interests, the masses in her sense of the term lack the transmission belts between the individual and the group that are guaranteed by stable political structures in democratic government and rely on an "adaptability and absence of continuity" (*Origins* 408) for their survival.

It is important to note, at this point, that the politics of mobility underwriting Arendt's theory of the masses is dual, calling attention both to their fickleness and to their desire for stability. Arendt emphasises the extent to which the masses, devoid of rational conviction and internal structure as they are, materialise as an effect of their ability to adapt to propaganda, which effectively endows them with meaning. For this reason, they constitute the perfect social mechanisms through which totalitarian movements safeguard the "perpetual-motion mania" that guarantees their existence, since they "can remain in power so long as they keep moving and set everything around them in motion" (408). At the same time the masses long for a "completely consistent, comprehensible, and predictable world" that will offset the fortuitousness that pervades reality (463). In promising a fixed and homogeneous world vision, fascist ideologies appear "like a last support in a world where nobody is reliable and nothing can be relied upon." They offer an escape route out of a reality that is experienced as painful through the "strict avoidance of contradictions that seems to confirm a man's identity outside all relationships with others" (615). Although "set[ting] everything in motion," therefore, fascism cancels out "the capacity for motion" that is foundational to the subject's ability to re-invent itself and its world (600). To Arendt, this idea of unpredictable "motion" differs markedly from the laws of movement dictated by nature and history which totalitarianism's total terror is designed to translate into reality (Canovan 28). These discourses of biological and historical determinism rely on the principle of non-contradiction to institute subjects and collectives as the result of natural or historical inevitability. In that sense, the frantic expansionism and "chaotic, nonutilitarian, manically dynamic movement of destruction" (Canovan 26) driving totalitarian regimes forward may be in fact construed as fostering a world of subjective and political immobility best represented through Arendt's description of the mass as a group of individuals squashed against each other and unable to move. Bands of iron, she writes, hold them "so tightly together that it is as though their plurality had disappeared into One Man of gigantic dimensions." Reducing the collective to a "single" thing, as mass discourses do, is equal to eliminating the space between individuals, "pressing men against each other," and thus destroying the "one essential prerequisite of all freedom which is simply the capacity of motion" (600).

In contrast to this, the political, in Arendt's anti-communitarian logic,[4] is allied with a public space of togetherness that is structured around the conflictual coexistence of heterogeneous viewpoints made possible through respect for the "spaces" of division within the collective and the retreat of the "common." As such, it operates in terms of a non-teleological temporality and movement best articulated in her theory of natality. As Arendt explains, totalitarian terror eliminates the "very source of freedom which is given with the fact of the birth of man and resides in his capacity to make a new beginning" (601); it slows down the movement induced by the birth of each human being, which, in a sense, begins the world anew. And the world, in Arendt's argument, is born again with every new individual arrival in a series of repetitions that come to alter the codes of the system in terms of which they become meaningful. Julia Kristeva identifies in this "act of refoundation" and continuous rebirth (of the world and the subject) the basis for a politics of plurality which is open to the experience of surprise and which can guard against totalitarian "massification" ("Refoundation" 353–54, 358).

TREASON AND GLOBAL ENGLISHNESS IN THE 1940S

Rebecca West's *The Meaning of Treason* is premised on its author's expressed desire to call the British public's attention to the political significance of a series of treason trials conducted in the late 1940s and lasting until the early 1960s. Starting with the trials during the mid 1940s of British fascists William Joyce and John Amery, the book proceeds to report on a series of espionage scandals and subsequent trials that shook Britain in the 1950s and 1960s. First serialised in *The Evening Standard* in the late 1940s,[5] her critical commentaries were intended to alert a wide readership to the changing mechanisms of political treachery and the power games of the Cold-War era in which post-war Britain had already become embroiled as one of its keenest players. Clearly, West's project in analysing home-grown fascism is to call attention to national treason as a form of political evil whose hold on the popular imagination has begun to wane.

It should be noted from the outset that West's understanding of treason is far from uncomplicated. To be sure, her condemnation of treachery in *The Meaning of Treason* is for the most part unequivocal, coming to the fore through emotionally-charged commentary on the legal proceedings and questions of sovereignty, citizenship, allegiance, origins and belonging. It comes as a surprise, then, that in the concluding pages of the book, West remarks that

> All men should have a drop of treason in their veins, if the nations are not to go soft like so many sleepy pears. Men must be capable of imagining and executing and insisting on social change if they are to reform or even maintain civilization, and capable too of furnishing the rebellion which is sometimes necessary if society is not to perish of immobility. (413)

Clearly bearing the imprint of her modernist appreciation of textual duplicity,[6] this passage presents West as sharing Hannah Arendt's recognition that a politics of mobility underwrites the politics of change necessary for maintaining civilised societies free from evil. Still, this is, at best, an unexpected conclusion for West to reach, having just spent 400 pages extolling the gains involved in maintaining political and social stability by means of eradicating treason from the system. What largely accounts for the ambivalent inscription of treachery in her work, as well as West's revised assessment of the relationship between mobility and political reform, is a mixture of oppositional preoccupations that structure her text and post-war political outlook: on one hand, a deep concern for justice and improved social relations and, on the other, an even deeper anxiety experienced in the face of an emerging world order where the social, national or racial categories of the past can no longer be easily accommodated.

Treason, it is useful to remember, is a register that presupposes a structure of national and cultural loyalty. It assumes a community whose limits are definable and whose books assign clear roles to citizens and sovereigns. To exist as a (political) category, treason needs to materialise within the juridico-political space opened up by the law of sovereignty upholding the modern nation-states. And the logic of rule behind modern sovereignty, as Giorgio Agamben reminds us via the work of Carl Schmitt, is defined always in relation to an outside, an exemption, which helps constitute the realm of the sovereign by being included in it, yet always in a clear, orderly hierarchy (*Homo* 15–18). To be sure, it is stable frontiers that confer legibility and legitimacy on any claim to citizenship and national belonging. By contrast, the restructuring of British society, following the chaos and madness left behind by the Second World War (West, *Meaning* 139), takes place within a system of international relations marked by transnational, post-independence mobility and cultural cross-overs. What alarms West is the realisation that treason, while originally situated in the margins of the political order, now gradually begins to infiltrate the domain of mainstream politics and enters "an unlocalizable zone of indistinction" (Agamben 19). Even more threateningly, rather than operating solely within the bounds of official (covert or overt) ideological antagonisms, treason in 1950s Britain seems to have accrued cultural legitimacy in the eyes of a population either indifferent to or unable to decode the semantic nuances and differential dynamics of treachery. In West's own ironic admission, there are many English people who "would have felt acutely embarrassed" by lieutenant Terence Waters' story of bravery in the Korean War, feeling "more at ease with many of the traitors in this book," since "treason has a certain style, a sort of elegance, or, as the vulgar would say, 'sophistication'" (*Meaning* 288–89) that old-fashioned, patriotic heroism lacks. To the uneasy West, the American scientist's frivolous response to the suspicion of treachery—consisting in his gossiping away valuable knowledge to a Russian official—evacuates the (national, political or cultural) "outside" of any meaningful existence.

In light of this, it is no accident that English treason legislation, which dates from the reign of Edward III, has been rarely used in the last fifty years. The laws used to prosecute the crime have grown so dusty with neglect that the legal textbook *Blackstone's Criminal Practice* stopped including the Treason act of 1351 in the 1990s ("Could UK Taleban Fighters be Tried for Treason?"). It appears that in the multicultural, multiracial and multiethnic Britain of the late twentieth and early twenty-first centuries, treason lacks a clear definition, an audience and a reason for being.[7] In this climate of loosening sovereign ties, locating the traitor is at times an impossibility. Rebecca West's hard political line on the question of treason, her very invocation of the discourse of treason, to be precise, is a measure of her uneasiness and suspicion before a world organised around ambient warfare and unlocatable, because constantly mobile, enemies.

A certain kind of mobility in the structure of warfare is already evident in the war tactics of World War II. Yet it becomes far more pronounced on the ideological battlefields opened up by espionage practices during the Cold-War era. Consider, for example, the case of William Joyce, the notorious "Lord Haw Haw," whose court case constitutes the first and perhaps best-researched and most-appreciated piece of investigative analysis in West's book.[8] Joyce was indicted on three counts of high treason, all of which revolved around his fascist broadcasts over the radio from Nazi Germany in the years between 1939 and 1945. What helped materialise his "treasonous" intentions was the radio technology available at the time, which enabled his voice to slip into thousands of British households, invoking the intimacy of a friend sitting in front of the family hearth, yet slippery, undetected, unstoppable and uncontrollable in its effects. Joyce was tried and hanged on account of his voice, the last man in Britain to go to the gallows for treason in the system's final attempt to stabilise and silence a voice that already stood metonymically for treason. Both (treason and the voice) were by now on the move and in need of containment.

Though considered by most a polarised ideological structure, the Cold War that figures in West's narrative is shown to rely on espionage strategies that have left behind the clear-cut battle lines of World War II, and have initiated a secret and undeclared, almost rhizomatic kind of warfare. West is clearly annoyed and worried. In her coverage of a number of espionage trials in the 1950s, communist spies are shown to organise themselves in obscure networks; constantly on the move, they go forward and back on themselves, they change camps, compromise their loyalties (as is the case with double agents) and, worst of all, most of them remain uncaptured and escape punishment. If the concept of treason in its most basic configuration invokes the inside/outside problematic in calling attention to the "enemy within" the national community, the structures of espionage that West uncovers dismantle the dichotomy by rendering the detection of the enemy almost untenable. Writing about the "War on Terror" in the early twenty-first century, Nikos Papastergiadis draws our attention to the "dispersed structure of terrorist warfare that has developed in response to the mobile technologies of globalisation" (Margaroni and Yiannopoulou 21). Following similar tactics of dispersal, espionage strategies in the 1950s and 1960s disorientate the ideologies surrounding citizen loyalty and promote an understanding of evil as fundamentally mobile, multilocational and often unlocatable.

Rebecca West responds to the perceived threat to British national sovereignty by attempting to re-codify the meaning of treason. The task that she assigns herself is clearly an interpretive one, her challenge being to recast the concept of treason as a readable, decodable category. There is little doubt that West's narrativisation of treason, her lengthy analyses of courtroom and personal drama in widely-circulating magazines or her irritation at the secrecy surrounding some of the trials all constitute progressive political statements. They are committed to the principles of a democratic politics whose openness is a measure of its "narrati*visibility*," the site, and sight, of a "shared meaning-making" (Dayal 8). Where she fails her best political instincts is in cancelling out the imaginary and differential dynamics motivating the sign in the name of a relentless pursuit of facts. Instead of her narrative assuming, or aiming to construct, a polis as a site of *inter-est*

(Kristeva, "Hannah Arendt, or Life is a Narrative" 52), an intermediate space in which every act of narration contributes, through its "ever-renewing strangeness" (70), to the rebirth of the subject, it forecloses semantic (and subjective) unpredictability and seeks to compensate for cultural transformation by situating truth in the muddled-up, fictional landscape that her less observant co-citizens mistake for reality. How else can one read West's attempt to extract treason from the "world of fancy," dream or image-making (as in films) and re-invest it with the factual credibility of a railway accident or a jewel robbery (*Meaning* 273–74)?[9] Contributing to the gradual conservative twist in her socialist, feminist and narrative politics, West's efforts to stabilise the referent suggest a vision of the polis, and especially of the national collective, as a site devoid of the self-generating strangeness and consequent interlocking plurality of different perspectives that makes the political for Arendt the space of subjective and collective survival. Survival is certainly also crucial to West's project, except that its call to close off the political, and to a large extent cultural, borders of Britain seems to rest on exclusionary mechanisms of identification with the motherland that seek to protect English culture from disruptive outside influences and differences. In this sense, West's stabilising readings of treason may be read as her attempt to make the idea of a coherent, and at the same time morally upright, Englishness meaningful.

Nowhere is her "commitment to the national" more attentively pursued than in West's psycho-biographical profile of William Joyce. While publicly probing into his private life, thoughts and fascist motivations, West is engaged in more than rigorous investigative journalism. Her need to underscore the "irony" with which his case and death were tinged from the start (17), Joyce having been hanged, to all intents and purposes, for betraying a country that was never legally his own since he owed the King of England only "temporary allegiance" (26),[10] is undercut by her anxious dismissal of his "right" to claim allegiance to England. What is at issue, more perhaps than the patriotic premises of his fascism, is the invocation of England and the English sovereign as the target of his identificatory investment in the first place. In what makes for a fascinating reading of the temporal logistics that formed the core of the prosecution's case against Joyce, West spends tens of pages disproving his claim to be "a young man of pure British descent" (*Meaning* 20). She dwells with vigour on his Irish roots (*Meaning* 16, 20, 113), the treachery that runs in his family blood (his father betrayed his people by being an Anglophile [18, 50]) and the disturbing artificiality of his presence (25, 40), all of which automatically invoke the clear, honourable, face of an authentic Englishness at the opposite end. And though genuine in her anti-fascist critique and her anti-Nazism, West presents British fascism at times as a marginal problem that touched British society of the 1930s only superficially. The fascist parties of Sir Oswald Mosley and William Joyce did not number, it is suggested, sufficient members to make them truly dangerous for the political stability of the country and certainly failed to attract really "distinguished" supporters from the upper classes (72).

Subtly invoked as it may be, the cultural and racial superiority of the English constitutes a strategic assumption in West's construction of Englishness and lends legitimacy to her claims. Unlike interwar (and even wartime) inscriptions of Englishness, that seek to uncover patterns of national self-understanding in terms of class and local divisions (an upper-class, or rural, or industrialised Englishness, for example),[11] West's imaginary projections onto the national collective resonate with global overtones. They are intent on articulating an "ethics of Englishness" that materialises on the stage of global exchange, as in West's narrative England is constantly pitted against Ireland, Italy, Russia and America to achieve self-definition. In this way evaluative judgments on other races and peoples create a sense of national culture that is both "comprehensible and habitable" (Gilroy, *Empire* 97). Robert Young has recently argued that "global Englishness" emerged during the expansion of the British Empire in the nineteenth century. "Englishness was defined," Young remarks, "less as a set of internal cultural characteristics attached to a particular place, than as a transportable set of values which could be transplanted, translated and recreated anywhere on the globe" (232). The emptying or universalisation of Englishness took place in the colonies, according to Young, and developed largely for the sake of the English diaspora. Likewise, West's treatise on treason promotes Englishness as a set of "transportable values," yet its immediate site of reference is the very "territory" of England which is becoming increasingly globalised and culturally varied in the late 1940s and 1950s. With the arrival of the *Empire Windrush* at Tilbury in June 1948, the country enters a new phase of historical development marked in equal measure by the gradual dismantling of the British colonial empire and the influx of racially and culturally diverse immigrants from the colonial periphery. Giving rise to a sense of national discomfort that emerges in the face of waning cultural and racial homogeneity, immigrant movement into the metropolitan centre extends and accentuates the feeling of national crisis experienced during the war and contributes to England's self-perception as an imperiled culture, what Paul Gilroy describes as "the morbid culture of a once-imperial nation that has not been able to accept its inevitable loss of prestige in a determinedly postcolonial world" (*Empire* 117).[12] Though not directly addressing Britain's postcolonial experience of difference(s of colour and culture) on its own soil, West's compensatory response to the possible deterritorialisation of Englishness is, nonetheless, articulated and made intelligible in the context of the nation's generalised cultural reaction to England's increasingly uneasy self-understanding as a decentred transnational "home." Her challenge to fascism and "the giant inconvenience of Communism" (*Meaning* 195) taps into the English public's post-war, post-imperial confusion in order to codify both political and cultural differences as threats. There is, indeed, little evidence in *The Meaning of Treason* that

West's defence of English valour, honour, integrity and justice, the rule that the occasional aberration of a traitor only serves to confirm, conjures up Englishness as the "incorporative identity" that "could involve other peoples, religions and cultures," which Robert Young sees developing in the nineteenth century (237).

I am more inclined to identify in West's text signs of what Paul Gilroy has called "post-imperial melancholia," England's, that is, unwillingness to engage with the brutalities marking its imperialist ventures and its inability to mourn the passing of a coherent and distinctive national culture (*Empire* 97–98). Nowhere in *The Meaning of Treason* can one detect clear signs of an awareness that the ideological structures within which her re-articulation of treason and Englishness is couched are suspect, contributing to and sustaining Britain's past imperial evils and present decolonisation conflicts, which proliferate and gain momentum in the 1950s.[13] Unlike her progressive stance in *Black Lamb and Grey Falcon* (1942), where West openly identifies racism with (mostly Nazi and partly British) imperialism, her reflections on treachery remain curiously silent about the evil smudges on the clear face of honourable Englishess, the great unsaid acting as the moment of national "oblivion" that is foundational in turning others into "holes of oblivion." In this respect, contrary to her recognised political activism, West fails to perform what to Hannah Arendt is the most important political act, which is to own up to the horrors of historical and contemporary experience. "We can no longer afford," writes Arendt in the summer of 1950, "to take that which was good in the past and simply call it our heritage, to discard the bad and simply think of it as a dead load which by itself time will bury in oblivion" (*Origins* xxvii). Arendt relates this individual and collective disavowal of horror to the human being's refusal to confront its state of non-belonging, lack of unity and fundamental mobility. In her vocabulary, refusing to accept the human being's unpredictability effectively eliminates the individual, renders "all men . . . equally superfluous" (*Origins* 624) and generates a mass mentality that supplants the individual will to act and thus engage in transformative politics.

Unexpected though it may be for a narrative so openly political in its critique of fascism, West's ambivalent inscription of treason assigns to Englishness the dubious traits that Arendt attributes to the totalitarian masses. Through repeated slippages in her narrative identifications, she constructs an idealised, perfectly comprehensible, predictable England unmarked by self-division and difference, an England that English people continue to cite and recycle with neurotic persistence to the present (Gilroy, *Empire* 97). In emptying Englishness of evil and ignoring the contemporary realities of race and imperialism, West reproduces in *The Meaning of Treason* fascism's need for uniform identity structures and anticipates late-twentieth century British multiculture's responses to questions of racial and cultural difference. West is certainly far from lending legitimacy to fascist ideologies and practices. Rather, her combat against fascism deploys Enlightenment principles (of the unitary character of subjective and collective identities) that release their potential for dangerous ethnocentrism when articulated on, and in relation to, the homely territory. In that sense, her narrative comes to lend support to Gilroy's claim that fascist racial hierarchies and biopolitical commitments are not only attractive to the aspirations of the social-democratic Left but they persist in mechanistic notions of national culture that have developed as a response to global mobility in the last fifty years (*Empire* 158–59). At the end of the day, West's treatise does not so much issue a call to rethink the idea of treason as create a framework within which contemporary readers may consider what is at stake in the persistent legacy of fascism in post-war global politics and, crucially, the stories that Western cultures have been telling themselves about their tolerant and liberal selves.

NOTES

1. See, for example, Julia Kristeva's biography *Hannah Arendt* (2001) and Richard H. King and Dan Stone's collection of essays *Hannah Arendt and the Uses of History: Imperialism, Nation, Race, and Genocide* (2007).
2. Arendt was perhaps the exception among white post-war intellectuals in constructing this intellectual genealogy. By contrast, there was a long line of black mid-century thinkers, such as W. E. B. Du Bois and Aimé Césaire, who vociferously argued that Europe's history of the slave trade and its colonial expansion harboured the intellectual seeds that would later make totalitarian atrocities possible.
3. Arendt's claim that the masses consisted mostly of economically and socially disenfranchised individuals is not backed up by historical evidence, according to Peter Baehr. His argument that fascism also drew supporters from the mainstream of political and social life, respectable citizens who "evinced a distinctive economic sectoral bias," unveils what is perhaps a homogenising tendency in Arendt's theory on the masses (17).
4. Ronald Beiner claims that Arendt's understanding of citizenship is not communitarian and is marked by an anxiety about identity-based politics (44, 56 n3).
5. The book was published in 1947 in the United States and in 1949 in Britain after serialisation in the *Evening Standard*. In 1963, it was updated to include scientific and diplomatic espionage (Glendinning 185, 187).
6. Recent critical commentary of West's writings challenges post-war biographical readings of her work—unduly concerned with the details of her private life, her illicit affair with H. G. Wells, her illegitimate child and liberal sexual conduct—by redirecting attention to West's modernist contribution to formal experimentation in her early novels, *The Return of the Soldier* (1918), *The Judge* (1922) and *Harriet Hume* (1929). See Scott; also Mackay, "Lunacy" 125–26.
7. This has continued to be the case until recently, when Britain began to consider reactivating the dormant legislation to prosecute British Taleban fighters (in 2001) or more recently British Muslim clerics (2005).
8. To many of the book's early critics, this was its most "solid" achievement. See Kalven 379; also Gault and Deininger.

9. I agree, in part, with Marina Mackay, who attributes Rebecca West's interest in treason to her fascination with the traitors' ability to construct alternative fictional realities that compensate for their disempowerment. It is also important, however, to call attention to her narrative's textual slippages that, as in this case, effectively reveal a tension in her account of treason's relationship to "fantasy" and reality, and, consequently, in her discursive positionings *vis-à-vis* the idea of treason itself ("Muriel Spark" 509, 517).
10. It emerged during the trial that Joyce was, in fact, an American citizen, the son of Irish parents who were initially naturalised American citizens and later British subjects who did not, however, renew their British citizenship.
11. See John Baxendale's account of J. B. Priestley's "I Had See a Lot of Englands" for an example of interwar and wartime discourses of Englishness.
12. When the first West Indian immigrants from Jamaica disembarked from the *Empire Windnrush* at Tilbury, the movement of people within the empire was still fairly unrestricted. The discomfort at the changing racial and cultural texture of England intensified in the last decades of the twentieth century, generating the need for tougher legislation that would effectively protect the (white) English from the racial immigrant threat. Edward Heath's 1971 Immigration Bill and the 1981 British Nationality Act effectively abandoned, according to Ian Baucom, territorial conceptions of nationality, based on the *ius soli* principle, to legislate in favour of a racialised conception of national identity (12). Substituting the genealogical principle of "patriality" for the law of the soil in the determination of nationality "effectively guaranteed that most of those who would qualify as patrials would be the children or grandchildren of whites who had moved abroad rather than the children of Indians, Pakistanis or Nigerians whose parents or grandparents had been born in the colonies" (12, 13).
13. I will only mention indicatively the Mau Mau Uprising in Kenya (1952–1960) and the Cypriot struggle for independence (1955–1959).

8 Geographies of Cultural Globalisation and Cosmopolitanisms of the Future

Joseph Michael Gratale

By its very nature the study of the processes associated with globalisation requires a mode of analysis which embraces a trans-disciplinary orientation. As Fredric Jameson notes, globalisation "falls outside the established academic disciplines, as a sign of the emergence of a new kind of social phenomenon" ("Preface" xi), lacking as it does a fixed disciplinary domain yet requiring theorisation which is neither too narrow nor overly generalised. In attempting to negotiate between these twin dangers, this chapter focuses on a particular aspect of globalisation known as cultural globalisation and considers the potential implications of its intensification for individuals and collectivities. To what extent does cultural globalisation create new possibilities of identification? And if we call globalisation "a new kind of social phenomenon," will it not be necessary to find ways of articulating new geographies of meaning? Finally, can the intricate processes of cultural globalisation facilitate the emergence of a postnational order in which the ideas of cosmopolitanism might play a leading role in the formulations of new political communities?

Given this discourse of "newness" that I seem to be utilising in reference to globalisation, perhaps some clarification is in order. While key characteristics of globalisation have certainly been around for centuries,[1] its development, according to Immanuel Wallerstein's world-system's analysis, is primarily capitalist driven and dates back to the beginning of the modern world economy during the long sixteenth century (*Historical Capitalism* 115). For the historical context that I am focusing on, the following point is essential: since the 1970s we have been experiencing an accelerated phase of global interconnectedness (Waters 186). Though seemingly obvious, this position does not represent a consensus view. Some regard globalisation with skepticism, holding that its impact on contemporary social structures is negligible, or that globalisation as a conceptual framework is fraught with dilemmas, and hence its actual existence "in question," to use Hirst and Thompson's phrase.[2] My use of the term derives from a number of perspectives, one being that of Roland Robertson, who suggests that globalisation refers both "to the compression of the world and [to] the intensification of consciousness of the world as a whole" (*Globalization* 8). Alternatively, it may be expressed as the linking of "distant localities in such a way that local happenings are shaped by events occurring many miles away and vice versa" (Giddens, *Consequences* 64). In addition to Robertson and Giddens, the work of David Held et al. fills in many gaps in terms of defining this contested concept. As they indicate, globalisation should be approached as "a process (or set of processes) which embodies a transformation in the spatial organization of social relations and transactions—assessed in terms of their extensity, intensity, velocity and impact—generating transcontinental or interregional flows and networks of activity, interaction, and the exercise of power" (Held et al. 16). This explanation captures the dynamics of globalisation, particularly its transformative qualities and its multifarious attributes. In acknowledging the spatial component, both definitions make clear that any theoretical treatment of globalisation will entail surveying and mapping the newly emergent geographies resulting from its processes and impacts.

SOCIAL LANDSCAPES

In *The Communist Manifesto*, Marx and Engels famously described the rapidly changing conditions transpiring in the industrialising countries of Western Europe. "All fixed, fast-frozen relations," they state, "with their train of ancient and venerable prejudices and opinions, are swept away, all new-formed ones become antiquated before they can ossify. All that is solid melts into air" (K. Marx 224). Although the excerpt was written in the middle of the nineteenth century, its contemporary relevance is striking,[3] especially the phrase "all that is solid melts into air," which has been picked up by several contemporary social theorists. In his work *Liquid Modernity*, Zygmunt Bauman makes use of the metaphors "fluidity" and "liquidity" to describe the nature of our present condition. As he sees it, any "dense and tight network of social bonds" represents a barrier for "global powers bent on dismantling such networks for the sake of their continuous and growing fluidity, that principal source of their strength and the warrant of their invincibility" (14).

Building on this metaphor of "liquid modernity," John Urry calls for new frameworks and methodologies to capture the essence of what he terms "mobile sociology" (*Global Complexity* 59). Global fluidity, he argues, is characterised by a number of varied qualities including unevenness, unpredictability, diverse viscosity, and a partial lack of structure (60). Urry also makes use of the concepts of *disjuncture* and *scapes*, terms developed by Arjun Appadurai, which provide a helpful framework for grasping the varied forms of global flows. As Appadurai explains, the "new global cultural economy" can best be understood through a deployment of a conceptual construct involving the following five designated scapes: ethnoscapes, mediascapes, technoscapes, financescapes and ideoscapes ("Disjuncture" 296). Each designated prefix embraces a specific domain. For example, an ethnoscape refers to the mobile persons or groups which comprise the world's population, including, among others, tourists, refugees, immigrants, business travelers and guest workers. An ideoscape concerns the realm of ideology which "consists of a concatenation of ideas, terms and images" (299). Likewise Manuel Castells' work on the "information age," particularly his metaphor of the "network society," have been pivotal. Collectively, the insights of Appadurai, Bauman, Urry, Robertson and Castells, among others, have provided a new set of analytical tools for investigating the global present.

A number of theorists have put forward the argument that disciplines such as sociology are in dire need of re-conceptualisation. The concept of "society," for instance, is obviously a foundational element in this discipline. As Wallerstein points out, no concept "is more pervasive in modern social science than society, and no concept is used more automatically and unreflectively than society, despite the countless pages devoted to its definition" ("World-Systems" 137). To illustrate this problem, consider the following definition of "society" in a standard sociology textbook.[4] A society, it suggests, is a "fairly large number of people who live in the same territory, are relatively independent of people outside it, and participate in a common culture" (Schaefer 433). What relevance does such a concept have today, ignoring as it does the various contexts of the local and the global, the layered, dynamic and juxtapositional arrangement of contemporary relations? As Urry argues, sociology "will not be able to sustain itself as a specific and coherent discourse focused upon the study of given bounded or 'organised' capitalist societies" (*Global Complexity* 3). Other theorists go even further. Ulrich Beck, for instance, calls social science classifications "zombie categories," by which he means "living dead categories which blind the social sciences to the rapidly changing realities inside the nation-state containers, and outside as well" (Beck 24). The deployment of concepts such as "liquidity," "flows" and "scapes" counters the territorialised and structured modes of social analysis so long a part of social science methodologies; what is needed in the twenty-first century, suggests Urry, is a "sociology beyond societies" *(Sociology* 211).

NATIONAL IMAGININGS

> What does it mean, at the end of the twentieth century, to speak . . . of a "native land?" What processes rather than essences are involved in present experiences of cultural identity? What does it mean to write as a Palestinian? As an American? As a Papua-New Guinean? As a European? (Clifford, *Predicament* 275–76)

In questioning the relevance of such a concept as "society," there emerges the imperative to provide new paradigms for the social interactions of the individual, and of the collective. Does the same hold true, however, for the category of the nation-state and national identification? Clearly, James Clifford's queries have a greater resonance than ever, given the frequency of celebratory discourses of an emerging postnational order. Are, however, national forms of individual and collective identification just another "zombie category"? According to Benedict Anderson, the nation "is an imagined political community . . . because the members of even the smallest nation will never know most of their fellow-members, meet them, or even hear of them, yet in the minds of each lives the image of their communion" (6). Anderson's "national imagining" is appealing in its exposure of the constructed and invented qualities of the nation; despite being a formation of identity, the solidarities that are assumed to exist lack depth and meaning. While this may very well be the case, something else is blatantly clear about national identification: its persistence. Although a number of factors and forces have been working against various forms of nationalism, it still remains pervasive and relevant to many for a variety of reasons, including identification, ideology, emotional and sentimental appeal, and its necessity as a prerequisite for the processes of modernisation. This durability of national solidarities is manifested in "strident local forms of religious nationalism, of consciousness of social homogeneity and collective myths of shared tradition and common destiny" (Niezen 177). So while the nation may be "imaginary," the view that "nations matter"[5] can also be uttered with equal certainty. Craig Calhoun sees nationalism as meaningful "in part because it has offered such a deeply influential and compelling account of large scale identities and structures in the world—helping people to imagine the world as composed of sovereign nation-states" (8). In short, statements about the arrival of a postnational order are certainly premature. What is also apparent is not only that globalisation is capitalist driven, but also nation-state driven. The continued preeminence of the nation-state is part of the logic of globalisation, which "extends the regime of uneven development as it exists between developed and developing nations" (Radhakrishnan 89). In other words, some countries benefit more from particular aspects of globalisation than others. At the same time it is impossible to ignore the way the status of the nation-state has been altered irrevocably, and in some cases undermined, by the processes of globalisation.[6]

The current diffusion of globalist practices and processes ultimately operates to counter the strategies utilised in fomenting a collective national consciousness, specifically, efforts to create unified communities through homogenised cultural practices. As Bauman remarks, the "nation-state, after all, owed its success to the suppression of self-asserting communities; it fought tooth and nail against parochialism, local customs or 'dialects,' promoting a unified language and historical memory at the expense of communal traditions" (*Liquid* 173). The nationalist project, therefore, seeks to create a fixed-static identity and to undermine any pluralistic positioning of the nation. This "constructed" reality of the nation can also be found in other types of identification. As Christopher Lasch has noted, in a world where disposability is pervasive, "identities can be adopted and discarded like a change of costume" (qtd. in Bauman, "Pilgrim" 23). Unlike the "solidity" of the nation, identity moves about like a fluid, mirroring the de-territorialised mobilities of contemporary scapes. This mobile quality is utilised by Stuart Hall, who writes that "identities are never unified and, in late modern times, increasingly fragmented and fractured; never singular but multiply constructed across different, often intersecting and antagonistic, discourses, practices and positions" (Hall, "Introduction" 4). These "transformative" properties of identity discussed by Hall and other cultural theorists require contextualisation and historicisation. At this present historical juncture the intensification of global interconnectedness and global flows has markedly impacted on "*creating and proliferating* cultural identity" (Tomlinson, "Globalization" 161). Therefore, identities or pluralised forms of identity are a reflection of a spatial and temporal regime which is susceptible to modification. Despite claims that globalisation has made geography irrelevant due to the conquest of time and space, I take the view that new geographies are needed to account for the newly emergent cartographies of socio-cultural relations. To this end, I want now to turn to a particular paradigm and focus on the realm of culture and what many refer to as cultural globalisation.

THE CULTURAL DOMAIN

To attempt to map the flows of the "new global cultural economy," as Appadurai terms it, would be far too ambitious within the scope of this chapter. Instead, I will more modestly set out to do the following: discuss the main competing analyses and critiques of cultural globalisation, articulate what I view as the beneficial aspects of this set of processes for the individual and the collective, and finally, consider the potential connection between cultural globalisation and the emergence of a cosmopolitan consciousness. The initial step, therefore, is to elucidate my use of the concept of culture.[7] On the basis of Raymond Williams's helpful and lengthy explanation, culture in the context of this chapter refers to "a particular way of life, whether of a period, a group, or humanity in general . . . [and] the works and practices of intellectual and especially artistic activity" (90). The anthropological approach of Clifford Geertz supplements Williams's definition: "believing with Max Weber, that man is an animal suspended in webs of significance he himself has spun, I take culture to be those webs and the analysis of it to be therefore not an experimental science in search of law but an interpretive one in search of meaning" (Geertz 5). Such a view of culture as "webs of meaning" is helpful for the context of globalisation, which both directly and indirectly promotes fluidity and pluralism of identity as opposed to fixed, single-layered forms of identification. One further element to complement what is mentioned previously concerns the geographical dimension of culture. Besides conducting analyses of the beliefs, ideas, and practices of a given locale or place,[8] the study of culture should also "investigate the connections and disconnections, the circulations and movements, the ups and downs that make a culture a living culture above and beyond its singular location" (Oswell 9).

A cultural analysis of the global (cultural globalisation) involves moving beyond singular locations and given geographical situations. While history is replete with examples of different civilisations and polities exchanging cultural practices, beliefs and artifacts, the contemporary period is unprecedented (applying Held's framework) in the extensity, intensity, velocity and impact of cultural contact and interconnectedness. Determining and interpreting both the overall nature and specific facets of this interplay between cultures and globalisation is a contested enterprise. One approach, which is usually referred to as the cultural imperialism thesis,[9] is actually a collection of discourses which focus on a number of socio-cultural phenomena ranging from the mass media to critiques of modernity to nationalist discourses and analyses of global capitalism.[10] In short, proponents of the cultural imperialism thesis are convinced that the world is experiencing a greater degree of cultural convergence. They also believe that the "world is becoming more uniform and standardised, through a technological, commercial and cultural synchronisation emanating from the West" (Pieterse, *Globalization as Hybridization* 45). Mike Featherstone argues that there is a "process of conquest and unification of the global space. The world becomes a singular domesticated space, a place where everyone becomes assimilated into a common culture" (*Undoing* 6). The implication is that national and local cultures are being penetrated and undermined by the strategic dissemination of Western cultural practices which are themselves part of the economic system of global capitalism. The United States is clearly a key protagonist in this process of cultural imperialism; the discourse of cultural imperialism is often synonymous with the presumed "Americanization" of global culture. It is claimed that this is made possible by "transnational corporate cultural domination," specifically through the vehicle of global media corporations (Schiller 39) which promote American mass culture and consumer capitalism. Many would cite the examples of Hollywood, Disney, McDonalds, Microsoft, and Coca-Cola, to name just a few. Whether referring to cultural imperialism as Westernisation or Americanisation, the end result is cultural homogenisation and/or global cultural synchronisation.[11]

One of the problems with the cultural imperialism model is its assumption of an existing global culture, Westernised or not, in the first place. Rather than homogeneous and unified, the concepts of Westernisation and Americanisation surely involve an inherently pluralistic notion of collective cultural identity. The view that a national culture such as that of the US is unaffected by "outside" cultural influences is clearly flawed; this myth of impenetrability ignores the realities of cultural diffusion. Believing that nations are "hermetically sealed, territorially self-contained or internally undifferentiated" (Bender 3) makes less sense now than ever, given the fluidity of the global cultural economy. There is an assumption in the cultural imperialism thesis which suggests that particular local or traditional cultures are somehow timeless (Sharp 84), remaining unchanged throughout history and managing to maintain discrete boundaries. The discourse of "Westernisation" also overlooks another factor which essentially privileges a Western-Eurocentric perspective. As Appadurai has noted, there are many localities that feel threatened by other types of cultural penetration. For the inhabitants of "Irian Jaya, Indonesianization may be more worrisome than Americanization, as Japanization may be for Koreans, Indianization for Sri Lankans, Vietnamization for the Cambodians, and Russianization for the people of Soviet Armenia and the Baltic republics" (*Modernity* 32). The end result, therefore, of the cultural imperialism position is an underestimation of local dynamics and an overestimation of global forces.

"NEW WORLD" GEOGRAPHIES

The notion of disjuncture put forward by Appadurai, which emphasises the increasingly nonisomorphic flows of global culture through the scapes which comprise his formulation (*Modernity* 37), along with various postcolonial critiques offers understanding of the *unevenness* of contemporary global social relations. Any discussion of the benefits of global flows and transnational interconnectivity must be tempered by acknowledging global inequalities which persist, despite the celebratory tone of certain globalist discourses. Notwithstanding the claims of particular popular treatments of globalisation, the world is not flat. ("Everywhere you turn," suggests Thomas Friedman, "hierarchies are being challenged from below or transforming themselves from top-down structures into more horizontal and collaborative ones" [45].) At the political and economic levels, new unevennesses or relationships "structured in asymmetry" (Radhakrishnan 1) are emerging. Place, far from becoming irrelevant, as Friedman might suggest, continues to be highly significant. While globalist discourses utilise the metaphor of a shrinking planet, situational differences from "the uneven distribution of natural resources to the unequal availability of opportunity, [indicate that] place remains a powerful arbiter" (De Blij 3).[12]

This failure to recognise the inherent inequalities of global geographic distributions of prosperity, opportunity and equality represents a misreading of globalisation as a one-dimensional phenomenon.[13] The same applies in the realm of cultural dynamics, where the cultural imperialism thesis implies an understanding of culture as a unified whole. For example, the claim that there is a single global culture that is part of an "actual world society" (Lechner and Boli 25) seems to assume that cultural influence is uni-directional, moving from the core developed countries to countries of the developing periphery. The thesis of cultural convergence ignores the "countercurrents—the impact nonwestern cultures have been making on the West . . . and the reception of western culture" (Pieterse, *Globalization and Culture* 69). Obvious examples would be in cuisine, fashion and music, where significant impacts on western practices and styles have been occurring. In addition, it downplays the network-oriented basis of the cultural economy, which disrupts the spatial arrangement of the core-periphery model. Other theorists focus on the specific dialectical relationships which emerge when one culture trait or system encounters another—the complexities, in other words, of the global-local nexus. Robertson has developed this dialectic, which he describes as the interpenetration of the global and the local, the universal and the particular ("Glocalization" 30). The term "globalization" can thus be regarded as something of a misnomer in its failure to encapsulate the local dimension; hence Robertson's use of the term "glocalization" (30). In the meeting of the global with the local, a range of factors and variables determines how a given artifact or practice of culture will be received. Appadurai has also made a case for the importance of the interplay of the global and the local. His view of the global cultural economy recognises not only its complexity and layered qualities but also its disjunctive order, which intensifies due to the speed, scale and volume of global cultural flows (*Modernity* 37). So while culture moves in multiple directions, it is also experienced in an uneven way on the receiving end.

The reception of "foreign" cultural influences at given locations occurs neither in a void nor in a de-contextualised setting. Cultural imperialism assumes the passive acceptance and unreflective stance by inhabitants of foreign cultural practices. Tomlinson points out that as it moves from one location to another, culture always "involves interpretation, translation, mutation, adaptation, and 'indigenization' as the receiving culture brings its own culture resources to bear, in dialectical fashion, upon 'cultural imports'" (*Globalization* 84). Through this kind of particularisation, novel aspects of culture are redefined and filtered for local needs. In this process of negotiation a given cultural practice or repertoire might be rejected for a variety of reasons, including the role of nationalist-oriented responses to supposed threats to national cultural identification; in turn it might serve as a catalyst for the promotion of local-national cultures.[14] We see this for example in the "slow food" movement, the rediscovery of indigenous cultural traditions, and policies of linguistic preservation.

This process of relativisation of cultural meaning alluded to previously poses interesting possibilities for individual and collective identity formations. As the processes of "glocalization" fundamentally realign our social world interactions, identity formation is generated or "constructed within, not outside [this] discourse" (Hall, "Introduction" 4). Historicising identity within the flows and networks of cultural globalisation requires concepts that reflect that fluidity and complexity. Giddens, for example, speaks of social reflexivity, in which individuals "reflect" on their life conditions which have undergone radical transformations due to the loss of long-embedded structures, institutions and traditions resulting from accelerated globalisation (*Sociology* 123). Individual and collective social reflexivity disrupt the fixities of both culture and identity and encourage acknowledgement of their fluidity. Paul Gilroy captures this dynamic in his comments on black political culture, suggesting that it has been more preoccupied with the "relationship of identity to roots and rootedness than in seeing identity as a process of movement and mediation that is more appropriately approached via the homonym routes" (*Black Atlantic* 19). The outcome of the "changing same" of culture and identity, Gilroy suggests, is one that is "creolized, syncretized, hybridized and chronically impure" ("Diaspora" 335).[15]

The term hybridisation describes "the mixture of phenomena which are held to be different, separate; hybridization then refers to a *cross-category* process" (Pieterse, "Globalization as Hybridization" 55–56).[16] Applying this concept to the cultural field destabilises the belief that national cultures are non-syncretic constructs and instead advances the view that all cultures are a result of inter-cultural contact and are engaged in a process of negotiation with other cultures. The cultural hybridisation perspective also undermines discourses centered on the hegemonic stance that a global culture results from processes of cultural homogenisation. Fredric Jameson asks: "Is it a matter of transnational domination and uniformity or, on the other hand, the source of the liberation of local culture from hidebound state and national forms" ("Preface" xiii)? Rather than framing the issue as a choice between cultural homogenisation and national-local cultural paradigms, the integrative configuration of the perspectives mentioned previously provides the basis for new cartographies to locate, trace and elucidate the de-territorialised mobilities and cultural complexities of the present. These new geographies, which have only begun to be accounted for, essentially call for a revision of our methodological and conceptual approaches to socio-cultural phenomena. Also, it necessitates thinking beyond older concepts of "society" and the nation-state, as well as challenging binary dichotomies of globality and localism. What then is there to envision beyond contemporary socio-political arrangements? As Bauman asks: after the nation-state—what? (*Globalization* 55).

THE COSMOPOLITAN IMAGINARY

> [C]ulture and cultural identities, which at the broadest level are civilization identities, are shaping the patterns of cohesion, disintegration, and conflict in the post-Cold War world . . . [T]he most important distinctions among peoples are not ideological, political, or economic. They are cultural. (Huntington 20–21)

> *The Satanic Verses* celebrates hybridity, impurity, intermingling, the transformation that comes of new and unexpected combinations of human beings, cultures, ideas, politics, movies, songs. It rejoices in mongrelization and fears the absolutism of the Pure. *Mélange*, hotchpotch, a bit of this and a bit of that is *how newness enters the world.* (Rushdie 394)

These quotes represent two quite different viewpoints on cultural relations and cultural identification. For Samuel Huntington globalisation has intensified discord and conflict between different cultures or "civilizations," to use his term. These collective identities "clash" with others in an attempt to maintain their identity in the face of globalising trends. Salman Rushdie's model, on the other hand, acknowledges that encounters and reactions to difference facilitate identity reconstruction as part of a process that is never quite complete. Gilroy's "routes," Hall's "fractured and fragmented" identities and Giddens' "social reflexivity" all make the case that contemporary socio-cultural contexts create "indefinite, changing, unknowable identities" (Niezen 1). Homi Bhabha writes:

> What is theoretically innovative, and politically crucial, is the need to think beyond narratives of originary and initial subjectivities and to focus on those moments or processes that are produced in the articulation of cultural differences. These "in-between" spaces provide the terrain for elaborating strategies of selfhood—singular and communal—that initiate new sites of collaboration, and contestation, in the act of defining the idea of society itself. (1–2)

In challenging binary oppositions, Bhabha, echoing Rushdie and others, creates a third space which in positional terms is less stable and replete with ambivalence. This state of being for individual and collectivity alike, which animates shifting solidarities and pluralities of identification, as I see it, is one of the more important consequences of cultural globalisation.[17] Taken a step further and in response to Bauman's question about what will follow the nation-state, can we contemplate that the transformative powers of cultural globalisation can serve as a catalyst for the emergence of a global imaginary?

While the relevance of the nation-state and the collective identity of the nation remains (and will no doubt continue to remain) strong, another layer of identification beyond the nation also seems not only feasible but desirable. Many connect cosmopolitanism[18] to a global business elite, a hyper-traveling minority and ideas of global democracy, universal human rights and world citizenship, or alternatively present the cosmopolitan "as dabbling rootlessly in a variety of cultures . . . as [a] voyeur, parasite" incapable of making commitments to places and individuals

(Featherstone, "Cosmopolis" 1). One of the problems with contemporary discourses of cosmopolitanism is that it tends to be used in a multitude of ways, from vague and universalistic to narrow and limited in scope. For some it represents a political ideology, for others it is a philosophical or legal project, while for others it is a matter of socio-cultural orientation.[19] We must also be cognizant of the fact that cosmopolitanism has not been realised yet. Simply because the condition of globality exists today, it "ought not to be mistaken for an existing mass-based feeling of belonging to a world community (cosmopolitanism) because the globality of the everyday does not necessarily engender an existing popular global political consciousness" (Cheah 31). So despite the prevalence of discourses about global "connectivity" and "interpenetration," we seem to lack certain attachments and solidarities at the global level, solidarities which have long been a part of the history of the nation-state experience. Irrespective of this, however, one can not overlook the efforts of a plethora of social groups, organisations and the masses in general, campaigning at various levels for human rights, social justice and protection of the environment. "The aim is to globalize democracy," one observer notes, "and to democratize globalization" (Martell 216). The political upheaval of early 2011 in the Arab states of North Africa and the Middle East is an example of how mass protests can usher in change in places that have seemed impervious to democratisation. To the surprise of many, governments have collapsed, parliaments have been dissolved and dictators have fled. Egypt's eighteen-day revolt stands out as an example of what massive collective action can achieve.[20] One wonders if a country such as China can remain politically intact with the diffusion of digital communications and the circulation of images of mass protests taking place in various corners of the world.[21]

Another serious challenge that cosmopolitan theory must face is coming to terms with what some have credited to be cosmopolitanism's success: the ability to mediate between the "universal and the particular, the global and the local" (Vertovec and Cohen 4). For example, how should human rights be promoted at the global level? Will universalistic positions about reason, what is just and unjust, conflict with local traditions? To some, a cosmopolitan vision is too reminiscent of Western imperial relationships with the colonised Other, or even worse, part of a long tradition of Western utopian thinking out of touch with the complex socio-political realities of the present. Niezen is correct to ask the following question: "how do liberal societies accommodate, assimilate, or dominate these illiberal societies that flout the principles of individual freedom and the dignity of the person?" (169). Is consensus possible under such conditions? Will given localities and collectivities be denied the right to practice their traditions under a global cosmopolitan regime which proclaims the principles of cultural universalism? As Vertovec and Cohen suggest, cosmopolitanism can negotiate between this binary relationship. Whereas the pivot of the nation-state can extend only so far from its local-particularistic position of exclusivity, a cosmopolitan consciousness, as inherently ambivalent, is better suited to accommodate both national societal patterns and the discourses of universalism. In the realm of "global politics beyond the nation-state," it is this *gravitational convergence* present in cosmopolitanism that offers appealing political possibilities.

Despite apparent obstacles to the application of cosmopolitan ideas, it seems evident that there are more compelling reasons why the need for new ways of thinking about community is imperative. My use of the term cosmopolitanism is close to that of Ulf Hannerz, who describes it as "an orientation, a willingness to engage with the Other . . . [an] intellectual and aesthetic stance of openness toward divergent cultural experiences, a search for contrasts rather than uniformity" (239). Considering the extent of racial bigotry, ethnic-based violence, anti-immigrant feeling and the persistence of extremist-nationalist ideology in the world today, there is an urgent need to create alternative modes of thinking and solidarities to counter divisive mentalities. As Rob Wilson remarks, a cosmopolitical option seeks to stimulate "new cultures of global/local mixture whose hope-generating resources can be marshaled to serve better ends than the xenophobic hegemony of mononations, monoraces, and monocreeds" (360).[22] One of the outcomes of cultural globalisation towards this end is that it deterritorialises culture; it pries culture away from the fixed spatialities of the nation-state and acknowledges the circulating, fluid nature of cultural diffusion. Mobility is manifested not only through the capitalist, the business person and the traveler, but also through migrants or guest workers, immigrants, refugees and diasporas. To destabilise cultural boundaries is to undermine ethnic enclaves and relational communities, as well as the dichotomy between insider and outsider, local and non-local.

A cosmopolitan orientation need not be centered only on the global-local nexus. In terms of geographic scale, there is also the relevance of regional dynamics. If we can speak of re-spatialising cultural configurations, why not consider the same for political and economic attachments and solidarities? Some examples of this are the regional identifications associated with the European Union project of integration or that of the African Union, ASEAN, MERCOSUR, NAFTA, CARICOM, and COMESA. The EU, for example, as a complex supranational organisation, represents an interesting case in both current practices and future potential. As Maurice Roche notes, Europe's division "between a formation of commonality and one of differences" (219) epitomises the desire to harmonise the universal and the particular.[23] Could such a model be applied elsewhere in other regions of the world to compensate for the shortcomings of the nation-state paradigm? It would seem that part of the myriad of problems faced by Africans might be solved by weakening the solidarities of the nation-state and encouraging collective identification on a larger scale. This point is made by Manthia Diawara, who sees the regional imaginary as an essential strategy for the political, economic and cultural development of countries plagued by stagnation and fragmentation due to particular antagonisms. He states:

> What is urgent in West Africa today is less a contrived unity based on an innate cultural identity and heritage, but a regional identity in motion that is based on linguistic affinities, economic reality, and geographic proximity, as defined by the similarities in political and cultural dispositions grounded in history and patterns of consumption. (Diawara 124)

To say this is to call not for a rejection of the national scale, but merely for recognition of the nation-state's limitations. The logic of a cosmopolitan consciousness is that the local, national, regional and global stand side by side.[24]

The application of cosmopolitan policies and practices need not be contingent upon the disappearance of the nation-state. While many cosmopolitans speak of this as a necessity, I have emphasised throughout that the nation may remain an important site of identification and that the cosmopolitan vision embraces the notion of multiple allegiances linked with the emergence of a global consciousness. A long-term result, however, might well be the weakening of the national imaginary.[25] Furthermore, since cosmopolitanism values pluralism and difference, there is no reason to exclude the permeation of multiple *cosmopolitanisms* that are diverse and a product of given social contexts.[26] While we face collective problems that require transnational solutions, this should not exclude the role of localised action. In most cases the various scales (local, national, regional and global) will need to work parallel to each other if particular challenges such as the environment, human rights, nuclear proliferation and economic inequality are to be addressed in a satisfactory manner.[27] To put it another way, who or what will prevent the next Srebrenica, Rwanda or Darfur? In the end it will take individual localities working in unison with other localities within their respective regions in cooperation with given global institutions to find collective solutions to collective challenges in an intertwined set of relations Held refers to as our "overlapping collective fortunes" ("Culture" 58). What this will necessitate is what Castells describes as a culture of communication protocols. As part of the global network society, protocols of intercultural communication will develop "on the basis of the common belief in the power of networking and of the synergy obtained by giving to others and receiving from others . . . thus ending the ancestral fear of the other" (*Communication* 38).

The problems we face collectively at the beginning of the twenty-first century clearly require a greater scale of collaboration dependent upon new structures and mechanisms for dealing with the complex emergent networks and geographies of power associated with the conditions of globalitiy.[28] For example, we might envisage the waning of American hegemonic power in the world, with the real possibility of an emergent multipolar structure at the level of international relations. Increasing flows and exchanges of culture between localities impact on our perceptions of individual and collective identification, making it no longer feasible to remain fixed solely on the territorialised boundaries of the nation-state and its corresponding component of national culture. The *cosmopolitanisms* of the future, grounded in addressing global challenges and geared toward fomenting a global consciousness, will better enable the multitude of localities which comprise our world to contend with our shared predicaments.

NOTES

1. There is much debate among historians and social scientists regarding the "starting point" of globalisation. Did it exist during antiquity or was it the product of the early modern period? Perhaps it emerged during the nineteenth century or the post-World War II era? Did it emerge in the East or was it the product of the West's development? This issue is taken up by A. G. Hopkins, who emphasises "the importance of understanding the historical dimensions of globalization" (13).
2. Paul Hirst and Grahame Thompson challenge assumptions about the "newness" of contemporary global economic integration and see globalisation as "largely a myth" (2).
3. Further on it becomes evident that Marx and Engels seem to be describing specific characteristics of global capitalist designs: "The need of a constantly expanding market for its products chases the bourgeoisie over the whole surface of the globe. It must nestle everywhere, settle everywhere, establish connections everywhere" (K. Marx 224).
4. Richard T. Schaefer, *Sociology: A Brief Introduction* (7th ed., 2008).
5. This is a phrase used by Craig Calhoun in the title of his book *Nations Matter: Culture, History, and the Cosmopolitan Dream* (2007).
6. Very briefly the effects of globalisation would include the following: increased migration and mobility, increased contact between cultures, the weakening of national sovereignty in the political and economic realms and the growing appeal of alternative post-national forms of individual and collective identification.
7. Raymond Williams's assertion that culture "is one of the two most complicated words in the English language" (*Keywords* 87) certainly still applies, especially considering its contested nature and long historical trajectory as a concept.
8. James Clifford is clear on this in his analysis of twentieth-century anthropological discourses and practices. He states: "Localizations of the anthropologist's objects of study in terms of a "field" tend to marginalise or erase several blurred boundary areas, historical realities that slip out of the ethnic frame" ("Traveling" 99).
9. According to Joanne P. Sharp, cultural imperialism is the "use of political and economic power to spread the value systems, ideas, and institutional forms of a foreign culture on a native culture" (84).
10. John Tomlinson notes that there exists a degree of "artificial coherence" in the cultural imperialism thesis in that there are a "variety of different articulations which may be in tension with each other, or even mutually contradictory" (*Cultural Imperialism* 9).

11. This conclusion is supported by a number of theorists such as Benjamin Barber and George Ritzer. The former speaks of a "McWorld" of cultural uniformity made possible through "an entertainment shopping experience that brings together malls, multiplex movie theaters, theme parks, spectator sports arenas, fast food chains and television into a single vast enterprise that . . . transforms human beings" (Barber 97). In his work, Ritzer also utilises a cultural homogenisation framework in which he deploys the term "McDonaldization." Through this process, the "principles of the fast-food restaurant are coming to dominate more and more sectors of American society as well as the rest of the world" (1). Other theorists have used labels such as Coca-Colonization and Disneyization.
12. Doreen Massey's concept of the power-geometry of time-space compression is helpful in this context of power relations and location. "For different social groups and different individuals," she states, "are placed in very distinct ways in relation to these flows and interconnections" (qtd. in Sharp 100).
13. It is also essential to recognise that resistance to globalising tendencies can be applied through the very tools and applications of globalisation itself. The anti-globalisation movement, for example, organises strong resistance to aspects of global capitalism. As Leslie Sklair comments, such groups aim at "disrupting capitalism locally and finding ways of globalizing these disruptions, while seizing the opportunities to transform it that democracy provides" (306–7).
14. Ronald Niezen observes that given localities may respond to "de-localisation" by rediscovering and re-establishing "lost cultures, to 're-localise' identities in a supposedly original, pure form" (40).
15. This is taken from Gilroy's discussion of the African Diaspora, which he terms the "Black Atlantic."
16. A problem with this term is that it reminds one of colonial discourse and imperialist forms of knowledge which sought to racially categorise colonised populations according to pseudo-biological theories. Pieterse recognises another problem in that if we acknowledge that all cultures are hybrid, then hybridisation "is in effect a tautology: contemporary accelerated globalization means the hybridization of hybrid cultures" (*Globalization and Culture* 82).
17. As Paul Hopper explains, "globalization can facilitate this transition because its processes and manifestations enable us to experience a plurality of cultural influences and to gain multiple attachments and sources of allegiance" (175).
18. Cosmopolitanism has a long history stretching back to the ancient world, particularly ancient Greece, and experienced a re-emergence during the European Enlightenment of the eighteenth century. Due to intensified globalisation over the past thirty years, cosmopolitanism has continued to attract increasing interest.
19. David A. Hollinger provides an illustration of the multiplicities of cosmopolitanisms which exist. "On my desk at one time recently," he states,

    > I had books and articles espousing vernacular cosmopolitanism, rooted cosmopolitanism, critical cosmopolitanism, comparative cosmopolitanism, national cosmopolitanism, discrepant cosmopolitanism, situated cosmopolitanism . . . cosmopolitan patriotism, cosmopolitan nationalism, cosmopolitan democracy, and cosmopolitan post-colonialism. (228)
20. Besides the speed of regime change in Tunisia and Egypt it is also revealing to note its diffusion throughout the Arab world. Clearly one can not overlook

the role that digital technology and communication networks are playing in mass political mobilisations at the present time.

21. Slavoj Žižek has commented that there "is a kind of poetic justice in the fact that the final result of Mao's Cultural Revolution is the current unmatched explosion of capitalist dynamics in China" (*Violence* 209). The Chinese authorities have erected "walls" to prevent the flow of digital information into the country. While successful in the short-term, it is hard to believe that China can remain linked to the world economically but disconnected in terms of socio-political reforms.
22. The recent mass protests taking place in Spain and Greece in response to austerity programs and rising unemployment are examples of solidarities formed by different national groups due to a shared economic plight and popular rebellion. These collectivities of protesters gathering in urban public spaces are for the moment without visible party affiliations, operating at the level of *spectacle* or as a social happening. There is the potential, however, that these protests can develop into a serious socio-political mobilszation of the masses.
23. The 2010–11 eurozone crisis does however register some concern and clearly indicates that current integration is lacking in many areas, including fiscal policy. Whether or not national leaders in the EU and other supranational organisations can unhinge themselves from national interests and individual agendas for the collective good remains to be seen.
24. Geographers have been addressing the spatial dimensions of such relations and have explained "the interaction of processes, structures and agents at different scales of analysis" (Murray 19).
25. Keeping in mind the complexities of cultural globalisation and the newly emerging cultural geographies, Warrick E. Murray reminds us that identities and culture are increasingly located "in dispersed networks" in which various diasporas, for example, play a key role in maintaining national cultural identifications (259).
26. As Held notes, just "as there is not one form of liberalism or one single way to conceptualize democracy, there is not one unified or monolithic understanding of cosmopolitanism" (*Cosmopolitanism* 14–15).
27. In terms of environmental politics, Joan Martinez-Alier gives the example of environmental justice in which the "local is connected to the global in a generalized movement of resistance. Thus, Oil-Watch unites local environmental groups in tropical countries threatened by the oil industry from Mexico, Ecuador, and Peru to Nigeria, Indonesia, and Timor" (324).
28. Capitalist core countries have been compelled to incorporate voices from the developing world through the organisational framework of the G-20 which includes such countries as South Africa, India, Indonesia, Argentina and Brazil.

9 "Touching Everyone"

Media Identifications, Imagined Communities and New Media Technologies in the Case of Madeleine McCann

Nicola Rehling

When, in 2007, the four-year-old Madeleine McCann went missing while on holiday in Portugal with her parents, who had left her and her twin brother and sister in their unlocked apartment while they dined with friends in a tapas bar, few could have predicted the media frenzy this still unsolved case would unleash. Within a few weeks, it was possible to talk of the "Maddification" of Britain, akin to the "Dianafication" of Britain that followed the death of the equally photogenic, white, blonde Princess ten years earlier. Photographs of Madeleine McCann soon became one of the most mass reproduced images in the last decade, and a short film appealing for help was even screened at the FA cup final and seen by an estimated 500 million people (Addly). Large rewards were offered by wealthy businessmen and women, including Richard Branson and J. K. Rowling, reaching the figure of £2.6 million, while *The News of the World* alone offered £1.5 million for her safe return. Gordon Brown sought reassurance from his Portuguese counterpart about the case while in discussions about the EU treaty ("Brown Thanks Portugal"). The national cricket team sported yellow ribbons, the England rugby team wore "Look for Madeleine" T-shirts, David Beckham made a well-publicised televised address, and the MCanns were granted an audience with the Pope. Newspapers, magazines, TV and radio programs, internet sites and blogs dissected minute details of the case, fabricated elaborate scenarios when no facts were available, with particular focus placed on the culpability of the parents, Gerry and Kate McCann, whose every action fast became a national addiction. Many British tabloids devoted headline space to the case almost every day for six months, and for a few weeks the *Sky News* website even had the name Madeleine appearing as a menu option alongside "business," "politics" and "weather" (Freeland). The so-called "quality" press, equally parasitically, made much mileage out of scrutinising what they deemed the tabloids' hysterical obsession with the story, as well as navel-gazing about the state of British journalism, even as their own articles re-narrativised the popular press's fascination, albeit for a different implied reader. The story also attracted significant attention in the rest of Europe, as well as the US, with Madeleine's face appearing on the cover of *People* magazine, and the McCanns invited to appear on Oprah Winfrey's talk show (Addly). As *Newsnight* presenter Kirsty Wark aptly put it, "It is hard to think of a story that has had so much coverage for so long, with so few facts" (qtd. in Botzas).

At the risk of hyper-realising the case further, this chapter examines mass media responses to the McCann case, particularly in British newspapers, asking what it was about the story of an individual missing child and her parents that prompted such interest on an unprecedented scale. As Gerry McCann himself put it, referring to the huge affective power the case wielded, Madeleine's disappearance "touched everyone" (qtd. in Enright). A quintessential example of the personalised, melodramatic and unresolved narratives that the popular media love best, the story offered numerous points of collective identification for media consumers and users. With parenthood providing a "universal" concern, the story formed the perfect vehicle through which the popular press could engage in inclusive rhetoric, construct a community of readers, and fulfill their self-appointed role as purveyors of normative, "common sense" values (Conboy, *Tabloid Britain* 9), while affirming the individualistic values of neo-liberalism. The white, middle-class, British status of the McCanns was essential in this regard, providing an ideal means of inscribing hegemonic norms, particularly those concerning nation, class, gender (especially motherhood) and the nuclear family. Moreover, with almost everyone having something to say about the McCanns, and indeed doing so in a variety of media modes, the case also offers a paradigmatic means of thinking through the changing relationship between mass media texts and consumers/users, highlighting the emergence of what some media theorists have termed "participatory culture" (H. Jenkins). While feverish online discussions and DIY media creations on the topic of Madeleine McCann might not exemplify the invigorated public sphere for which Jürgen Habermas has famously yearned, or the extended democratic space, empowered citizenship or nourishing virtual communities that many cybertheorists have attributed to the internet, such participation certainly refutes any notion of mass media audiences as passive consumers. At the same time, in that the popular media largely determine which stories get mass airing, and work hard to provide the interpretative lens through which those stories and collective media identifications are shaped, the case also raises questions about the role played by the political economy of media production in what Manuel Castells has famously termed the "Information Age."

The Madeleine McCann case contained all of the ingredients of a riveting "who-dunnit" narrative, and was a gift to the popular press, which increasingly blurs the borders between news and entertainment (Conboy, *The Press* 138). Here was a middle-class couple in a foreign locale, whose child had disappeared under mysterious circumstances, but had been sighted in as diverse, exotic climes as Morocco, India and South America. Then, an "arguido," an official suspect, was announced—Robert Murat—the only evidence being, it later transpired, that a journalist had found his willingness to help suspicious and had promptly informed the police. Then, while the nation was split between pouring out sympathy for the McCanns and castigating them for leaving their children unattended, Kate McCann was swiftly pulled in for questioning, booed by the crowd gathering outside the police station, named, along with her husband, an "arguido," and then offered a plea bargain of two years imprisonment if she admitted to inadvertently over-sedating her daughter. The majority of British popular newspapers, and with them public opinion, did a massive *volte-face*, and, despite the lack of any conclusive forensic evidence, revelled in the possibility of the McCanns being murderers. The case now offered the kind of "monsters lurking behind the façade of middle-class respectability" drama which would not be out of place in an episode of *Desperate Housewives*. Stories then abounded that the McCanns and their friends, the "tapas seven" as they became known, were "swingers"—demonstrating the deep-seated need to mark this "ordinary" couple as deviant all along. Responses were largely polarised: while some newspaper columnists, readers, viewers and bloggers protested the McCanns' innocence, others expressed anger and betrayal, often in vitriolic terms. Public knowledge was largely constructed by the media, which was itself fed by conjecture from the Portuguese tabloids and leaks from the Portuguese police, since under Portuguese laws of judicial secrecy details of an ongoing investigation cannot be disclosed. This, combined with the demands of 24/7 cable news and internet sites, which require a constant feed of news, inevitably "mak[ing] verification more of a problem" (Tumber 19), left plenty of opportunities for speculation, for "solving" the mystery. For weeks in Britain, everyday conversation, TV programs, radio programs and call-ins, internet sites, blogs and chat rooms were dominated by one overwhelming question—did the McCanns do it? With Madeleine still not found (at the time of writing), and no one charged, lack of closure worked to sustain narrative desire, unlike similar high profile cases of missing children, such as the 2002 Soham murders, where the bodies of the two ten-year-old girls were found within two weeks.[1]

The obsession with the McCann case also exemplifies the media maxim that the majority of us respond most readily and passionately to individualised, familiar stories. The unpleasant truth, as Johann Hari noted in *The Independent*, is that a story about thousands of nameless, faceless children being kidnapped in the Congo every year simply fails to produce the same affective response because it cannot provide points of easy identification. The tabloids cultivated intimacy with Madeleine, collapsing boundaries between public and private through rhetorical strategies such as the use of the diminutive form "Maddie," reportedly none too popular with the McCanns, who used her full name in all their interviews, website and campaign material. These "individualizing narrative paradigms," as Fredric Jameson has noted in a different context, not only elicit easier identification, but also provide emotional security (*Geopolitical* 41). For instance, the demonisation of a lone child-snatcher—the kind of individualistic articulation of a social problem that characterises neo-liberal discourse (Buck-Morss 71)—is more palatable and reassuring to most of us than contemplation of the collective social forces that might facilitate such a crime, such as the opportunities for human trafficking provided by global capitalism and the market-driven EU "freedom of movement." As I have noted elsewhere, Theodor Adorno is right to argue that any privileging of an individual in mass culture "already succumbs to ideology" (65), which is precisely why so many political theorists on the left who attempt to reconceptualise collectivity, such as Giorgio Agamben, Roberto Esposito and Jean-Luc Nancy, have called for an end to the "search for a proper identity in the already improper and senseless form of individuality" (Agamben, *Coming* 65; Rehling 9–12).[2]

Individualisation strategies were also evident in the melodramatic treatment the case received in the popular media. In his influential *The Melodramatic Imagination: Balzac, Henry James, Melodrama, and the Mode of Excess* (1976), Peter Brooks defined melodrama as "the indulgence of strong emotionalism; moral polarisation and schematisation; extreme states of being, situations, action; overt villainy, persecution of the good, and final reward of virtue; inflated and extravagant expression; dark plottings, suspense, breathtaking peripety" (11–12). The McCann case was treated precisely in this manner, not only as regards the moral polarisation and didacticism with which it was narrativised (especially in relation to parenting, a point I will return to), and the concomitant "retrieval and staging of virtue through adversity and suffering" (L. Williams 15), but also the media's deployment of "rhetorical excess," which for Brooks is a defining characteristic of the mode. This excess included melodramatic headlines (examples from *The Sun* include: "Paedo ring snatched Maddie"; "Wish you were here Maddie"; "Cops' final bid to solve Maddie"; "Anguished mum opens heart"); articles trading in melodramatic archetypes such as the innocent, virtuous child and the evil child-abductor; dramatic expressions of moral indignation; photographs of Madeleine, accompanied by poignant commentary stressing her beauty and innocence; and stills or footage of Kate McCann, such as close-ups of her shaking and tense hand clasping her husband for support, shots of her biting back tears, bowing her head or clutching her daughter's cuddly toy—examples of what Brooks regards as the "muteness" of the mode, where words "appear to be not wholly adequate to the representation of meanings, and the melodramatic message must be formulated through other registers or signs" (56).

For Brooks, the attraction of melodrama is that, in a post-sacred era, in which pre-modern, unifying, communal bonds have dissolved, it offers a means of "making the world morally legible" (43) though can only now do so in individualised terms (16). The stylistic excess finds a language for the inexpressible, and the "heightened dramatization" of the mode performs a didactic function (ix). In this Manichean universe, characters have no interior depth but rather represent ethical imperatives or psychic signs (35). With the nuclear family a site of intense primal bonds, but increasingly under threat as an institution, it is perhaps inevitable that it is repeatedly chosen for melodramatic treatment, not only in Hollywood films, which so often, as Geoffrey Nowell-Smith puts it, screen the difficulty experienced by subjects to find "a place in which they can both be 'themselves' and 'at home'" (73), but also in the British popular press, which, as Martin Conboy observes, commonly treats "the primal roles of Son, Mother, Baby and Dad" with melodramatic hyperbole (*The Press* 173).

This melodramatisation of family roles could also be seen as indicative of the shift from class-based politics to identity-based politics, in which a weightier role is given to "cultural" matters "broadly defined to encompass 'feelings,' 'differences,' 'lifestyles,' and 'affectivity'" (Webster 6)—what Michel Maffesoli has termed "an empathetic 'sociality' which is expressed by a succession of ambiences, feelings and emotions" (11). Even though most tabloids still construct themselves as offering a voice to the marginalised working classes (*The Sun*, for instance, despite being a subsidiary of Rupert Murdoch's News Corporation, advertises itself as "The People's Paper"), this resides in rhetoric, not ownership (Conboy, *The Press* 181). The institution of the family is regulated and idealised by the popular press since it provides an arena in which ethical imperatives can be explored in support of the status quo, unlike potentially more divisive issues such as class inequality, the ethics of global capitalism and immigration, issues which these papers still address, but which offer fewer opportunities for speaking for "the people." In this respect, presenting the McCann case as a family melodrama allowed the popular press to appeal to a wide spectrum of diverse readers linked by the shared concern of parenthood, to construct their version of "the popular," and, in the process, reaffirm their self-appointed role as "a key and subtle purveyor of normative assumptions to a mass audience" (Conboy, *The Press* 183). As Conboy notes, despite differences in political allegiances, most popular papers reaffirm "common-sense" norms, with sufficient engagement with oppositional voices to "[allow] the hegemonic process its proper reciprocity" (16). Subjecting the McCann case to melodramatic treatment provided opportunities for hegemonic norms (expressed as ethical obligations rather than ideological operations) to do with parenting, family values, gender and nation to be asserted and put in the service of "the normalization of certain modes of belonging" (Conboy, *Tabloid Britain* 9).

With the phrase "every parent's worst nightmare" reverberating in columns and editorials, it was the trope of parenting that opened up identificatory and affective investment for most journalists, readers and viewers. For example, Booker prize winner Anne Enright admitted in a remarkably honest (and much-maligned) article which scrutinises her own morbid fascination with the case that disliking the McCanns simply made her feel like a better parent: "Distancing yourself from the McCanns is a recent but potent form of magic. It keeps our children safe." The story, in other words, shored up parental egos and bolstered normative, collective discourses about how "proper" parents behave. In turn, it unleashed widespread discussion in diverse media forums on the culpability of the McCanns, with some 17,000 internet users going as far as to sign an online petition for social services to investigate them.

The story thus fed into the current obsession with "good" and "bad" parenting that fuels the sales of many tabloids, particularly the *Daily Mail*, which constructs itself as representing middle England, often in overtly traditionalist, backward-looking discourse. Marriage and the nuclear family are reified, while other manifestations of reproduction or sexuality are posited as social problems (Wykes 235) in discourses that demonise non-traditional family structures and link the fate of the nuclear family with the fate of the nation. The McCanns were in many respects what is considered "ideal" parents (middle-class, educated, professional, happily married, religious), thus providing the popular press with a framework which allowed it to shape "an idealized version of the ordinary people," a "normative process" which "build[s] upon these discourses of the people and can target them emotionally, economically and politically, claiming to speak on their behalf" (Conboy, *The Press* 8). For example, the *Daily Mail,* a tabloid with the highest female (mainly lower middle-class) readership of all daily newspapers in Britain (172), initially contained many sympathetic articles that repeatedly used the first-person plural in their rhetorical address. For instance, Allison Pearson wrote that "[t]his kind of thing doesn't usually happen to people like us." Here, the use of the first-person plural addresses a middle-class readership that can fully identify with the McCanns, making no bones about the fact that if such a tragedy befell someone *unlike* "us," such as a welfare-dependent or lesbian mother, it would fail to produce the same shocked incomprehension or affective dissonance. As Martin Conboy notes, such inclusive rhetoric is "the strategy which the popular press employs to maintain a relationship which is hegemonically negotiated in favour of the dominant power structures within society while keeping its readers relatively happy that their views and interests are represented" (*The Press* 13).

Similarly, in the same newspaper, journalist Jill Parkin repeatedly uses the first-person plural, which, in conjunction with her deployment of vernacular forms, promotes both inclusivity and intimacy:

> Time and again over the last few days we've heard it: "I would never have left a child like that." We say it, shake our heads, tighten the grip on our child's hand and thank the Lord we are not the parents of little Madeleine McCann.
>
> And so we should, because when we say it most of us are being hypocritical: there but for the grace of God—or chance—go all of us.

> We have all taken risks and we have all had a little uneasy voice deep inside as we took them, but right now we've all forgotten that. It's much more comfortable to think that someone's at fault, that a finger can be pointed at Kate and Gerry McCann.

Taking its role as "social educator" to heart (Conboy, *Tabloid Britain* 9), admonishing readers for their smugness but including the journalist in its plural address, this article discursively divests its readers of heterogeneity by appealing to shared behaviour and "common sense" values. In this respect it is a prime example of what Martin Conboy, drawing on Baudrillard, regards as the popular press's articulation of the "popular" at a time when organic, political communities have dissolved: "Once the rhetoric emerged from the people; now it is a simulacrum standing in for their loss" (*The Press* 140). The McCann case thus functions as an archetypal Debordian spectacle, "a social relation among people, mediated by images" (Debord 24).

Another such "imagined community," as Benedict Anderson has argued, is that of nation, and for Conboy "the confirmation of the existence of a national space and indeed a national identity" is another "performative function of the popular press" (*The Press* 157). Insofar as the McCann case involved a British couple abroad, it provided the opportunity to reaffirm prevalent discourses of national identity and superiority at a time when, as Manuel Castells argues, the nation-state has been exposed to "competition from sources of power that are undefined, and sometimes indefinable," such as "networks of capital, production, communication, crime, international institutions, supranational military apparatuses, non-governmental organizations, transnational religions, movements of public opinion, and social movements of all kinds, including terrorist movements," as well as "communities, tribes, localities, cults and gangs" (*Power of Identity* 357). This need to renarrativise nation, to stabilise its meanings through constant reiteration, ultimately, of course, belies the volatility and mutability of "Britain" as a category. For Conboy, the mobilisation of an older rhetoric of nation that is in fact addressed to a new and "virtual community" is "rooted in desperation" since the "predominantly white, male and patriotic nation hostile to Europe and sensitive to its past glories" that the popular press consistently constructs "stands for a nation that has ceased to exist" (*The Press* 160). Yet, it is economically imperative for the popular press, particularly when it is losing readership to other media formats such as cable TV and the internet, to reinforce a sense of cultural uniformity and a set of shared values (Alabarces, Tomlinson, and Young 563).

The McCann case provided prime opportunities for the narrativising of nation, often in nostalgic, colonialist discourse. The McCanns were initially represented as a British couple who had fallen victim not only to the evil act of a foreign abductor, but also to the bungling of the Portuguese police. For instance, after Jane Tanner, a friend of the McCanns, stated that she believed she saw Madeleine McCann's abductor, a headline in the *Daily Mail* read: "Tapas Nine Witness Says 'Mediterranean Man Took Madeleine'." She is then quoted as stating, "the man I saw was more local, or Mediterranean looking, rather than British. He had dark, almost black, long hair and had swarthy skin" (Wilkes and Allen). Here a threatening, ethnically and racially marked otherness is put in the service of consolidating an anachronistic notion of Britishness, one divested of ethnic and racial diversity, while simultaneously shoring up prevalent ideologies of white purity, moral superiority and universality. In the same newspaper, famed for its Euroscepticism and anti-immigration stance, Peter McKay, chiming with the sentiments of many other tabloid journalists, wrote: "Viewed from here, from day one the Portuguese investigation seemed clumsy and amateur." This article, which ran with the headline "How the McCann Case Highlights Our True Attitude towards EU Membership," acted as a springboard for the paper to reassert its anti-EU stance, with the first-person plural assuming reader consensus (though readers' comments following the online article underscore that this inclusivity is rhetorically constructed rather than actual).

The McCanns attracted mass media interest not only because of their status as "Brits" aboard, but also because they were middle-class doctors (albeit from working-class backgrounds). Without doubt, initially their class status helped foster media sympathy, even though many commentators (and people I conversed with) felt that "they should have known better"—the suggestion being that the white, middle-classes are usually more responsible parents than their working-class counterparts. For instance, India Knight in the *Sunday Times*, using an intimate, second-person address, states that Mark Warner resorts are usually populated by "recognizable types," "none of them the kind of people who wallop their weeping kids in Sainsbury's. You heave a sigh of relief. 'Everyone is like us,' you think. 'Nothing bad could happen here'" ("Every Mother's Nightmare"). While this article is sympathetic to the McCanns, whom she describes as a "normal" family, "just like ours," who did what "more or less everyone else I know has" done (Knight herself excepted), the mystery of the story as it was dissected in the popular media, blogs and message boards revolved around why well-off, middle-class parents would leave their children unattended when baby-sitting facilities were readily available.

At the same time, the more liberal press, such as *The Guardian* and *The Independent*, critical of the tabloids and conservative broadsheets, addressed readers able to perceive this class bias, discursively constructing a more discerning, sophisticated readership (Campbell; Freeland; Wilby). For instance, as Peter Wilby summarised: "Feckless single mothers in high-rise flats may be denounced for leaving their children 'home alone.' The McCanns are churchgoing professionals from suburban Leicester and therefore not to blame." For these newspapers, the McCann case cemented their own community of readers and policed the borders of "quality" and "popular," news and entertainment, as is evident in *The Guardian*'s Simon Jenkins's observation about the case: "There is nothing [the British media] finds too vulgar or too prurient for its wandering, penetrating lens."

Of course, what these accounts were decrying and simultaneously confirming is the unhappy fact that some individual bodies count more than others in mass media representations. This is precisely the point made by former Metropolitan Police Chief Sir Ian Blair in relation to the Soham murders when he accused the mainstream media of "institutional racism." His assertions that "nobody can understand why that dreadful story became the biggest story in Britain," and that "the reporting of murders in ethnic minority communities appears not to interest the mainstream media" (Steele) were met with such forceful condemnation that he was forced to apologise for causing offence to the victims' families. Yet, if we compare the so-called "Maddie" effect to the space devoted in the British media to similar cases occurring at the same time, whose victims were not as British or white or middle-class or simply as photogenic as Madeleine McCann, the McCann case functions as a textbook illustration of Blair's point, though class and nation would seem to be equally as important criteria as race. For instance, Mari Luz Cortés, a Spanish child (since found dead) who, in January 2008, went missing from a location just a ninety-minute drive from the McCanns' resort, received nowhere near the media attention, either in Spain or Britain, as Madeleine McCann, and those that covered the case most often noted similarities and differences, or the McCanns' expressions of support. The fact that Mari Luz Cortés was from a deprived neighborhood and a Roma family fuelled speculation that her disappearance might be the result of a family feud, thus providing a ready-made, socially legible narrative explanation that was not available in the McCann case.

Equally instructive is the case of Shannon Matthews, who went missing from her home in the Moorside estate in Dewsbury in February 2008. The family and residents attempted similar collective action to the McCanns, namely a poster and T-shirt campaign, but, like the Cortés family, lacked comparable financial resources. Most attention from the tabloids, however, focused on the fact that Shannon Matthews' mother, Karen Matthews, was benefit-dependent and had had seven children by five different men. Much like Fiona MacKeown, whose fifteen-year old daughter was found murdered in Goa in February 2008 after she had allowed her to stay there alone, failure to conform to the nuclear family model (Fiona MacKeown had nine children with different fathers, lived in a caravan in a field in Devon and had a lifestyle frequently described as "hippy") was deemed "proof" of irresponsible parenting. What followed was a form of "class tourism," as many popular newspapers relished describing the perceived social and moral deprivation of the Moorside estate, with *The Sun*'s headline, quoting a road-sweeper, proclaiming "Estate is Like a Nastier Beirut" (Taylor). While it might seem paradoxical for a newspaper addressing a working-class readership to discuss the Mathews case in these terms,

Conboy notes that the popular press frequently draws on the Victorian distinction between the deserving and undeserving poor (*Tabloid Britain* 17); moreover, the quote from the road-sweeper illustrates how the popular press "borrows the people's voice" and "exploits the heightened effectiveness of popular culture to close down popular discourses to a restricted political agenda largely supportive of the status quo" (*The Press* 170). Yet, such assumptions were not limited to tabloids, with Melanie Reid from *The Times* assuring readers, "[t]hese children are not like our children," adding, "[t]heir parents are not adults we would recognise as adults." This time, no rich businessmen or women came forward to offer rewards and *The Sun* offered only £20,000, with the total reward reaching £25,000.

As with the McCann case, *The Independent* and *The Guardian* foregrounded this class bias, most often by comparing media coverage of the two cases. For instance, Beatrix Campbell wrote:

> Both stories dramatise the distribution of virtue and blame that fixes the working class and the middle class in moral hierarchies . . . Karen Matthews has acted appropriately throughout: she was waiting for Shannon at home; she contacted the police as soon as she had exhausted all the obvious locations. And yet, our eye is drawn to her poverty, numbers of partners, cans of lager going into her household. Everything about Ms Matthews' life has been up for scrutiny.

Once Shannon was found in the base of the bed belonging to her step-father's uncle, and Karen Matthews was charged with perverting the course of justice and child neglect amid allegations that the fake abduction was a "Maddie-style" stunt to extract money from the media and the *Find Madeleine Campaign*, this worked to confirm the class assumptions that had governed much initial reporting, unleashing self-congratulatory articles in many tabloids that justified family values in the face of what was deemed the anti-family "left." The *Daily Mail*, for instance, under the headline of "Downfall of a Decent Clan: What the Shannon Family Tree Reveals about the Social Breakdown of Britain" charted a family tree of the Matthews family which stated which members of the family had been imprisoned or criminally charged (Pendlebury). In the *Daily Mail*, Conservative party leader David Cameron decried the Matthews case as "a verdict on our broken society"—an assertion never made in relation to the McCanns, even when they were named as formal suspects. Karen Matthews' conviction also provoked a lengthy article in *The Guardian* which criticised "class warriors on the blogs" and journalists like Campbell for the "politically correct" "insidious argument" that "Shannon was being neglected by the press because of where she came from, that her parents were being judged for their lifestyle" (Adams). The fact remains, though, that the Shannon Matthews case captured the popular media's attention more fully once it validated classist assumptions than when Karen Matthews appeared a victim.

What connected the media interest in all these British cases was a rigorous interrogation of femininity and maternity which worked to consolidate normative gender roles. Despite initial sympathy, as time wore on, like Fiona MacKeown, Kate McCann was accused of not grieving sufficiently, not being traumatised enough, not corresponding to prevalent notions of female frailty. Both women, indeed, were proactive in the case, with Fiona MacKeown refusing to accept the Indian police's first verdict of accidental death, with Indian authorities later forced to admit that her daughter's murder had been covered up by local police. Suspicions that Kate McCann might be implicated in her daughter's death were also raised by the fact that she did not seem sufficiently distraught. Accusations leveled at Kate McCann were also culturally bound. Many Portuguese journalists felt that the fact the McCanns were emotionally restrained, had put their children to bed so early (the usual British 7 p.m. bedtime) and hadn't taken their children with them to dine, as most Portuguese do, implied a lack of parental affection. Once Kate McCann was named an "arguido," and public sympathy shifted to outrage, every aspect of her behavior was scrutinised, in both the popular media and online chatter, such as her clothes (being too well dressed), her clutching of Madeleine's "Cuddle Cat," her jogging expeditions, not crying enough, and, more implicitly, being too beautiful.[3] While Gerry's controlled, corporate-like (to use Enright's analogy) addresses to the media were also criticised, they were more compatible with prevalent assumptions about masculinity and male repression. Moreover, despite the assumption that a man had snatched Madeleine, there was no interrogation into the relationship between masculinity and violence, but rather an obsessive regulation of female and maternal behaviour.

It soon became apparent that the McCanns themselves, rather than Madeleine, had become the story, with articles on topics such as Gerry McCann's anger at the suggestion he was not Madeleine's biological father, or Kate McCann's experience of post-natal depression, occupying headline space. But this was also a side-effect of their active solicitation of the mass media. Refusing to inscribe themselves into the more culturally legible role of passive victims, the McCanns, their relatives and friends set about building a media campaign to keep Madeleine in the public eye. Here, their economic status and social connections were essential. They had the financial resources to stay in Portugal and not return immediately to work, and enlist the help of a PR agency, a media spokesman and a private detective agency.

However, it was not just a case of financial and cultural capital. Indeed, Gerry McCann himself, in attempting to explain the "Maddie" phenomenon, perceptively underscores the role played by new media technologies: "Of course the world has changed in terms of information technology and the speed of response, you know, in terms of the media coming here and us being prepared [. . .] to some extent to use that to try and influence the campaign" (qtd. in Enright). For instance, the case of Ben Needham, who went missing in the Greek island of Kos in 1991, offers a remarkably similar scenario to the McCann case, with its British subjects, foreign locale, and police suspicion that the family members were suspects;[4] however, the same media technologies were simply not available to the family. Gerry McCann's sister, on the other hand, started a chain email which quickly circulated. The McCanns also set up a website (http://www.findmadeleine.com), which received 50 million hits in its first day (Addly). The website itself offers details on Madeleine and her family, a family photograph album, as well as "Gerry's blog," an example of the reterritorilaisation of public and private spaces in web culture. The site also gives details of their Find Madeleine Campaign, related events, and their work with other non-governmental organisations. There is a link "how to help" which instructs users in how to give donations, buy wristbands or T-shirts, or download campaign posters (in numerous languages), which make clever use of Madeleine McCann's indelible singularity—the fact her pupil runs into her iris. The site contains video clips, such as "Don't You Forget About Me," with a voiceover by actress Zoë Wanamaker, as well as wallpaper downloads for computer desktops. It thus offered interactive formats that allow visitors to participate in the ongoing search for Madeleine.

Participation was not limited to this website. The McCanns had to name their website the "official" one because countless similar websites had sprung up on the web. Over 200 groups were set up on Facebook, with "Please remember Madeleine McCann is still missing" currently tolling over 57,000 members (along with some less supportive groups such as "I am sick to death of hearing about Madeleine McCann"—a reminder of the role of aggression as well as compassion in establishing collective identifications). YouTube also hosts homemade videos about Madeleine McCann made by people who have never actually met her, followed by comments by viewers such as "I miss you" or "come home to us," as well as some nastier, disparaging comments about the video-maker and, predictably, the McCanns themselves. The volume of vicious online commentary generated further traditional media response, such as that of India Knight, who berates the "heartless abuse heaped on Kate McCann," and quotes online entries such as: "The parents are a disgrace. They were on the razz every night after leaving their children in the crèche all day every day. Much wanted children? More like little fashion statements that they couldn't be bothered to look after properly. The children unfortunately got in the way of their 'me time'" ("Madeleine McCann: You Are All Guilty"). Arguing that on the whole the British press "acted pretty responsibly," Knight chooses to blame not the media, which, she states, is regulated and strives for objectivity, but "the public": "The public, through the internet, can—and does—say anything, no matter how degrading or toxic, and keeps on saying it until, by a sort of insane osmosis, it stops being an outright lie and becomes a half-truth." The fact that many popular newspapers were forced to pay out damages to the McCanns and Robert Murat certainly undermines Knight's assertion about responsible reporting. Her analysis also follows regressive conceptions of the "public," reminiscent of Le Bon's or Freud's view of the "mass" as a contagious, irrational force that overthrows social restrictions, in this case through the anonymity not of the crowd but of cyberspace, accompanied by a desire to police the increased access to the public sphere granted by new media technologies.

Indeed, with the McCann case, readers, audiences and users were not passively absorbing the story as handed down by the mass media; rather, they were actively involved in creating meanings, as well as allegiances and networks, in new media modalities. The McCann case, in other words, headlined at a time when, with the creation of user-friendly technologies, neither specialised technical skills nor financial capital are required for "average consumers to archive, appropriate, and recalculate media content" (H. Jenkins 1), fulfilling "a public desire to participate within, rather than simply consume, media" (150). While this shift from the consumption of monologic discourse to the modular, interactive and polyphonic discourse of participatory media mirrors many aspects associated with face-to-face communication (Warnick qtd. in Howard 501), the difference is that this discourse is published in the public domain.

Many cybertheorists have extolled this participatory aspect of the World Wide Web, pointing to its potential to extend democratic possibilities and social participation. Often these accounts refer to Jürgen Habermas's influential *The Structural Transformation of the Public Sphere* (1962), which argues that the commercialisation of the mass media has turned the public into consumers of information rather than actors in the social sphere. From the 90s onwards, many scholars noted that the types of discussion enacted in internet forums and blogs had the potential to reinvigorate the public sphere by encouraging participation in debates, allowing more marginalised, oppositional voices to be heard without institutional "gatekeepers," and forging new modes of citizenship, affective bonds and communities.[5] For instance, in his seminal *The Virtual Community: Homesteading on the Electronic Frontier* (1993), Howard Rheingold speculates on the "capacity to challenge the existing political hierarchy's monopoly on powerful communications media, and perhaps thus revitalize citizen-based democracy." More pessimistic accounts, on the other hand, have attributed to web culture increased atomisation, social seclusion, a withdrawal from the public sphere to the privacy of the home and a concomitant loss of social responsibility.[6] However, recent accounts are less polarised and suggest that both trends are simultaneously at work, since internet cultural production is as unstable, multiple and hybrid as other cultural forms. Alongside online petitions, independent media, collective political mobilisation (the power of which was evidenced with the role played by social media and networking sites during the Arab Spring 2011 popular uprisings), one can find more institutional sites, mainstream media, abundant online gossip, computer games and commercial sites. Such diversity was evident in responses to the McCann case: while much online commentary did not evidence a revitalised public sphere or empowered citizenship, other responses such as home-made clips on YouTube, groups on Facebook, chain emails and internet sites are indubitably forms of social participation and collective action. Moreover, the sheer volume of media participation the case generated is indicative of the desire to be a member, however fleetingly, of an online community. While there is much debate as to whether virtual communities are comparable to off-line communities, whether they act as compensation for the fragmentary nature of our lives and the lack of organic communities under late capitalism (Fernback 39–40; Rheingold; Turkle 177–78), or whether they are more transitory modes of belonging than that suggested by the term community, with its connotations of consensus, assimilation, permanence and geographical proximity (Carroli 360), what is certain is that online responses to the McCann case facilitated modes of belonging and collective encounters, however ephemeral, through "mutual production and reciprocal exchange" (H. Jenkins 137).

That said, it is also essential to accentuate that "[t]he interactive audience is not autonomous; it still operates alongside powerful media industries" (H. Jenkins 135). With respect to the McCann story, "knowledge" was originally disseminated by more traditional mass media, which supplied information and interpretations that media users went on to rearticulate, appropriate or reproduce. These responses certainly refute the concept of mass media imposing itself on passive mass audiences in the manner famously delineated by Adorno and Horkheimer in their critique of the "culture industry." As cultural studies theorists such as Stuart Hall argued long before the emergence of interactive media, audiences respond actively and critically to media content, and the notion of people as passive "cultural dupes" is "a deeply unsocialist perspective" (Hall, "Notes" 67). However, Hall also insists that "there is *no* whole, authentic, autonomous 'popular culture' which lies outside the field force of the relations of cultural power and domination" (67). Indeed, despite increasing challenges, the powerful organisations that control offline news content still dominate online news sources (Wilson and Peterson 451). With this in mind, web responses to the case and concomitant cultural production cannot simply be read as an expression of the voice of the "people," since *initial* mass media attention was generated not only by the McCanns' innovative campaign, but also, as I hope to have shown, by the opportunities the story offered for the popular media to shore up their political economies by consolidating their community of readers/viewers, reaffirming prevalent social norms and re-articulating the "popular." But the surprise expressed in traditional media at the extent of internet participation in the case certainly signals a definite cultural shift: the entry of participatory media culture into the quotidian. Hence the paradigmatic status the case acquired.

Five years after Madeleine McCann's disappearance, the story has died down but has by no means disappeared. In March 2008, the McCanns were headline news again when, after libel suits, the *Daily Express* and *Daily Star* newspapers offered a front page, headline apology for their suggestions that the McCanns had been involved in Madeleine's disappearance. The *Daily Express* alone paid £550,000 to the Find Madeleine appeal. In May 2009, the McCanns dominated headlines when they released a digitally-enhanced, age-processed picture of Madeleine, showing how she would look at age six. Even in 2011, Kate McCann's book *Madeleine,* her first-person account of events published on Madeleine's eighth birthday (the original date changed by the McCanns to avoid a media clash with the Royal Wedding), not only hit the headlines, but was serialised by *The Sun*.

On the website, Kate McCann has stated:

> My feeling is that the publicity surrounding Madeleine's abduction was *not* inappropriate. Every child in such a situation should receive this same amount of attention, but it shouldn't be down to the family to instigate it. The public awareness of Madeleine's plight has at the very least, highlighted cases of other missing children and the extent of the problem as a whole, and from that we can take a small bit of comfort.

While some have asked whether the obsessive media attention might have endangered Madeleine's life, Kate McCann hopes that some collective good can come out of their individual tragedy. However, while responses to the case in new media technologies underscored that knowledge and cultural production is not the exclusive preserve of the mainstream media, the case also confirmed that not "every child" does receive the same attention, not only because many families lack the necessary cultural and financial capital, but also because social hierarchies and prevailing social norms determine which individual stories are deemed worthy of mass media representation, and which will struggle to be heard.

NOTES

1. In August 2002, Holly Wells and Jessica Chapman went missing while out buying sweets. After a high-profile missing persons hunt lasting thirteen days, their bodies were found and their school caretaker, Ian Huntley, was convicted of their murder.
2. For such theorists, the constitutive alterity of both the self and the other problematises traditional concepts of the "individual" as well as "community," since "[b]eing in common," "an integral part of being oneself" (Douzinas 99), inevitably "closes [individual subjects] off from their identity with a line, which traversing them, alters them" (Esposito 139). See Rehling 10–12. See also Parkin-Gounelas, "Helping Yourself," for an excellent review essay on these authors.
3. *The Guardian*'s Cristina Odone put it as follows: "Kate McCann is guilty. Madeleine's mother has been charged with looking composed and controlled, pretty and slim. Her lower lip doesn't wobble, her highlights are perfect, her

tummy is flat. She is guilty, in other words, of not conforming to type. It's not murder, but it's a crime: robbing the public of what it wants."

4. I am grateful to Maria Vara for alerting me to this point.
5. For a useful summary of internet studies, see Stevenson.
6. See Stevenson.

10 Swarm Intelligence
Blogging and On-Line Subjectivities

Holger Briel

FRAMING THE QUESTION

Over the last few years, blogging (the writing and disseminating of short pieces of electronic text) has become an important part of online communication. According to Blogpulse.com, a technology webpage, on the 15th of June 2011 there existed 163,327,404 blogs worldwide (in 2010 49% of them were American). The average blog is 11.1 months old (Papacharissi 25) and, if labour hours are calculated, the time spent blogging would add up to 150,000 full-time jobs. This is twice the number of accredited journalists in the US (Quiggin 77). Another convincing example of the pervasiveness of blogs is the fact that many Google searches have begun leading to blogs. If for the last fifteen years searches tended to lead to databases, these have now been co-opted by blogs—or, indeed, have become blogs. Furthermore, most internet users are bloggers or, at least, micro-bloggers. Most people online write taglines on their Gmail and Skype accounts, compose short emotional make-up lines on Facebook ("What are you doing now? Enter text here"), or engage in more or less elaborate attempts at individuality on MySpace. In one way or another, all these activities relate to the blogging phenomenon, to mediated communication between e-individuals and e-masses.

Yet blogging also continues to have many detractors. A case highlighting the darker side of online living was the suicide on the 2nd of October 2008 of Korean actress Choi Jin-sil, who had apparently been so distraught about negative comments left on her personal homepage that she decided to take her own life. In the wake of this event, Korean authorities debated the stricter regulation of cyberspace (Veale). There is also the question of quality, with the trivia factor irritating many potential and actual blog readers. Most blogs do not deal with rigorously-constructed exchange, nor do they function as news breakers. Rather, they seem to have appeared as compensation for the loss of face-to-face exchanges in traditional social settings such as family meals or friendly get-togethers and are a result of today's fragmented and multifaceted social structures.

Blogging also represents a significant threat to professional journalism, due perhaps partly, as Geert Lovink claims, to the fact that printed and broadcast messages have lost their aura and audience in a postmodern age (Lovink 1). Mainstream media are still fighting back, if not in the US, certainly in Europe. Here is the view of a *Neue Zürcher Zeitung* columnist, S.B, on 25 March 2008: "[Journalists] are specialists in leaving things out. Because readers do not pay money to read, but rather to be able to afford non-reading, in order to have the certainty that by not reading they have not missed anything" (S.B. "Web 2.0."). At least according to this columnist, blogs are no substitute for the old media, not even for aura-less mass media. Another perception challenge blogs encounter could be termed the "writing for writing's sake" phenomenon. This means that there are so many blogs in existence that their sheer number might prevent some readers from even entering the market. As one commentator has put it, "never have so many people written so much to be read by so few" (Boxer).[1]

Blogs have begun to exert a strong influence on their readers. An example is the influence of bloggers on the image of politicians. According to a 2007 study, one particular UK political blogger, Iain Dale, exerted 15% of the BBC's and almost 60% of *The Guardian*'s influence on the image of Britain's Conservative party leader David Cameron (Madsen). Now this might not seem to be much, but it is worth remembering that such influence has been acquired within the space of a mere few years. Blogs are not only influential in politics, but have begun to infiltrate all aspects of life. In August 2008, JupiterResearch conducted a survey of online consumers, with 25% of the questions posed relating to blogs and how they may or may not influence consumer behavior. This clearly demonstrates that blogs have begun to exert much more power than any other online medium. According to Rob Crumpler, CEO of BuzzLogic, "blogs rival search as a navigation tool, which has really interesting implications for advertisers. Blogs are becoming trusted guides, steering users who are seeking very specific information to places of interest online" ("Blogs Influence Purchases").[2]

Despite some worries about their shape and content, the fact remains that blogs are here in force, making an important point about the way humans and their societies are changing. Subjectivity, deconstructed by postmodernism, is now resurfacing in blogs in a different guise, that of the swarm or networked multitude. Typical examples are the pages of Wikipedia, to which hundreds of thousands of writers have flocked to combine their texts in order to present collective encyclopaedic knowledge. The individual blogs of the blogosphere can be viewed in a similar vein, as a product of a specific moment in the history of technology, portending a mass culture change in the making, a breaking-through of the barrier between the producer and the consumer, creating a multitude of "producers" (Bruns and Jacobs 6). Whereas previously the "flock" had connotations of an assemblage of passive and mindless individuals who have given up their particular faculties, now it has taken on a more active and intelligent role. This is a significant development, given that blogs arose out of a Western individualist culture which until recently was not particularly keen on collectivist activities.

In what follows, the way in which blogs shape their writers' and readers' subjectivities will be more closely analysed, starting with their precursors and continuing on to their significance for today's (online) societies and communicative practices. This will then lead to a discussion of how online communicative practices have radically begun to question older concepts of identity.

THE ORIGINS OF BLOGS

Blogging can be more specifically defined as the distributed, broad-based practice of content production, with a reverse chronology of frequently updated uploads (Bruns and Jacobs 5). Typical features of blogs are the reverse chronology in which they appear and were developed, permalinks, the linking to other individual blog entries (itself a political act) and the so-called blogroll, a list of and links to other blogs to which the blogger is favourably inclined.

Despite these common features, the blogosphere is not a united, homogeneous space. Rather, it is heterogeneous and vast, and in this vastness has perhaps become a victim of its own success. There are of course a large number of different blog genres, such as liveblogs, videologs, podcasts and collaborative blogs. However, many of these are merely dependent on different media for recording and dissemination, making the field rather more manageable. Thus it could be said that in terms of their origins, there exist three partial precursors for blogs, one a mass media phenomenon, one very individualist, and one a particular mode of communication.

Blog Precursor 1: Newspapers and Electronic Mass Media

Perhaps the main precursor of many blogs is the newspaper, still the preferred print mass medium. Besides carrying information, newspapers like blogs are already interactive, even two-way media, albeit on a small scale. Readers were and are able to contribute to newspapers via Letters to the Editor or Op-Ed pages. However, editors still have the last word on the publication of any such material. Blogs are becoming serious competitors for newspapers in terms both of public appeal and of the speed with which they deliver their message. To a large extent, the delivery speed lies at the heart of newspapers, and while almost all of them nowadays have web pages updated more frequently than their printed issues, even that does not seem to be enough to satisfy the demand for constant up-dating. Thus, a number of papers have completely dropped their print versions and are now only available online. Others have experimented with chargeable areas in their online editions, but so far these have remained at the experimental level. The *New York Times* tried to charge for some of its content, but abandoned the charge in 2007, as only 227,000 subscriptions were sold. It soon became clear that advertising revenue would be much higher than any income generated from subscriptions (Sandoval). More recently, print media have pinned their hopes for survival on the Apple iPad, as this platform allows for access fees through its Apps features. It remains to be seen, however, whether this will reverse the seemingly overwhelming trend towards free content. Moreover, many blogs can now compete with newspapers in terms of professionalism of layout and seriousness of reporting. A typical example is the *Huffington Post*, the number one blog in the world, at least according to "Technorati Top 100." These blogs have achieved semi-professional status, bringing with it, however, the danger of becoming indistinguishable from the mass media they had set out to criticise in the first place. Nevertheless, they still represent a serious threat to traditional media and are one of the main reasons why print journalism is undergoing crisis. And indeed in 2008, the *Huffington Post* gave up calling itself a blog in favour of an "internet newspaper." Finally, in February 2011, it was sold to AOL for the sum of $315 million ("AOL buying Huffington Post").

The most prominent blogs are usually media blogs, gate watchers or citizen journalist blogs, where the impact has been immense. These bloggers have helped to create new digitally encoded public spheres, micro public spheres (Gold, "Weblogs" 113). An example from Germany is the *Bild* blog, which exercises a gate-watcher function in relation to one of Europe's largest tabloid newspapers, *Bild*. In existence since June 2004, it has won the most important German press prize, the Grimme prize. The most famous European blogger is arguably Beppe Grillo, who has enthralled millions with his blog in Italy and beyond, demonstrating that political blogging is not only an American phenomenon. A significant moment came for the medium when sometime around 2002 or 2003, the tables turned; whereas before bloggers had watched the media as gate watchers, now the media began watching the bloggers. This has led to the present situation, where most newspapers feature parts of their own blogs in the newspapers themselves. In terms of electronic mass media, one could also point to public access, community and open TV channels which allow individuals to "broadcast" their message, although due to the elaborate and expensive technology necessary, access is usually limited to a few.[3] Having been cottage industries at the time of their inception in the late 1960s, these channels received a huge boost in the 1970s and 1980s due to the fact that in many countries, most notably the US, Canada, Australia, Austria, Luxembourg and Germany, government agencies in charge of the airways requested broadcasting spaces for citizens from cable and satellite operators in return for their own broadcasting licences. Flagship examples are the *Manhattan Neighborhood Network (MNN)*, *Roger's Television* in Ottawa or the *Offener Kanal Berlin* (Briel). However, by and large, and echoing the problems of print journalism, it seems their heyday has passed and much of their amateur and community-oriented energy has migrated online, to YouTube or, indeed, to blogs.

Blogs therefore carry within themselves the opportunity to outdo old journalism. They are able to respond more quickly to new developments, can create microlocal content through managed citizen journalism, are issue based, and can easily create vast databases. Whether all this leads to better-quality journalism in both online and traditional mass media, as Tremayne believes (269–70), remains open to debate.

Blog Precursor 2: Diaries

While media blogs are among the most read, it is generally agreed that the overwhelming number of online blogs are of a more personal character, dealing with daily trivia. Typically exemplified by aggregators such as http://www.livejournal.com, their *raison d'être* is to inform the world about personal goings-on; as they are the overwhelming majority, they are referred to as the "long tail" of the blogosphere, the millions of blogs read only by the few. With these, the movement is away from mass media audiences and topics towards private, personal experiences. Writers of such blogs are of course aware of the fact that, as for the diarist, the gain derived from the exercise lies with the writer more than with the reader. But whereas traditional diaries often fetishise secrecy (small locks, elaborate hiding places, etc.), blogs parade and are dependent on their accessibility. In both cases, however, the reasons for writing were and are much more diverse than the popular view recognises. They range from memory support to catharsis, self-analysis, self-hypnosis, thought and faith-support to creating a location in the dislocation of the world (Holm 11).

From its inception, diaristic practice has in fact always had an appeal to an audience. Its beginnings can be traced to the Roman emperor Marc Aurel (121–180 AD) and his "Notes" (*Hypomnematiá),* (literally, something to remember, worth remembering or that ought to be remembered, things that address oneself). In 1559 Aurel's text was re-issued under a new title, *Tà eis heautón* (that which belongs to one person, belongs to me, text for himself). This subtle shift in meaning would become even stronger with a later Latin edition, whose title weakens this self-referentiality and adds a biographical touch: *De seipso seu vita sua* (On himself or his life) (Butzer 94–96). Thus, already the first diary undermines the assumption that diaries are written for oneself alone. Nor are they the unmitigated guarantors of truth and/or authenticity. For instance it has been proven that Columbus faked his on-board diary in order to maintain morale. With Columbus we also enter the era of the logbook proper. The "log" of the logbook had first been introduced by mariners attempting to chart their way in unknown waters. Quite literally, it was a piece of wood tied on a rope and lowered into the sea several times a day to ascertain water depth. These were then recorded, "logged" in the ship's "logbook." As the practice became common, logbooks would be standardised and become a space for personal entries. But, as the example of Columbus shows, not all logbooks could be trusted.[4]

One stricture binding Western diaristic practice is a disciplined, economic model (of time).[5] This becomes obvious from a second genealogical strand of diaries which, like the ship logbook, increased in importance during the Renaissance. In many shops and trading offices, daily books were beginning to be kept to record the incoming and outgoing of goods. Later on these books were standardised into calendars, again with space for personal entries. In the seventeenth and eighteenth centuries, this economic model was then transferred into the personal, spiritual realm with the daily writing and reading of uplifting texts in spiritual calendar books. One basis of this pietistic usage is the Latin phrase *carpe diem*, seize the day, hence the early name of such texts, "diurnal" and then later on "journal."[6]

Here the gain would be the recording of personal growth, with one of its enduring qualities being the daily repetition of such diary writing. This can be illustrated by an experiment initiated by the culture ministry of the Soviet Union in 1963. On the 27th of September of that year, all artists in socialist and communist states were requested to write a diary entry. The East German writer Christa Wolf continued this tradition up until 2000, writing a diary entry every 27th of September. In an earlier diary entry from 1961, she had already expressed an inkling of what would be the result of her entries: "Am ehesten hält sich das Gerüst des Tages" (Mostly, what remains is the scaffolding of the day) (Wolf 17). Days would differ; circumstances change, but the basic day-to-day remained the same. It is this "scaffolding of the day" that has allowed diaries to be both individualistic yet also similar and predictable when it comes to formalist criteria, such as the typical reasons for writing given on the first page or excuses for interruptions in the flow of writing. All diaries contain such formulae at one point or another in their textual structure.

Diaries are part of what Foucault called "Technologies of the Self," a form of care directed primarily towards oneself. However, this care of the self does stretch to others as well, as a self is unthinkable without the other. (This raises questions of identity discussed at greater length by other contributors to this volume.) While diaristic practice might first and foremost be directed towards oneself, even this self-directed writing is already a reading. As the Swiss author Max Frisch writes: "Schreiben heißt sich selbst lessen" (To write means to read oneself) (qtd. in Holm 30). A diary always already appeals to an other, at first during the actual writing process, and then again in a later reading, either by the author or by others. All written texts demand a reading; a person writing is writing as if she were another, constantly watching herself writing. A good example of this estrangement or doubling are the diaries of Franz Kafka, which show that in writing a diary, one is neither oneself nor alone (Holm 78).

Moving on to electronic texts, one of the first electronic media diaries and proto-blogs was the text written by the German writer and sometimes *Vanity Fair* contributor Rainald Goetz, which appeared on the internet in 1998–1999 as *Abfall für Alle* (Trash for All), a tongue-in-cheek title already hinting at the long tail of qualitatively questionable blogging material. Another project worth mentioning here is that of Gordon Bell, whose *MyLifeBits* aims to capture his life digitally and continuously. This he attempts to achieve by recording everything he experiences with a head-mounted camera and microphone and scanning into the computer all his correspondence, thereby creating a vast archive of his life, like a digital voluntary *Truman Show*.

While there exist an infinite number of online diaristic blogs, their academic exegesis is still in its infancy. One area worthy of attention is the relationship between gender and blogs. The general rule that women write diaries and men don't seems to have been turned on its head in cyberspace; at least in the Western world, many more men write blogs than do women. How gender is performed in these blogs is still under-researched.[7] Another area that requires attention is the cultural specificity of blogs. In general it must be noted that not much emphasis has been given to the multiculturality of the blogging phenomenon, which no doubt has to do with the up until now overwhelming US presence on the web. But starting in 2007, the largest number of blogs was written in Japanese (37%). This has had profound implications for generalisations about blog cultures. Thus Sarah Boxer reports on the difference between US and Japanese blogs: "Most of [the Japanese blogs] are polite and self-effacing—'karaoke for shy people'," and thus very different from a typical American blog (Boxer). The predominance of Japanese blogs is a striking fact; add to this that in 2008 China surpassed the US in internet connections and it becomes clear that much more research on the internationalisation of blogs and their underlying multicultural foundations remains to be done.

Diaries and blogs share the need for continuous, regular updates, the interlacing of the private and the public and the need of the writer to address some other. However, important differences between the two genres remain. While most diaries are a means of ritualistic, slowly preformed *(self-)preservation*, most blogs are performative, vehicles for instantaneous *(self-)presentation*. Blogs are deeply entrenched in and formative of a mediasphere in which the archive has been relegated to the background, as was the case with the genesis of printed texts. But real-time is frail and precious, a complaint that also reverberates throughout the blogosphere. As Laurence Sterne noted two and a half centuries ago in *The Life and Opinions of Tristram Shandy, Gentleman,* Tristram had to learn that the writing down of one's life eats up the living of it, its performance (Sterne). In correlation to this and in its extreme form, blogging can also become a way of life standing in the way of life itself.

Blog Precursor 3: Oral Communicative Practice

The two precursors of blogs discussed so far are both writing based, and indeed, most blogs are written. It might not be immediately obvious, then, that the oral communicative practice is a precursor to blogs as well and has had a profound impact on them. In his seminal *Orality and Literacy: The Technologization of the Word (*1982), Walter Ong traces the historic turn from oral to chirographic culture. This change, Ong argues, involved a different kind of memory storage, exemplified by Plato's rejection of the poets (i.e. those who were previously charged with retaining and reciting the collective memory of the people) from his Republic and the distancing of the originator of a thought from the receiver, who merely reads the other's text without the context present in face-to-face communication. According to Derrida's theory of *différance*, this is also one of the reasons for the necessary inconclusiveness of texts. With print, words became more firmly embedded in space and time and thus became objects (Ong 123, 118). All writing is thus "limotrophic," situated on the border and encompassing both the life-world and its opposite.

For Ong, there also exists a second orality, that of electronically transmitted words via radio, TV and telephone, which like the first orality, creates certain highly-bonded user groups, but is transmitted through technological means. In Chapter 3 of his book, he lists a number of psychodynamic factors which for him differentiate orality from chirography. They are:

(i) In orality, expression is additive rather than subordinate.
(ii) It is aggregative rather than analytic.
(iii) It tends to be redundant or "copious."
(iv) There is a tendency for it to be conservative.
(v) Expression is agonistically toned.[8]
(vi) It is empathic and participatory rather than objectively distanced.
(vii) It is situational rather than abstract.[9]

When examining blogs, it becomes apparent that actually all of these requirements which Ong had stipulated for orality are applicable to blogs' textual structure as well. What differentiates blogs from other forms of rapid oral communication, though, is that, unlike the equally biased opinions of talk radio (Tremayne 264), it is not the spoken word that is used, but rather the written word. It would therefore seem that we have here entered a *third stage of orality*, in which the written word is treated as if it were oral. This would be the case not only for blogs, but also for chat rooms and other short message systems. Blogs and all their e-cousins are therefore able to avoid what Günter Österle has called the problematic "transportation crisis of intensity" ("Transportkrise der Intensität") (103) of other written texts, precisely because so much of their identity hinges on characteristics of oral speech, particularly its rapidity and intensity. Blogging is thus able to combine the emotional with the Socratic ideal of measured textual discourse (in a very broad sense) and could be called the digital extension of the oral tradition (Wiener qtd. in Lovink 10).

Weblogs thus stem from three distinct realms of communicative practices between the individual and the collective, one public, one private, one oral:

(i) The newspaper column, in which one and the same person publishes something at fixed intervals.
(ii) The *journal intime*, in which a given person writes primarily personal notes to him/herself (although this supposed auto-referentiality is simultaneously a call for communication with others) (Gold, "Einführung" 6).
(iii) The linguistic ductus of oral communication.

TECHNOLOGICAL CONDITIONS

There is another important issue to consider in relation to the formation of blogs: that of technology. In electronic written communication, Christa Wolf's previously mentioned "scaffolding" would perhaps need to be replaced by another word, one used by Heidegger: I am thinking here of his "enframing," the *Ge-stell*. He writes: "We now name that challenging claim which gathers man thither to order the self-revealing as standing-reserve: 'Ge-stell' (enframing)." And he continues:

> Enframing means the gathering together of that setting-upon that sets man upon man, i.e., challenges him to bring forth, to reveal the real, in the mode of ordering, as standing reserve. Enframing means that way of revealing that holds sway in the essence of modern technology and that is itself nothing technological. (Heidegger)

What Heidegger is describing here in his characteristic way is the state of mind of modern humans who have relegated (some of their) cognitive and communicative functions to technology, a technology always in the making, always beckoning, always promising, but never fully delivering. And at any given time, particular features of this technology can be found on such scaffolding, such shelves, especially when it comes to the structure of our days, which are becoming ever more technologically mediated.

In blogging, certain technological prerequisites are obvious: a computer, some sort of power supply, software and internet access. Software that even twenty years ago was groundbreaking has today become so common and/or obsolete that it has almost been forgotten. In the context of blogging, however, one piece of software stands out: hypertext, the ability to link one document with another by merely clicking on an electronic word or symbol. Hypertext's potential for fiction was quickly detected by writers like Michael Joyce, whose *Afternoon, a Story*, written in 1986 and published on the internet in 1990, is generally regarded as the first example of the genre. Much fiction and art has followed suit. In blogging, hypertext is used for in-text and blog roll linking, but it really encompasses the whole idea of the "inter"-net, of the interlinking of ideas, products and avatars.[10] De-centralised rapid sharing and distribution are after all two of the main functions of the World Wide Web.

It is this kind of enframing that differentiates online from offline diaries. Technology has allowed for the easy dissemination of personal musings in an unprecedented way. However, Heidegger's concern that the human usage of technology lacks extensive understanding of what it is that is being used and that the Gestell has in effect begun to dominate humans also has relevance in the blogosphere. One of the reasons why blogging became so successful was the fact that shortly after 2000 blog aggregators began to appear, thus standardising blogging web pages. Bloggers did not have to worry about the formats of their blogs anymore; all they had to do was fire away. This standardisation, on the other hand, in-formed bloggers, made them a cog in the internet machine and took away their ability to format their input. Because of the ease of use of such aggregators, their "enframing" capabilities were hardly ever challenged. Instead of having to create an archive for oneself (e.g. a diary), archives had become prefabricated. The enframing had reached the *journal intime*, further challenging the precarious balance between public and private.

Computer usage ranges from the most official to the most private, depending on what kind of software program and setting one chooses. While at work, clicking on an EBay auction, reading personal emails, surfing for information about holidays, etc., introduces the personal into the professional/public; conversely, when sitting at home writing personal emails or chatting, work intrudes in the form of an email or a Skype message/call. These are all aspects of the further linkage and diffusion of e-private and e-public. Continuous availability has become the expected norm. The mere closeness of applications on a desktop computer erodes the difference between public and private. Blogging by its very nature participates in the further blurring of these boundary lines.

TECHNO-SOCIAL IMPLICATIONS: NARRATIVITY AND SWARM INTELLIGENCE

In connection with hypertext and blogging, the philosophical tenets of postmodernism can be applied in ways its proponents might not originally have envisaged. A case in point here is Jean-François Lyotard's challenge to the *grands récits* of ideology. Lyotard's texts were certainly helpful in debunking ideological encrustations and exposing the ways in which such *récits* legitimised knowledge and power. Meta-narratives, he argued, were dispersed into "clouds of narrative language elements," leading to "the obsolescence of the metanarrative apparatus of legitimation" (xxiv). But, perhaps unwittingly, one effect of the postmodern move was that the very process of narrativistic enclosure of texts itself became suspect, putting into question the idea of narrativity *per se*, whether it applied to written texts, to films, or to the breaking up of textual media, the movement away from the material and spiritual corpus of the book and towards the micro-contents of blogs.[11] (This shift from homogeneity to heterogeneity has become a mainstay of postmodern discourse and has also been picked up by such post-postmodern thinkers as Alain Badiou and Giorgio Agamben.)[12] And indeed, blog books (an attempt to give coherence to the heterogeneous) do sell rather poorly; just as graffiti rarely work in the museum, blogs do not work in book form.

A seemingly dissenting voice to the endorsement of the loss of narrative is that of the philosopher Paul Ricoeur, who has contributed much to the field of general narratology. His conviction is that narrative has an exceptional capacity to describe and survive the passage of time. At first sight, it would seem that Lyotard's rejection of (ideological) narratives is incompatible with Ricoeur's argument. Yet it could be argued that while traditional narratives are becoming weaker, narrativity *per se* is alive and well, albeit in fractured forms. A single weblog might be irritatingly petty or unsophisticated. However, if viewed as a semantic block within the larger blogosphere, it might begin to make more sense. Within the blogosphere, one blog will invariably belong to a thread of other blogs, all of which shed light on each other. So, rather than speaking of the end of narrative, one might speak of the creation of a new kind of interactive culture, a passing of time checked by various *threads* of communication.

This break-up of longer, sited narratives is already in full swing. Nowadays, for many people a typical Saturday night no longer necessarily implies going to the cinema, a pub or a club, but rather sitting at home watching an eclectic group-agreed mix of YouTube offerings, often closely duplicating the rankings of the items on the "most viewed" list. This activity goes hand in hand with interruptions due to the necessity of everyone present checking their Facebook, MySpace and Skype accounts, their downloads and other Web 2.0 interfaces. We are therefore witnessing a patchwork of rapidly changing proto- and micro-narratives and the demise of much of the narrative *longue durée*. With the advent of mobile computing, this might change once again, strengthening the trend towards people being somewhere and somewhere else at the same time in virtual form. As such it is one more example of how more and more people are assuming virtual or ghost-like identities. If, as has been argued, people thought ghosts had been banished with the advent of electricity and its effect of eternal light, the opposite could be said to be true. Because of electricity, we have more ghosts than ever before—on the television and cinema screens, on Skype, as the voice from our mobile telephones, as an email writer and as a blogger.[13]

While most blogs are perhaps not the harbingers of a culture many might wish for, their potential for effecting radical social change is indisputable, creating as they do something akin to a swarm intelligence, where the overall entity of many individuals develops a mind of its own, similar to a flock of birds, a swarm of bees or a herd of zebras. For an animal group, such swarm behaviour may be a matter of life and death.[14] Similarly not the individual blogger but rather the collection of bloggers may take on a political force of unexpected dimensions, as the events at the beginning of 2011 in North Africa and the Middle East have demonstrated. In addition, peer-to-peer file sharing has sparked off a large debate on intellectual property and property rights as a whole,[15] forcing media owners to rethink their sales strategies and producing a significant culture change from hoarding to sharing, from ownership to cloud participation. This technologically-enabled swarm mentality is one of the main innovations of today's internet, with bloggers creating larger and larger networks from below. Within this context the blogger's identity is defined as the capacity to construct links between various content chunks. In this way, blogs fulfil several social tasks at once: they contribute to the deconstruction and demystification of traditional media and the technosphere surrounding them, and they create participatory authorship (and sometimes action) through the description and creation of new realities (Bruns and Jacobs 20).

BACK TO THE "SELF"? CONTENT CREATION AND CONTENT LOSS

One valid objection to the increasing importance of (intelligent) linking might be that it always presupposes material to link to. However, with the arrival of Web 2.0 and its philosophy of social networking, we have begun moving into a cloud of ever-changing yet also ever-present content, making the activity of collecting unnecessary, even anachronistic. This might have serious repercussions for subjectivity as well. We are no longer able to define ourselves through what we might have collected; rather, we define ourselves through our links, through the number of connections we are able to make online. If a few years ago many were worried about the rapid disappearance of web content, today, with more and more memory available, these fears turn out to be unfounded. Content is always available somewhere in this cloud. This is undoubtedly an important historical phenomenon, as plentiful, even over-abundant and over-determined content bombards our senses as never before. As such, the need materially to "own" content becomes less relevant. Everything is there, continually streamed, updated, accumulated, but visible only for a moment in the forefront before disappearing into the milky white of the distance. Potentially, this has ramifications even for our memory archives, which become less and less necessary as long as we have a working Content Management System (CMS) available. Anecdotal evidence suggests that a diminishing attention span is significantly related to sustained internet usage (Hoffman; Carr).

Perhaps this situation also puts to rest one of the dichotomies Walter Benjamin pointed out in 1936 in "The Work of Art in the Age of Mechanical Reproduction." In this text, Benjamin observed that one of the main differences between the reception of photographs and that of films was that while one had all the time in the world to inspect and analyse a photograph, what was necessary to understand a film was presence of mind, a rapid understanding of the changes from frame to frame. With the internet as a huge reservoir of old, new and rapidly-changing content, perhaps we can have it both ways now, understanding the rapid changes while at the same time existing in a "poliverse" of ever-increasing yet always available content. As such, bloggers could be regarded as important pathfinders in this computer-generated cloud.

Geert Lovink describes the emergence of e-subjectivities in the following way: "We are moving from living, analyzing and imagining contemporary culture as an information society technically underwritten by the computer, to inhabiting and imagining relays of entwined and fragmented techno-social networks" (227). The apt name for such a culture would be *thread culture,* with individual threads practising a communal, politicised lifestyle reminiscent of 1960s communes, or of the 1980s Sausalito WELL, the first bulletin board and online community. Many of the previously named phenomena seem to indicate that online societies are moving in this direction.[16]

This development might also shed light on some of its accompanying dangers. One of the potentially most serious charges against it is that the change from a diary-oriented individualist perspective towards a collective blogging and sharing perspective gives sway to Foucault's technologies of the self, ever more mediated, threatening individual ethics or aesthetics—media-presencing at the expense of human agency. While the internet must hinge on the findable (as Bernhard Siegert puts it, "What is, is posted" [qtd. in Lovink 84]), at least some truths must also lie in the unlinkable. This is not to say that we should (or could) return to a modern subjectivity believing in its own indivisibility. Rather, it ought to compel us to question this alleged monolithic identity via the new media, applying a new sense of agency in a postmodernist setting, along the lines of a Hegelian sublation.

As we move into a new era of shared knowledge imbued with a more thoroughly constructed aesthetics, older authenticities are questioned and deconstructed and new subjectivities are created and disseminated. Blogs are able to stoke community-oriented energy on an unprecedented level through swarm phenomena, taking full advantage of cloud computing and Web 2.0 social phenomena, and are at the forefront of technosocial change capable of effecting the democratisation not only of the technosphere but of our offline lives as well.[17]

NOTES

1. See also Blood.
2. See also Wright and Page, which examines the way women flock to blogs for information.
3. In this regard, community radio was more successful, especially on a global level, precisely because the technological entry requirements were set much lower than with community TV.

4. A writer who applied the log metaphor to his collage texts was Walter Kempowski, whose massive 10-volume *Echolot* (sonar, echo-sounder) chronicles a collective diary of Germany from 1943–1945. The wordplay on echo and log evidences the mutual deixis of time and place. His text also points to the fact that one alternative reading of the word *weblog* is "we log," a communal communicative activity.
5. Non-Western diaristic practice probably began in the eleventh century with Ibn Banna, who is said to have written the first modern diary in the Arabic world. Other non-European traditions include *The Pillowbook* of Japanese courtesans (depicted in the 1996 Peter Greenaway film of the same name) and Asian travel journals. All of these have in common that they do not insist as much on a strict chronology as do their Western counterparts. The discipline of the latter is nicely illustrated by one of the greatest ever diary writers, Samuel Pepys. On the 14th of January 1666 he writes with a certain regret "that I have to write my diary before I kiss a woman or drink wine" (Pepys).
6. The economic model becomes even clearer in the German language where one meaning of *carpe diem* is "den Tag auskaufen", literally, to buy/gain as much as possible from a day.
7. One notable exception is Van Doorn et al. (143–58).
8. One other difference between journalism and blogging should also be mentioned here. Many blogs are (in)famous for their jargon and tone (their "snarky" or "emo[tional]" language). Many of them also contain an element not usually found either in news journalism or in many diaries: the majority of blogs contains humorous elements, however distorted they might be. This imbues the public discourse with small idiosyncratic snippets aimed at creating a different atmosphere from usual news journalism. As such, this change in language register underlines the demarcation line between present-day journalism and blogging.
9. See Art Bingham's noteworthy review of Ong's text.
10. However worthwhile linking practices might be, inherent in them is also a certain danger: namely that they do not contribute to a renaissance of communication, but rather to its apartheid. Tendentious blogs (of which there are many) will in all likelihood only link to other blogs which share their ideas, thereby undermining the opportunity for a wider and more broad-based dialogue.
11. A good example of this is provided by the film industry itself during the 2008 US screen writers' strike. While the strike did eventually get script writers a salary raise, it proved to be far more beneficial to the studios. During the strike they had to find replacements for their usual aired fare. In so doing, they realised that screen writers had become more or less obsolete, that their audiences were quite happy with more action, more reality shows and less narrative.
12. Both Badiou and Agamben are grounded in postmodernism and its skepticism of subjectivity and homogeneity, but attempt to move beyond this impasse. In his *Being and Event*, Badiou takes up the heterogeneities of postmodernism, but goes beyond Lyotard in attempting to rescue the notions of truth and subject in the heterogeneity of sets and events. Agamben's *Homo Sacer: Sovereign Power and Bare Life* builds on Foucault and sees human subjectivity as an effect, but also as a possibility and/or potentiality. Thus, the move from bare life to qualified life takes an individual into the political and moral realm and allows for agency.
13. I would like to thank the performer and academic Alev Adil for her contribution to this point.

14. This is convincingly demonstrated in the video "Falcon Attack: Peregrine Divebombs Flock of Starlings," available on YouTube. It shows a large flock of starlings reforming themselves into ever-changing shapes to evade the attack of a peregrine falcon. It is not surprising, then, that one of the most recent internet browsers is called Flock, the Social Web Browser which promises to keep you updated with all the social web appliances you might subscribe to.
15. Cf. the work of Lawrence Lessig, whose ideas on intellectual property rights and wrongs continue to reverberate throughout the blogosphere.
16. One example of such a quasi-communal blog is the "Digg Blog," which updates blog stories within seconds of their appearance.
17. I would like to thank my students at the Management Center Innsbruck and at the University of Nicosia who, with their projects, knowledge and inquisitiveness, have significantly contributed towards the shape and content of this chapter.

Epilogue

Pluralities to Come

Ruth Parkin-Gounelas

The old romantic saying had it that two's company, three's a crowd—until, at least, the Rolling Stones brought us cynically into atomistic modernity with "get off my cloud / Don't hang around 'cause / *Two's* a crowd." As Freud understood very well, arithmetical schemata are a determining factor in human sociality: narcissistic ones, intersubjective twos and Oedipal threes. And it is no accident that many of the political philosophers and psychoanalysts referred to in this book have been preoccupied with mathematics, set theory in particular.[1] From Deleuze and Guattari's series and Lacan's mathemes to Badiou's ontology of numbers, various permutations and combinations of the "singular" and the "multiple" have formed the basis for discussions of human collectivity, in the process de-stabilising the relationship between the two terms and calling their distinction into question.

Underlying many of these discussions is a return to the old question of whether a whole (or group) is more than the sum of its (individual) parts. Set theory uses what Cornelius Castoriadis calls an "identitary-emsemblist" logic, one able to distinguish and count its individual units as "distinct and definite objects that can be collected together to form wholes" (Castoriadis 227). Social institutions depend on such a logic—in fact "society" is inconceivable without it (just think of a juridical system without the capacity to count and name its citizens). But intuition (and recent sciences like psychoanalysis and quantum physics) lead us beyond this logic to postulate what Castoriadis calls a "magma of social imaginary significations" (344) which always precedes or escapes the identitary-ensemblist logic of set theory. The magma is another name, perhaps, for what Ernesto Laclau here calls the radical heterogeneity of socio-political demands, which may temporarily unite to achieve a moment of (imaginary) unity but which are always in excess of their collective expression. This line of thought, as we have seen, follows directly from the cue given by Jacques Lacan in the mid 1950s. Discussing Freud's "Group Psychology" essay, Lacan spoke of "the 'inmixing' [*immixtion*] of subjects," an unconscious phenomenon that takes place between two subjects whereby, via speech (and hence community) they are turned into something quite different from what they were. This, he speculates, may be the best way of thinking about the concept of the crowd (*Seminar II* 100).[2] The modern period, Ernesto Laclau argues, is characterised by an "irreconcilable plurality" of the social.

Reconciliation, then, should not be the central issue when we attempt to re-think the plurality of the collective in relation to individual demands. While we are all undoubtedly hard wired to look out for Number One, twentieth-century history has shown that the ideology of singularity (whether individual "identity" or national or ethnic unity) is in serious trouble. Another way of putting this would be to say, with Slavoj Žižek, that "the fundamental feature of today's society is the irreconcilable antagonism between Totality and the individual" (Žižek, *Parallax* 26).[3] With striking cross-cultural agreement, contemporary analysts on the left are recommending the replacement of individualisms and Totalities not by some utopian communitarianism (or even less by a fascist notion of "organic community") but rather by a "singular plurality" (to use Jean-Luc Nancy's term [Nancy, *Being*]) capable of confronting our own otherness both to others and to ourselves. Singular plurality targets "proper" individuality, suggesting as it does in several European languages the idea of identity as one's "own," one's "property," a product of capitalist identity politics. As the chapters in this book demonstrate, group behaviour is in urgent need of reconceptualisation after its relegation to the sidelines by postmodern discourse in the wake of post-Romantic individualism and the reaction against fascist crowds. Judging from a certain set of publications around the turn of the new millennium, one might be excused for thinking that human collective meaning and action are doomed to imminent extinction. In *Identity in Question* (2009), which describes "the new individualism" of self-fashioning ("DIY selfhood") in global consumer culture, Anthony Elliott and Charles Lemert substantiate their views on the basis of books with titles like *The Closing of the American Mind*, *Bowling Alone*, *The Lonely Crowd*, *The Minimal Self*, *The Fall of Public Man*, *The Corrosion of Character* and *Death Sentence: The Decay of Public Language* (Elliott and du Gay 37–64). Against this line of argument, *The Psychology and Politics of the Collective* calls for a different approach with a set of theoretical tools capable of analyzing in terms not of either-or but of both-and. Human collectives (whether the small group, the crowd or the global mass) can neither be dismissed as "mindless" nor idealised as "mindful" (functioning according to exclusively rational motives). The deconstruction of the dichotomy between the universal and the particular—impossible but necessary, as Ernesto Laclau argues here—may enable us to counteract the irresistible illusions of self-identity. A sovereign/leader is (implicitly or explicitly) both integral and a potential danger to any group structure. At the same time, acknowledgement of the power of horizontal, participatory crowd action does not necessarily instate group activity as idealised democratic behaviour. Poised on the interface between affective and rational behaviour, as well as that between nature and culture, collectivity tests out fundamental shifts in recent thought from disciplines as disparate as philosophy and biology, literature and technology.

This book began by invoking Godwin on the significance of the relation between the individual and the group in order to suggest that this relation tends to demand re-assessment and re-structuring at times—like ours and Godwin's—of radical social transformation. It is a measure of just how much social theory has changed, however, that whereas for Godwin the function of the human sciences was to elevate the human by distinguishing it from the non-human, particularly the animal, today the concept of the human is undergoing major qualification and rarely appears without a prefix (post-human, anti-human, super-human).[4] The Enlightenment attempt to separate humans from other related forms is now being reversed, starting with the debates around the "animal question" in which Agamben, Derrida and others have engaged.[5] In *L'aperto: L'uomo et l'animale* (2002; *The Open: Man and Animal* [2004]) Agamben argues that since World War I, as it has become increasingly obvious that European nation-states are no longer capable of taking on historical tasks, all we have left is the "very factical existence of peoples" (Agamben, *Open* 76), bare life in the form of our animality. The demise of the "anthropological machine," he states, means that "the total humanization of the animal coincides with a total animalization of man" (77). The comparative study of animal behaviour (ethology) has run parallel with this trend, resulting in scores of studies of the sophisticated collective practices of other creatures, from birds to baboons.[6] With this recognition of the inter-implication as well as the comparability of the lives of humans and other animals, the need to understand our herd or swarm behaviour can hopefully be returned to with new insight and less distaste.

This is equally (perhaps even more) the case with that other encroaching form, the machinic. Several of the chapters in this book have explored the ways in which new digital information and communication technologies are re-shaping humanity in terms both of our self-perception and of our collective behaviour. It has long been recognised that if the hand is already a tool, then the distinction between nature and culture is a dubious one at best. Similarly, given our individual and group dependence on the mediation of electronic devices, it is becoming increasingly difficult to describe the human being in isolation from its prosthetic appliances (mobile phones, laptops, ipads). Much attention has been paid recently to "the Singularity," a California-based project researching the moment (predicted to be around 2045) when technological change will have become so rapid and profound that it will bring about "a rupture in the fabric of human history" (Grossman 21).[7] Its point of departure is the undeniable fact that the rate of technological development is accelerating exponentially; for example, the average cell phone today is about a millionth the size and price of and a thousand times more powerful than an advanced personal computer of forty years ago (Grossman 27). At this rate, it is far from inconceivable that nanotechnological implants may soon be assisting our basic physical and mental processes, including the extension of life by repairing the damage of ageing. And as the old belief that human intelligence will always outstrip artificial intelligence is crumbling under the weight of new evidence, it is highly likely, as biotechnology futurologists like Raymond Kurzweil maintain, that computers will keep on developing to the point where they will take over their own development (Grossman 22). Counter-intuitive as this may be, a Singularitarian would argue, these cyborganic predictions are hard to refute in the face of the reality of recent space-time compressions: "Five years ago we didn't have 600 million humans carrying out their social lives over a single electronic network. Now we have Facebook" (Grossman 27). Blogging, as Holger Briel argues here, is not only demystifying and democratising the technosphere around us but is employing participatory practices which are contributing to the construction of new forms of reality.

If the distinction between human- and machine-kind is becoming difficult to maintain, what happens to the concept of democracy, conceived originally by the Greeks as the power of the people over themselves? Many of the chapters in this volume have examined the shifts in the concept of democracy in the digital age, whether it functions as a meaningful rallying cry in recent mass uprisings, or as an "empty signifier." Others have explored the impact of these technologies on leadership, the way new bottom-up, participatory modes of organisation via the internet are creating different patterns (some would say illusions) of agency and control. In a book entitled *Démocratie dans quel état?* (2009), which includes presentations by Agamben, Badiou, Nancy, Rancière, Žižek and others, Plato is invoked in the exploration of the inherent contradictions in the idea of democracy, as well as its radical potential. For Badiou, the "interminable twilight" of democracy today, in the form of parliamentary capitalism, continues nevertheless to call up what he sees as its original Platonic sense—not of a homogeneous "life of the people," but rather the "communisms" which are now being invented (Agamben, Badiou et al. 25). For Žižek, the fetish of democracy in the West today, whereby sheltering behind the ballot box exempts us from protest against injustice, leads inevitably to a "utilitarian, pragmatic inertia" (Agamben, Badiou et al. 146). The critique of the democratic form, he agrees with Badiou, is the truly risky philosophical imperative today, the one that poses problems altogether more difficult than acknowledging the extent of the injustices of global capitalism (Badiou and Žižek 90). For Žižek the question is not so much whether a state is democratic or not, but rather the form of power wielded by its sovereign. After all, he reminds us, it was as a result of more or less free elections that Hitler came to power. The external figure of the sovereign is integral to any political structure in the same way that the analyst is integral to the analytic relation (there is no such thing as self-analysis). So in speaking of power, it's less a question of knowing whether it is democratically legitimate or not than one of understanding the character of the "totalitarian excess" associated with the leader (Agamben, Badiou et al. 146).

This volume has called into question a celebration of democracy as that which places individual liberty before everything else. As an alternative foundation for community, singular plurality (Laclau's the "people") offers enormous challenges. Indeed, the material conditions for such a politics remain vague—although here, it could be argued, we are in good company, as Plato's ideal of the philosophical city has frequently been called utopian. If the fairest and most workable conditions for human collectivity remain largely to be invented, this soft revolution is nonetheless, and none too soon, generating a great deal of collectivel energy.

NOTES

1. Set theory, "naively" defined by Cantor as "a collection into a whole of definite and distinct objects of our intuition or of our thought" (Castoriadis 223), has been of enormous influence in theories of human collectivity and sociality. Lacan once jokingly claimed to have reduced all psychoanalysis to set theory (Fink 155), and used ones, twos and threes to delineate his views on collectivity:

   > *Tres faciunt collegium* [Three people constitute a (decision-making) body] . . . collectivity is defined as a group formed by the reciprocal relations of a definite number of individuals—unlike the *generality*, which is defined as a class abstractly including an indefinite number of individuals. (Lacan, *Écrits* 174)

2. In the following seminar, Lacan spoke about "the fanning out, the blossoming of the different identifications of the *ego*" (*Seminar II* 167).
3. Žižek is here discussing Adorno's analysis of the antagonistic character of the notion of society, "the split between . . . the Anglo-Saxon individualistic-nominalistic notion and the Durkheimian organicist notion of society as a totality which pre-exists individuals" (Žižek, *Parallax* 26). His own solution to this irreconcilability is what he calls "the parallax Real," which is alone able to account for the multiplicity of appearances or symbolic fictions (26).
4. Many contemporary philosophers, Badiou and Žižek among them, regard "the displacement of the human" as the central challenge of today (Badiou and Žižek 82).
5. See Derrida, *Animal*; also Santner, *On Creaturely*.
6. A characteristic example here is Dorothy L. Cheney and Robert M. Seyfarth's *Baboon Metaphysics: The Evolution of a Social Mind*.
7. The word "singularity," borrowed from astrophysics, refers to a point in space-time (e.g. inside a black hole) at which the rules of ordinary physics do not apply (Grossman 23).

Contributors

Holger Briel is Associate Professor of Media and Communication at the University of Nicosia, Cyprus. He is the author of *Adorno Und Derrida: Oder Wo Liegt Das Ende Der Moderne?* (Peter Lang, 1993). He has also published articles and books on media theory and philosophy, cultural studies, European media systems and visual literacy. His latest book is *Glocalisation: Electronic Media in South Eastern Europe* (Blesok, 2008).

Joseph Michael Gratale is an Associate Professor at the American College of Thessaloniki, Greece, where he teaches courses in the Department of Humanities and Social Sciences. He has published several articles and book reviews on topics such as travel narratives and colonial discourse theory, as well as aspects of globalisation theory, cultural globalisation and American history and culture.

Sean Homer is Associate Professor of English Literature at the American University in Bulgaria. He is the author of *Fredric Jameson: Marxism, Hermeneutics, Postmodernism* (Polity Press, 1998); *Jacques Lacan* (Routledge, 2005) and is co-editor (with Douglas Kellner) of *Fredric Jameson: A Critical Reader* (Palgrave, 2004). His recent publications include "Retrieving Kusturica's *Underground* as a Critique of Ethnic Nationalism" (*JumpCut* 51 [2009]) and "The Voice as *Objet a* in Tony Gatlif's *Gadjo dil*"' (*Psychoanalysis, Culture and Society* 15.1 [2010]).

Ernesto Laclau is Emeritis Professor of Politics at the University of Essex and Distinguished Professor of Humanities and Rhetorical Studies at Northwestern University. He is the author of numerous books including: *On Populist Reason* (Verso, 2005), (with Judith Butler and Slavoj Žižek) *Contingency, Hegemony and Universality* (Verso, 2000), *Emancipation(s)* (Verso, 1996) and (with Chantal Mouffe) *Hegemony and Socialist Strategy* (Verso, 1985). *Laclau: A Critical Reader* (ed. Simon Critchley and Oliver Marchant) was published by Routledge in 2004.

Mandy Merck is Professor of Media Arts at Royal Holloway, University of London. Her next book is provisionally titled *The Melodrama of Celebrity*. Previous books include *Further Adventures of the Dialectic of Sex* (co-edited with Stella Sandford, 2010), *Hollywood's American Tragedies* (2007), *America First: Naming the Nation in US Film* (2007), *The Art of Tracey Emin* (co-edited with Chris Townsend, 2002), *In Your Face: Nine Sexual Studies* (2000), *Coming Out of Feminism?* (co-edited with Naomi Segal and Elizabeth Wright, 1998), *After Diana* (1998) and *Perversions: Deviant Readings* (1993).

Josiane Paccaud-Huguet is Professor of Modern English Literature and Literary Theory at Université Lumière-Lyon 2 (France). She has published extensively on Modernist authors and in psychoanalytic journals. Her latest publications include *Rewriting/Reprising in Literature: The Paradoxes of Intertextuality*, a co-edited volume (Cambridge Scholars Publishing, 2009). She is the author of the chapter "Psychoanalysis after Freud" in Patricia Waugh's *Literary Theory and Criticism: An Oxford Guide* (Oxford UP, 2006).

Ruth Parkin-Gounelas is Emeritus Professor of English Literature and Culture at Aristotle University of Thessaloniki, Greece, as well as Life Member of Clare Hall, University of Cambridge. Co-editor since 1993 of *Gramma: Journal of Theory and Criticism*, the 2006 issue of which was *Objects: Material, Psychic, Aesthetic,* co-edited with Sean Homer and Yannis Stavrakakis. Books include *Literature and Psychoanalysis: Intertextual Readings* (Palgrave/Macmillan, 2001) and *Fictions of the Female Self* (Macmillan 1991).

Jina Politi, formerly Teaching Fellow in English, Churchill College, Cambridge, now Emeritus Professor of English Literature and Culture at Aristotle University of Thessaloniki, Greece. Book publications include *The Novel and its Presuppositions: Changes in the Conceptual Structure of Novels in the 18th and 19th Centuries* (Amsterdam, Hakkert), as well as nine books on English, Greek and Comparative Literature written in Greek and published by Agra. Essays on the historical novel appeared in *The Scottish Literary Journal.* Numerous essays ranging from Shakespeare to James Joyce have also been published in journals and volumes. In 1998 she was awarded by the Institute of Technology the prize for Excellence in Teaching and Research, in 2007 by the literary journal *Diavazo,* the Essay Prize for her book *On Sin, Passion, the Gaze and Other Matters,* and in 2011 by the Hellenic Authors Society the Dido Sotiriou prize for contribution to literary research.

Nicola Rehling is a Foreign Instructor at Aristotle University of Thessaloniki, where she teaches courses on literature, film and research methods.

Her research interests include feminist film theory, gender theory, critical race theory, popular cinema, media culture and contemporary British literature. She is the author of *Extra-Ordinary Men: White Heterosexual Masculinity in Contemporary Popular Cinema* (Lexington, 2009). She also edited *The Individual and the Mass*, a special issue of *Gramma: Journal of Theory and Criticism* 18 (2010).

Stephen Reicher is Professor of Social Psychology at the University of St. Andrews, Scotland, Fellow of the Royal Society of Edinburgh, an Academician of the Social Sciences and a scientific consultant to *Scientific American Mind*. He was formerly editor of the *British Journal of Social Psychology*. His work centres on the creation of social identities and their relationship to collective action. Books include (with Nick Hopkins) *Self and Nation* (Sage. 2001) and (with Alex Haslam and Michael Platow) *The New Psychology of Leadership* (Psychology Press, 2010).

Effie Yiannopoulou is Assistant Professor of English and Cultural Theory at Aristotle University of Thessaloniki, Greece. Her publications are in the field of twentieth-century women's writings and have appeared in book collections and international journals. She has co-edited *Metaphoricity and the Politics of Mobility* (Amsterdam and New York: Rodopi, 2006), *The Flesh Made Text Made Flesh* (New York: Peter Lang, 2007) and *The Future of Flesh* (New York: Palgrave Macmillan, 2009).

References

Adams, Tim. "She 'Loved Shannon to Bits.' But She Had Her Kidnapped. Inside the Dark, Dangerous World of Karen Matthews." *Guardian.co.uk* 7 Dec. 2008. 26 Mar. 2009 http://www.guardian.co.uk/uk/2008/dec/07/shannon-matthews-kidnap-trial.

Addly, Esther. "Neverending Story." *Guardian.co.uk* 2 June 2007. 24 Apr. 2008 http://www.guardian.co.uk/uk/2007/jun/02/ukcrime.comment.

Adorno, Theodor W. *The Culture Industry: Selected Essays on Mass Culture*. Ed. J. M. Bernstein. London: Routledge, 1991.

Aeschylus. *The Oresteia*. Trans. Robert Fagles. London: Penguin, 1979.

Agamben, Giorgio. *The Coming Community*. Trans. Michael Hardt. Minneapolis: U of Minnesota P, 2009.

———. *Homo Sacer: Sovereign Power and Bare Life*. Trans. Daniel Heller-Roazen. Stanford, CA: Stanford UP, 1998.

———. *The Open: Man and Animal*. Trans. Kevin Atrell. Stanford, CA: Stanford UP, 2004.

Agamben, Giorgio, Alain Badiou, et al. *Démocratie dans quel état?* Paris: La Fabrique, 2009.

Ahmed, Sara. *Strange Encounters: Embodied Others in Post-Coloniality*. London: Routledge, 2001.

Alabarces, Pablo, Alan Tomlinson, and Christopher Young. "Argentina versus England at the France '98 World Cup: Narratives of Nation and the Mythologizing of the Popular." *Media, Culture and Society* 23 (2001): 547–66.

Anderson, Benedict. *Imagined Communities: Reflections on the Origin and Spread of Nationalism*. London: Verso, 2006.

Anderson, Chris. *The Long Tail: How Endless Choice is Creating Unlimited Demand*. London: Random House, 2006.

Andreas-Salomé, Lou. *The Freud Journal of Lou Andreas-Salomé*. Trans. Stanley A. Leavy. New York: Basic Books, 1964.

"AOL buying Huffington Post for $315 million." 6 Feb. 2011. 29 March 2011 http://latimesblogs.latimes.com/technology/2011/02/huffington-post-aol.html.

Appadurai, Arjun. "Disjuncture and Difference in the Global Cultural Economy." *Global Culture: Nationalism, Globalization and Modernity*. Ed. Mike Featherstone. London: Sage, 1990. 295–310.

———. *Modernity at Large: Cultural Dimensions of Globalization*. Minneapolis: U of Minnesota P, 1996.

Arendt, Hannah. *On Violence*. San Diego, CA: Harcourt Brace, 1970.

———. *The Origins of Totalitarianism*. Intro. Samantha Power. New York: Shocken Books, 2004.

Badiou, Alain. *Being and Event*. Trans. Oliver Feltham. London: Continuum, 2007.

———. "The Communist Hypothesis." *New Left Review* (II) 49 (Jan.–Feb. 2008): 29–42.
———. *Metapolitics*. Trans. Jason Barker. London: Verso, 2006.
———. "Politics Unbound." *Metapolitics*. Trans. Jason Barker. London: Verso, 2006. 68–77.
———. *Theory of the Subject*. London: Continuum, 2009.
Badiou, Alain and Slavoj Žižek. *Philosophy in the Present*. Trans. Peter Thomas and Alberto Toscano. Ed. Peter Engelmann. Cambridge: Polity, 2009.
Baehr, Peter. "The 'Masses' in Hannah Arendt's Theory of Totalitarianism." *The Good Society* 16.2 (2007): 12–18.
Barber, Benjamin R. *Jihad vs. McWorld*. New York: Random House, 1995.
Barrows, Susanne. *Distorting Mirrors: Visions of the Crowd in Late Nineteenth-Century France*. New Haven, CT: Yale UP, 1981.
Baucom, Ian. *Out of Place: Englishness, Empire, and the Locations of Identity*. Princeton, NJ: Princeton UP, 1999.
Bauman, Zygmunt. "From Pilgrim to Tourist—or a Short History of Identity." *Questions of Cultural Identity*. Ed. Stuart Hall and Paul du Gay. London: Sage, 1996. 18–36.
———. *Globalization: The Human Consequences*. Cambridge: Polity, 1998.
———. *Liquid Modernity*. Cambridge: Polity, 2000.
Baxendale, John. "'I Had Seen a Lot of Englands': J. B. Priestley, Englishness and the People." *History Workshop Journal* 51 (2001): 87–111.
Beck, Ulrich. "The Cosmopolitan Society and its Enemies." *Theory, Culture & Society* 19 (2002): 17–44.
Beiner, Ronald. "Arendt and Nationalism." *The Cambridge Companion to Hannah Arendt*. Ed. Dana Villa. Cambridge: Cambridge UP, 2000. 44–62.
Bell, Gordon. *MyLifeBits*. 29 Mar. 2011 https://research.microsoft.com/en-us/projects/mylifebits/.
Bell, Gordon, and Jim Gemmell. "A Digital Life." *Scientific American Magazine* 18 (Feb. 2007). 29 Mar. 2011 http://www.sciam.com/article.cfm?id=a-digital-life.
Bell, Vaughan, Ethan Grech, Cara Maiden, Peter W. Halligan, and Hadyn D. Ellis. "'Internet Delusions': A Case Series and Theoretical Integration." *Psychopathology* 38 (2005): 144–50.
Bender, Thomas. "Introduction: Historians, the Nation, and the Plentitude of Narratives." *Rethinking American History in a Global Age*. Ed. Thomas Bender. Berkeley: U of California P, 2002. 1–21.
Benjamin, Walter. "The Work of Art in the Age of Mechanical Reproduction." *Illuminations*. By Walter Benjamin. Ed. Hannah Arendt. Trans. Harry Zorn. London: Pimlico, 1999. 211–44.
Bhabha, Homi K. *The Location of Culture*. London: Routledge, 1994.
"Bildblog." 29 Mar. 2011 http://www.bildblog.de.
Bingham, Art. Review of Walter J. Ong, *Orality and Literacy*. 29 Mar. 2011 http://www.engl.niu.edu/wac/ong_rvw.html.
Bion, W. R. *Experiences in Groups and Other Essays*. London: Routledge, 2000.
Birmingham, Peg. "Holes of Oblivion: The Banality of Radical Evil." *Hypatia* 18.1 (2003): 80–103.
———. "A Lying World Order: Deception and the Rhetoric of Terror." *The Good Society* 16.2 (2007): 32–37.
"Blogs Influence Purchases More than Social Networks." 3 Nov. 2008. 29 Mar. 2011 http://www.marketingvox.com/blogs-influence-purchases-more-than-social-networks-041776/.
Blood, Rebecca. "Weblogs: A History and Perspective." 7 Sept. 2000. 29 Mar. 2011 http://www.rebeccablood.net/essays/weblog_history.html.

Botzas, Senay. "Madeleine's Father Appeals for End to 'Wild Speculation.'" *The Independent* 26 Aug. 2007. 28 Mar. 2009 http://www.independent.co.uk/news/world/europe/madeleines-father-appeals-for-end-to-wild-speculation-463041.html.

Boxer, Sarah. "Blogs." *The New York Review of Books* 55.2 (14 Feb. 2008). 29 Mar. 2011 http://www.nybooks.com/articles/21013.

Brennan, Teresa. *The Transmission of Affect*. Ithaca, NY: Cornell UP, 2004.

Brett, Judith. "Competition and Collegiality." *Australian Universities Review* 40.2 (1997): 19–22.

Briel, Holger. "Virtual Communities: Public Access TV as Mediation between Individuals and the (German) State." *Field Studies: German Language, Media and Culture*. Ed. Holger Briel and Carol Fehringer. Oxford: Lang, 2005. 217–28.

Brockbank, Philip. "Introduction." *Coriolanus*. By William Shakespeare. Ed. Philip Brockbank. London: Methuen, 1976. 1–89.

Brooks, Peter. *The Melodramatic Imagination: Balzac, Henry James, Melodrama and the Mode of Excess*. New Haven, CT: Yale UP, 1976.

"Brown Thanks Portugal Over Madeleine McCann." *Politics.co.uk*. 23 Mar. 2009 http://www.politics.co.uk/news/foreign-policy/brown-thanks-portugal-over-madeleine-mccann-$475815.htm.

Bruns, Axel, and Joanne Jacobs, eds. *Uses of Blogs*. New York: Lang, 2006.

Buck-Morss, Susan. "The Second Time as Farce . . . Historical Pragmatics and the Untimely Present." *The Idea of Communism*. Ed. Costas Douzinas and Slavoj Žižek. London: Verso, 2010. 67–80.

Burke, Edmund. *Reflections on the Revolution in France*. Ed. Conor Cruise O'Brien. Harmondsworth, Middlesex: Penguin, 1979.

Butler, Judith, Ernesto Laclau, and Slavoj Žižek. *Contingency, Hegemony, Universality: Contemporary Debates on the Left*. London: Verso, 2000.

Butzer, Günter. "Sich selbst schreiben. Das Tagebuch als Weblog avant la lettre." *Absolut privat!?: Vom Tagebuch zum Weblog*. Ed. Helmut Gold, Christiane Holm, Eva Bös, and Tine Nowak. Heidelberg: Wachter, 2008. 94–96.

Cadava, Eduardo, Peter Connor, and Jean-Luc Nancy, eds. *Who Comes After the Subject?* New York: Routledge, 1991.

Calhoun, Craig. *Nations Matter: Culture, History, and the Cosmopolitan Dream*. London: Routledge, 2007.

Cameron, David. "David Cameron: There are 5 Million People on Benefits in Britain. How Do We Stop Them Turning into Karen Matthews?" *Mail Online* 8 Dec. 2008. 7 Apr. 2009 http://www.dailymail.co.uk/news/article-1092588/DAVID-CAMERON-There-5-million-people-benefits-Britain-How-stop-turning-this.html.

Campbell, Beatrix. "Who Do We Blame." *Guardian.co.uk* 14 Mar. 2008. 26 Mar. 2009 http://www.guardian.co.uk/commentisfree/2008/mar/14/whodo weblame.

Canovan, Margaret. "Arendt's Theory of Totalitarianism: A Reassessment." *The Cambridge Companion to Hannah Arendt*. Ed. Dana Villa. Cambridge: Cambridge UP, 2000. 25–43.

Carr, Nicholas. *The Shallows: How the Internet is Changing the Way We Think, Read and Remember*. New York: Norton, 2010.

Carroli, Linda. "Virtual Encounters: Community or Collaboration on the Internet?" *Leonardo* 30.1 (1997): 359–63.

Castells, Manuel. *Communication Power*. Oxford: Oxford UP, 2009.

———. *The Power of Identity*. 2nd ed. Malden, MA: Blackwell, 2004. Vol. 2 of *The Information Age: Economy, Society and Culture*. 3 vols. 1996–98.

Castoriadis, Cornelius. *The Imaginary Institution of Society*. Trans. Kathleen Blaney. Cambridge: Polity, 1987.

Cheah, Pheng. "Introduction Part II: The Cosmopolitical–Today." *Cosmopolitics: Thinking and Feeling Beyond the Nation*. Ed. Pheng Cheah and Bruce Robbins. Minneapolis: U of Minnesota P, 1998. 20–41.

Cheney, Dorothy L. and Robert M. Seyfarth. *Baboon Metaphysics: The Evolution of a Social Mind*. Chicago: U of Chicago P, 2007.

Chevalier, Louis. *Labouring Classes and Dangerous Classes in Paris during the First Half of the Nineteenth Century*. Trans. F. Jellinek. London: Routledge and Kegan Paul, 1973.

Chion, Michel. *The Voice in Cinema*. Trans. Claudia Gorbman. New York: Columbia UP, 1999.

Churchland, Patricia S. *Braintrust: What Neuroscience Tells us about Morality*. Princeton, NJ: Princeton UP. 2011.

Clifford, James. *The Predicament of Culture: Twentieth-Century Ethnography, Literature, and Art*. Cambridge, MA: Harvard UP, 1988.

———. "Traveling Cultures." *Cultural Studies*. Ed. Lawrence Grossberg, Carl Nelson, and Paula Treichler. London: Routledge, 1991. 96–116.

Cohen, Lenard J. *Serpent in the Bosom: The Rise and Fall of Slobodan Milošević*. Boulder, CO: Westview P, 2001.

Conboy, Martin. *The Press and Popular Culture*. London: Sage, 2002.

———. *Tabloid Britain: Constructing a Community Through Language*. London: Routledge, 2006.

Copjec, Joan. "The Anxiety of the Influencing Machine." *October* 23 (Winter 1982): 43–59.

———. *Imagine There's No Woman: Ethics and Sublimation*. Cambridge, MA: The MIT P, 2002.

"Could UK Taleban Fighters be Tried for Treason?" *BBC News*. 30 Oct. 2001. 12 Mar. 2007 http://news.bbc.co.uk/1/hi/uk/1627893.stm.

Dallmayr, Dred. *Margins of Political Discourse*. Albany, NY: SUNY P, 1989.

Damasio, Antonio. *Looking for Spinoza: Joy, Sorrow and the Feeling Brain*. London: Vintage, 2004.

Davis, Natalie Z. "The Rites of Violence: Religious Riot in Sixteenth Century France." *Past & Present* 59 (1973): 51–91.

Dayal, Samir. "Introduction." *Crisis of the European Subject*. By Julia Kristeva. Trans. Susan Fairfield. New York: Other P, 2000. 3–45.

De Blij, Harm. *The Power of Place: Geography, Destiny, and Globalization's Rough Landscape*. Oxford: Oxford UP, 2009.

Debord, Guy. *The Society of the Spectacle*. Eastbourne, East Sussex: Soul Bay P, 2009.

Deininger, Whitaker T. Review of *The New Meaning of Treason. The Western Political Quarterly* 19.1 (1966): 210–11.

Deleuze, Gilles, and Félix Guattari. *Kafka: Toward a Minor Literature*. Trans. Dana Polan. Minneapolis: U of Minnesota P, 1986.

Derrida, Jacques. *The Animal that Therefore I Am*. Trans. David Wills. Ed. Marie-Louise Mallet. New York: Fordham UP, 2008.

———. *Specters of Marx: The State of the Debt, the Work of Mourning, and the New International*. Trans. Peggy Kamuf. New York: Routledge, 1994.

Diawara, Manthia. "Toward a Regional Imaginary in Africa." *The Cultures of Globalization*. Ed. Frederic Jameson and Masao Miyoshi. Durham, NC: Duke UP, 1998. 103–24.

Dickens, Charles. *Hard Times*. Harmondsworth, Middlesex: Penguin, 1981.

Diefendorf, Barbara B. *Beneath the Cross: Catholics and Huguenots in Sixteenth-Century Paris*. Oxford: Oxford UP, 1991.

"Digg Blog." 29 Mar. 2011 http://digg.com.

Douzinas, Costas. "*Adikia*: On Communism and Rights." *The Idea of Communism*. Ed. Costas Douzinas and Slavoj Žižek. London: Verso, 2010. 81–100.

Drury, John, and Stephen D. Reicher. "Collective Action and Social Change: The Emergence of New Social Identities." *British Journal of Social Psychology* 39 (2000): 579–604.

______. "Collective Psychological Empowerment as a Model of Social Change: Researching Crowds and Power." *Journal of Social Issues* 65 (2009): 707–25

______. "The Intergroup Dynamics of Collective Empowerment: Substantiating the Social Identity Model of Crowd Behaviour." *Group Processes and Intergroup Relations* 2 (1999): 381–402.

Eissler, K. R. *Talent and Genius: The Fictitious Case of Freud Contra Tausk*. London: Allen Lane, 1971.

———. *Victor Tausk's Suicide*. New York: International UP. 1983.

Eliot, T. S. *Collected Poems 1909–1935*. London: Faber and Faber, 1949.

Elliott, Anthony, and Paul du Gay, eds. *Identity in Question*. Los Angeles: Sage, 2009.

Emler, Nicholas, and Stephen Reicher. *Adolescence and Delinquency: The Collective Management of Reputation*. Oxford: Blackwell, 1995.

Enright, Anne. "Diary." *London Review of Books* 4 Oct. 2007. 24 Apr. 2008 http://www.lrb.co.uk/v29/n19/enri01_.html.

Esposito, Robert. *Communitas: The Origin and Destiny of Community*. Trans. Timothy Campbell. Stanford, CA: Stanford UP, 2010.

Euripides. *Orestes. The Complete Greek Drama*. Ed. Whitney J. Oates and Eugene O'Neill, Jr. 2 vols. Trans. E. P. Coleridge. New York: Random House, 1938. II, 111–65.

"Falcon Attack: Peregrine Divebombs Flock of Starlings." 29 Mar. 2011 http://www.youtube.com/watch?v=b8eZJnbDHIg&feature=related.

Featherstone, Mike. *Undoing Culture: Globalization, Postmodernism and Identity*. London: Sage, 1995.

———. "Cosmopolis: An Introduction." *Theory, Culture & Society* 19 (2002): 1–16.

Fernback. Jan. "The Individual within the Collective: Virtual Ideology and the Realization of Collective Principles." *Virtual Culture: Identity and Communication in Cybersociety*. Ed. Steven G. Jones. London: Sage, 1997. 36–54.

Fink, Bruce. *Lacan to the Letter: Reading* Écrits *Closely*. Minneapolis: U of Minnesota P, 2004.

Foucault, Michel. "Technologies of the Self." 29 Mar. 2011 http://www.thefoucauldian.co.uk/tself.pdf.

Frankfurt Institute for Social Research, The. *Aspects of Sociology*. London: Heinemann, 1973.

Freeland, Jonathan. "Madeleine: A Grimly Compelling Story that Will End Badly for Us All." *Guardian.co.uk* 12 Sept. 2007. 28 Feb. 2009 http://www.guardian.co.uk/commentisfree/2007/sep/12/comment.ukcrime.

Freud, Sigmund. "Address Delivered in the Goethe House at Frankfurt." *The Standard Edition of the Complete Psychological Works of Sigmund Freud*. Trans. Angela Richards. Vol. 21. London: The Hogarth P, 1961. 205–12.

———. "Group Psychology and the Analysis of the Ego." *Civilization, Society and Religion*. The Penguin Freud Library. Trans. James Strachey. Vol. 12. London: Penguin, 1991. 91–178.

———. *Letters of Sigmund Freud 1873–1939*. Trans. Tania and James Stern. Ed. Ernst L. Freud. New York: Basic Books, 1960.

———. "Mass Psychology and Analysis of the 'I'." *Mass Psychology and Other Writings*. By Sigmund Freud. Trans. J. A. Underwood. London: Penguin, 2004. 15–100.

———. "Project for a Scientific Psychology." *The Standard Edition of the Complete Psychological Works of Sigmund Freud* Trans. James Strachey. Vol. 1. London: Vintage, 2001. 281–397.

———. "Psycho-Analytic Notes on an Autobiographical Account of a Case of Paranoia." *The Standard Edition of the Complete Psychological Works of Sigmund Freud.* Trans. Alix and James Strachey. Vol. 12. London: The Hogarth P, 1958. 1–82.

———. "The 'Uncanny'." *Art and Literature.* The Pelican Freud Library. Trans. James Strachey. Vol. 14. Harmondsworth, Middlesex: 1985. 335–81.

Friedman, Thomas L. *The World is Flat: A Brief History of the Twenty-First Century.* New York: Farrar, Straus and Giroux, 2005.

Gagnon, V. P., Jr. *The Myth of Ethnic War: Serbia and Croatia in the 1990s.* Ithaca, NY: Cornell UP, 2004.

Gallese, Vittorio. "The 'Shared Manifold' Hypothesis: From Mirror Neurons to Empathy." *Journal of Consciousness Studies* 8.5–7 (2001): 33–50.

Gandhi, Leela. *Affective Communities: Anti-Colonial Thought, Fin-de-Siècle Radicalism, and the Politics of Friendship.* Durham, NC: Duke UP, 2006.

Garrisson, Janine. *1572: La Saint-Barthelemy.* Brussels: Editions Complexe, 2000.

Gault, Robert H. Review of *The Meaning of Treason. Journal of Criminal Law and Criminology* 40.1 (1949): 74.

Geertz, Clifford. *The Interpretation of Cultures.* New York: Basic Books, 1973.

Giddens, Anthony. *The Consequences of Modernity.* Cambridge: Polity, 1990.

———. *Sociology.* 5th ed. Cambridge: Polity, 2006.

Gilroy, Paul. *After Empire: Melancholia or Convivial Culture?* London: Routledge, 2004.

———. *Against Race: Imagining Political Culture Beyond the Color Line.* Cambridge, MA.: Harvard UP, 2000.

———. *The Black Atlantic: Modernity and Double Consciousness.* London: Verso, 1993.

———. "Diaspora and the Detours of Identity." *Identity and Difference.* Ed. K. Woodward. London: Sage, 1997. 299–346.

Giner, Salvador. *Mass Society.* London: Martin Robertson, 1976.

Glendinning, Victoria. *Rebecca West: A Life.* London: Phoenix, 1998.

Glynos, Jason, and Yannis Stavrakakis. "Encounters of the Real Kind: Sussing out the Limits of Laclau's Embrace of Lacan." *Journal for Lacanian Studies* 1.1 (2003): 110–28.

Godwin, William. *Enquiry Concerning Political Justice and its Influence on Modern Morals and Happiness.* Harmondsworth, Middlesex: Penguin, 1976.

Goetz, Rainald. *Abfall für All: Roman eines Jahres.* Frankfurt: Suhrkamp, 2001.

Gold, Helmut. "Einführung." *Absolut privat*!?: *Vom Tagebuch zum Weblog.* Ed. Helmut Gold, Christiane Holm, Eva Bös, and Tine Nowak. Heidelberg: Wachter, 2008. 3–13.

———. "Weblogs." *Absolut privat*!?: *Vom Tagebuch zum Weblog.* Ed. Helmut Gold, Christiane Holm, Eva Bös, and Tine Nowak. Heidelberg: Wachter, 2008. 111–21.

Gold, Helmut, Christiane Holm, Eva Bös, and Tine Nowak, eds. *Absolut privat*!?: *Vom Tagebuch zum Weblog.* Heidelberg: Wachter, 2008.

Gordy, Eric. *The Culture of Power in Serbia: Nationalism and the Destruction of Alternatives.* University Park: Pennsylvania UP, 1999.

Goulding, Daniel J. *Liberated Cinema: The Yugoslav Experience, 1945–2001.* Bloomington: Indiana UP, 2002.

Grillo, Beppe. 29 Mar. 2011 http://www.beppegrillo.it.

Grossman, Lev. "Singularity." *Time* 21 Feb. 2011: 21–27.

Habermas, Jürgen. *The Structural Transformation of the Public Sphere: Inquiry into a Category of Bourgeois Society.* 1962. Cambridge, MA: MIT P, 1995.

Hall, Stuart. "Introduction: Who Needs Identity?" *Questions of Cultural Identity.* Ed. Stuart Hall and Paul du Gay. London: Sage, 1996. 1–17.

———. "Notes on Deconstructing 'the Popular'." *Popular Culture: A Reader.* Ed. Raiford Guins and Omayra Zaragoza Cruz. London: Sage, 2005. 64–71.

Halligan, Benjamin. "An Aesthetic of Chaos: The Blurring of Political Subtexts in Film Depictions of the Bosnian War." *The Celluloid Tinderbox: Yugoslav Screen Reflections of a Turbulent Decade.* Ed. Andrew James Horton. Shropshire, UK: Central Europe Review, 2000. 62–86.

Hallward, Peter. "Ethics Against Others." *Radical Philosophy* 102 (July–Aug. 2000): 27–30.

———. "Order and Event: On Badiou's *Logics of Worlds.*" *New Left Review* (II) 53 (Sept.–Oct. 2008): 97–122.

———. Review of "Alain Badiou, *De Quoi Sarkozy est-il nom?*" *Radical Philosophy* 149 (May–June 2008): 50–52.

Hannerz, Ulf. "Cosmopolitanisms and Locals in World Culture." *Global Culture: Nationalism, Globalization and Modernity.* Ed. Mike Featherstone. London: Sage, 1990. 237–51.

Hardt, Michael. "Foreword: What Affects Are Good For." *The Affective Turn: Theorizing the Social.* Ed. Patricia Ticineto Clough with Jean Halley. Durham, NC: Duke UP, 2007. ix–xiii.

Hardt, Michael, and Antonio Negri. *Multitude: War and Democracy in the Age of Empire.* New York: Penguin, 2004.

Hare, Paul G. "The United Kingdom's Research Assessment Exercise: Impact on Institutions, Departments, Individuals." *Higher Education Management and Policy* 15.2 (2003): 43–62.

Hari, Johann. "Distraught Parents and Terrified Children." *The Independent* 24 May 2007. 20 May 2008 http://www.independent.co.uk/opinion/commentators/johann-hari/johann-hari-distraught-parents-and-terrified-children-450051.html.

Haslam, S. Alexander. *Psychology in Organizations: The Social Identity Approach.* London: Sage, 2001.

Haslam, S. Alexander, Stephen D. Reicher, and Michael J. Platow. *The New Psychology of Leadership: Identity, Influence and Power.* London: Psychology P, 2011.

HEFCE (Higher Education Funding Council for England). *REF 2014*, Bibliometrics, 1. 6 May 2011 www.hefce.ac.uk/research/ref/biblio.

Heidegger, Martin. "The Question Concerning Technology." 29 Mar. 2011 http://www.culturaleconomics.atfreeweb.com/Anno/Heidegger%20The%20Question%201954.htm.

Held, David. *Cosmopolitanism: Ideals and Realities.* Cambridge: Polity, 2010.

———. "Culture and Political Community: National, Global, and Cosmopolitan." *Conceiving Cosmpolitanism: Theory, Context, and Practice.* Ed. Steven Vertovec and Robin Cohen. Oxford: Oxford UP, 2002. 48–58.

Held, David, et al. *Global Transformations: Politics, Economics and Culture.* Cambridge: Polity, 1999.

Hirschman, Albert. *The Passions and the Interests: Political Arguments for Capitalism before its Triumph.* Princeton, NJ: Princeton UP, 1977.

Hirst, Paul, and Grahame Thompson. *Globalization in Question: The International Economy and the Possibilities of Governance.* London: Polity, 1999.

Hobbs, F. D. Richard and Paul M. Stewart. "How should we Rate Research?" *BMJ* 332 (Apr. 29 2006): 983–84.

Hoffman, Allen. "Online Minds: How the Internet may be Shortening our Attention Spans." 2 July 2008. 29 Mar. 2011 http://www.nj.com/business/index.ssf/2008/07/online_minds_how_the_internet.html.

Hollinger, David A. "Not Universalists, Not Pluralists: The New Cosmopolitans Find Their Own Way." *Conceiving Cosmopolitanism: Theory, Context, and*

Practice. Ed. Steven Vertovec and Robin Cohen. Oxford: Oxford UP, 2002. 227–39.

Holm, Christiane. "Montag Ich, Dienstag Ich, Mittwoch Ich. Versuch einer Phänomenologie des Diaristischen." *Absolut privat!?: Vom Tagebuch zum Weblog*. Ed. Helmut Gold, Christiane Holm, Eva Bös, and Tine Nowak. Heidelberg: Wachter, 2008. 10–50.

Homer, Sean. "Nationalism, Ideology and Balkan Cinema: Re-Reading Kusturica's *Underground*." *Did Somebody Say Ideology?: On Slavoj Žižek and Consequences*. Ed. Fabio Vighi and Heiko Feldner. Newcastle upon Tyne, UK: Cambridge Scholars Publishing, 2007. 237–48.

———. "Retrieving Emir Kusturica's *Underground* as a Critique of Ethnic Nationalism." *Jump Cut: A Review of Contemporary Media* 51 (Spring 2009) 18 June 2011 http://www.ejumpcut.org/archive/jc51.2009/Kusterica/index.html.

Hopkins, A. G. *Globalization in World History*. New York: Norton, 2002.

Hopper, Paul. *Understanding Cultural Globalization*. Cambridge: Polity, 2007.

Horkheimer, Max. *Les débuts de la philosophie bourgeoise de l'histoire : Suivi de Hegel et le problème de la métaphysique*. Trans. Denis Authier. Paris: Payot, 1980.

Hough, Graham. *The Romantic Poets*. London: Hutchinson, 1968.

Howard, Robert Glenn. "The Vernacular Web of Participatory Media." *Critical Studies in Media Communication* 25.5 (2008): 490–513.

Huntington, Samuel P. *The Clash of Civilizations and the Remaking of World Order*. New York: Simon & Schuster, 1996.

Iordanova, Dina. *Cinema of Flames: Balkan Film, Culture and the Media*. London: BFI Publishing, 2001.

———. "Introduction." *The Celluoid Tinderbox: Yugoslav Screen Reflections of a Turbulent Decade*. Ed. Andrew James Horton. Shropshire, UK: Central Europe Review, 2000. 5–16.

Jameson, Fredric. *The Geopolitical Aesthetic: Cinema and Space in the World System*. London: BFI, 1992.

———. *Marxism and Form: Twentieth-Centruy Dialectical Theories of Literature*. Princeton, NJ: Princeton UP, 1971.

———. *The Political Unconscious: Narrative as a Socially Symbolic Act*. London: Routledge, 2002.

———. "Preface." *The Cultures of Globalization*. Ed. Fredric Jameson and Masao Miyoshi. Durham, NC: Duke UP, 1998. xi–xvii.

———. *A Singular Modernity: Essays on the Ontology of the Present*. London: Verso, 2002.

———. "The Vanishing Mediator; or, Max Weber as Story Teller." *The Ideologies of Theory, Essays 1971–1986, Volume 2: The Syntax of History*. London: Routledge, 1988. 3–34.

Jeffs, Nikolai. "Transnational Dialogue in Times of War: The Peace Movement in Ex-Yugoslavia." *Radical Philosophy* 73 (Sept.–Oct. 1995): 2–4.

Jenkins, Henry. *Fans, Bloggers and Games: Exploring Participatory Culture*. New York: New York UP, 2006.

Jenkins, Simon. "The British Media Does Not Do Responsibility. It Does Stories." *Guardian.co.uk* 18 May 2007. 26 Mar. 2009 http://www.guardian.co.uk/commentisfree/2007/may/18/comment.pressandpublishing.

Kalven, Harry, Jr. Review of *The Meaning of Treason*. *The University of Chicago Law Review* 16.2 (1949): 378–81.

Kempowski, Walter. *Das Echolot*. 10 vols. Munich: Knaus, 1993–2005.

Kennedy, James, and Russell C. Eberhart, with Yuhai Shi. *Swarm Intelligence*. San Francisco, CA: Morgan Kaufmann, 2001.

Kenyon, J. P. *Stuart England*. The Pelican History of England. Vol.6. Harmondsworth, Middlesex: Penguin, 1979.

Kershaw, Ian. *The "Hitler Myth": Image and Reality in the Third Reich*. Oxford: Clarendon P, 1987.

King, Richard H., and Dan Stone, eds. *Hannah Arendt and the Uses of History: Imperialism, Nation, Race, and Genocide*. New York: Berghahn Books, 2007.

Kitto, H. D. F. *Greek Tragedy*. London: Methuen, 1971.

Knight, India. "Every Mother's" Nightmare." *Times Online* 6 May 2007. 26 Mar. 2009 http://www.timesonline.co.uk/tol/comment/columnists/india_knight/article1752292.ece.

———. "Madeleine McCann: You Are All Guilty." *Times Online* 16 Sept. 2007. 26 Mar. 2009 http://www.timesonline.co.uk/tol/news/world/europe/article2459924.ece.

Koonz, Claudia. *The Nazi Conscience*. Cambridge, MA: Bellknap P, 2003.

Kristeva, Julia. *Hannah Arendt*. Trans. Ross Guberman. New York: Columbia UP, 2001.

———. "Hannah Arendt, or Life is a Narrative." *Crisis of the European Subject*. Intro. Samir Dayal. Trans. Susan Fairfield. New York: Other P, 2000. 49–94.

———. "Refoundation as Survival: An Interrogation of Hannah Arendt." *Common Knowledge* 14.3 (2008): 353–65.

———. *Strangers to Ourselves*. Trans. Leon S. Roudiez. New York: Columbia UP, 1991.

Kronja, Ivana. "The Aesthetics of Violence in Recent Serbian Cinema: Masculinity in Crisis." *Film Criticism* 30.3 (Spring 2006): 17–37.

Krstić, Igor. "Serbia's Wound Culture. Teenage Killers in Milošević's Serbia: Srđan Dragojević's *Rane*." *The Celluoid Tinderbox: Yugoslav Screen Reflections of a Turbulent Decade*. Ed. Andrew James Horton. Shropshire, UK: Central Europe Review, 2000. 89–102.

Lacan, Jacques. *Écrits. The First Complete Edition in English*. Trans. Bruce Fink. New York: Norton, 2006.

———. *Écrits* [Fr]. Paris: Éditions du Seuil, 1966.

———. *The Four Fundamental Concepts of Psycho-Analysis*. Ed. Jacques-Alain Miller. Trans. Alan Sheridan. Harmondsworth, Middlesex: Penguin, 1977.

———. *The Seminar of Jacques Lacan, Book I: Freud's Paper's on Technique 1953–1954*. Ed. Jacques-Alain Miller. Trans. John Forrester. Cambridge: Cambridge UP, 1988.

———. *The Seminar of Jacques Lacan, Book II: The Ego in Freud's Theory and in the Technique of Psychoanalysis 1954–1955*. Ed. Jacques-Alain Miller. Trans. Sylvana Tomaselli. Cambridge: Cambridge UP, 1988.

———. *The Seminar of Jacques Lacan, Book VII: The Ethics of Psychoanalysis 1959–1960*. Ed. Jacques-Alain Miller. Trans. Dennis Porter. London: Routledge, 1992.

Laclau, Ernesto. "Can Immanence Explain Social Struggles?" *Diacritics* 31.4 (Winter 2001): 3–10.

———. "Discourse and Jouissance: A Reply to Glynos and Stavrakakis." *Journal for Lacanian Studies* 1.2 (2003): 278–85.

———. "Glimpsing the Future." *Laclau: A Critical Reader*. Ed. Simon Critchley and Oliver Marchart. London: Routledge, 2006. 279–328.

———. *On Populist Reason*. London: Verso, 2005.

———. "Populism: What's in a Name?" *Populism and the Mirror of Democracy*. Ed. Francisco Panizza. London: Verso, 2005. 32–49.

Laclau, Ernesto, and Chantal Mouffe. *Hegemony and Socialist Strategy: Towards a Radical Democratic Politics*. London: Verso, 2001.

Lang, Berel. *Writing and the Moral Self.* New York: Routledge, 1991.
Lazić, Mladen, ed. *Protest in Belgrade.* Budapest: Central European UP, 1999.
Le Bon, Gustave. *The Crowd: A Study of the Popular Mind.* London: Fisher Unwin, 1896.
———. *Le déséquilibre du monde.* Paris: Flammarion, 1923.
———. *La psychologie politique et la défence sociale.* Paris: Flammarion, 1910.
Lechner, Frank, and John Boli. *World Culture: Origins and Consequences.* Oxford: Blackwell, 2005.
Lefebvre, Georges. *Études sur la révolution française.* Paris: Presses Universitaires de France, 1954.
Lessig, Lawrence. 29 March 2011 http://www.lessig.org.
Levi, Pavle. *Disintegration in Frames: Aesthetics and Ideology in the Yugoslav and Post-Yugoslav Cinema.* Stanford, CA: Stanford UP, 2007.
Levine, Mark, Amy Prosser, David Evans, and Stephen D. Reicher. "Identity and Emergency Intervention: How Social Group Membership and Inclusiveness of Group Boundaries Shapes Helping Behavior." *Personality and Social Psychology Bulletin* 31 (2005): 443–53.
Lovink, Geert. *Zero Comments: Blogging and Critical Internet Culture.* London: Routledge, 2008.
Lyotard, Jean-François. *The Postmodern Condition : A Report on Knowledge.* Trans. Geoff Bennington and Brian Massumi. Minneapolis: U of Minnesota P, 1984.
MacFarquhar, Larissa."Putting the Camp Back into Campus." *Lingua Franca* (Nov.–Dec. 1993): 6–7.
Mackay, Marina. "The Lunacy of Men, the Idiocy of Women: Woolf, West, and War." *NWSA Journal* 15.3 (2003): 124–44.
———. "Muriel Spark and the Meaning of Treason." *Modern Fiction Studies* 54.3 (2008): 505–22.
MacLeod, Donald. "The Hit Parade." *Guardian* Education. 14 June 2005: 3.
Madsen, Flemming. "Benchmarking the Influence of a Blog." 29 Mar. 2011 http://www.onalytica.com/blog/2007/07/benchmarking-influence-of-blog.html.
Maffesoli, Michel. *The Time of the Tribes: The Decline of Individualism in Mass Society.* Trans. Don Smith. London: Sage, 1996.
Magaš, Branka. *The Destruction of Yugoslavia: Tracking the Break Up 1980–92.* London: Verso, 1993.
———. "Kosovo between Yugoslavia and Albania." *New Left Review* (I) 140 (July–Aug. 1983): 62–91 (published under the psuedonym "Michele Lee").
Margaroni, Maria, and Effie Yiannopoulou. "Introduction: Theorizing Metaphoricity, Reconceptualizing Politics." *Metaphoricity and the Politics of Mobility.* Ed. Maria Margaroni and Effie Yiannopoulou. Amsterdam: Rodopi, 2006. 9–23.
Martell, Luke. *The Sociology of Globalization.* Cambridge: Polity, 2010.
Martinez-Alier, Joan. "Environmental Justice (Local and Global)." *The Cultures of Globalization.* Ed. Fredric Jameson and Masao Miyoshi. Durham, NC: Duke UP, 1998. 312–26.
Marx, Anthony W. *Faith in Nation: Exclusionary Origins of Nationalism.* Oxford: Oxford UP, 2003.
Marx, Karl. *Karl Marx: Selected Writings.* Ed. David McLellan. Oxford: Oxford UP, 1977.
Masson, Jeffrey Moussaieff, ed. *The Complete Letters of Sigmund Freud to Wilhelm Fliess 1887–1904.* Cambridge, MA: Harvard UP, 1985.
McCann, Kate. "About Missing Children." *Find Madeleine.* 24 Apr. 2008. http://www.findmadeleine.com/missingchildren.

McKay, Peter. "How the McCann Case Highlights Our True Attitude towards EU Membership." *Mail Online* 10 Sept. 2007. 30 Mar. 2009 http://www.dailymail.co.uk/debate/columnists/article-480882/How-McCann-case-highlights-true-attitude-EU-membership.html.

Miller, William Ian. *The Anatomy of Disgust.* Cambridge, MA: Harvard UP, 1997.

Milton, John. *Paradise Lost.* Ed. Merritt.Y. Hughes. New York: Odyssey P, 1935.

Monnerot, Jules. *Sociology and Psychology of Communism.* Trans. Jane Degras and Richard Lees. Boston: Beacon P, 1960.

Moscovici, Serge. *L'Age des foules.* Paris: Fayard. 1981.

Mouffe, Chantal. "Hegemony and New Political Subjects: Towards a New Concept of Democracy." *Readings in Contemporary Political Sociology.* Ed. Kate Nash. Oxford: Blackwell, 2000. 295–309.

Muir, Kenneth, ed. *Elizabethan and Jacobean Prose 1550–1620.* Harmondsworth, Middlesex: Penguin, 1956.

Murray, Warwick E. *Geographies of Globalization.* New York: Routledge, 2006.

Nancy, Jean-Luc. *Being Singular Plural.* Trans. Robert D. Richardson and Anne E. O'Byrne. Stanford, CA: Stanford UP, 2000.

———. *The Inoperative Community.* Trans. Peter Connor et al. Ed. Peter Connor. Minneapolis: U of Minnesota P, 2001.

Niezen, Ronald. *A World Beyond Difference: Cultural Identity in the Age of Globalization.* Oxford: Blackwell, 2004.

Nowell-Smith, Geoffrey. "Minnelli and Melodrama." *Home Is Where the Heart Is: Studies in Melodrama and the Woman's Film.* Ed. Christine Gledhill. London: BFI, 1987. 72–78.

Nye, Robert A. *The Origins of Crowd Psychology: Gustave Le Bon and the Crisis of Democracy in the Third Republic.* London: Sage, 1975.

Odone, Cristina. "It's Time to Play the Crying Game, Kate." *Guardian.co.uk* 21 Oct. 2007. 25 Mar. 2009 http://www.guardian.co.uk/commentisfree/2007/oct/21/comment.comment1.

Oesterle, Günter. "Das Tagebuch als Intervall." *Absolut privat*!?: *Vom Tagebuch zum Weblog.* Ed. Helmut Gold, Christiane Holm, Eva Bös, and Tine Nowak. Heidelberg: Wachter, 2008. 100–3.

Ong, Walter J. *Orality and Literacy: The Technologization of the Word.* New York: Methuen, 1988.

Oswell, David. *Culture and Society: An Introduction to Cultural Studies.* London: Sage, 2006.

Overy, Richard. *The Dictators: Hitler's Germany and Stalin's Russia.* Harmondsworth, Middlesex: Penguin, 2004.

Panksepp, Jack. "The Periconscious Substrates of Consciousness: Affectivity States and Evolutionary Origins of the Self." *Journal of Consciousness Studies* 5.5–6 (1998): 566–82.

Papacharissi, Zizi. "Audiences as Media Producers." *Blogging, Citizenship, and the Future of Media.* Ed. Mark Tremayne. London: Routledge, 2007. 29–38.

Parkin, Jill. "The Nightmare of the McCanns: There but for the Grace of God Go Us." *Mail Online* 23 June 2007. 26 Apr. 2009 http://www.dailymail.co.uk/news/article-453330/The-nightmare-McCanns-There-grace-God-us.html.

Parkin-Gounelas, Ruth. "From Burke to Neuroscience: The Nature of the Emotions." *Reconstructing Pain and Joy: Linguistic, Literary, and Cultural Perspectives.* Ed. Chryssoula Lascaratou, Anna Despotopoulou, and Elly Ifantidou. Newcastle, UK: Cambridge Scholars Publishing, 2008. 75–95.

———. "Helping Yourself to Heidegger." Review Essay. *The Individual and the Mass.* Spec. issue *Gramma: Journal of Theory and Criticism* 18 (2010): 223–32. http://www.enl.auth.gr/gramma.

Pearson, Allison. "98 Words that Broke My Heart." *Mail Online* 9 May 2007. 26 Mar. 2008 http://www.dailymail.co.uk/debate/columnists/article-453607/98-words-broke-heart.html.

Pendlebury, Richard. "Downfall of a Decent Clan: What the Shannon Family Tree Reveals about the Social Breakdown of Britain." *Mail Online* 16 Apr. 2008. 15 Mar. 2009 http://www.dailymail.co.uk/news/article-559949/Downfall-decent-clan-What-Shannon-family-tree-reveals-social-breakdown-Britain.html.

Pepys, Samuel. *Diary*. 29 Mar. 2011 http://www.pepysdiary.com.

Pick, Daniel. "Freud's 'Group Psychology' and the History of the Crowd." *History Workshop Journal* 39 (1995): 39–61.

Pieterse, Jan Nederveen. "Globalization as Hybridization." *Global Modernities*. Ed. Mike Featherstone, Scott Lash, and Roland Robertson. London: Sage, 1995. 45–68.

———.*Globalization and Culture: Global Mélange*. Lanham MD: Rowman and Littlefield, 2004.

Politi, Jina."The Gibbet-Maker." *Notes and Queries* 38.1 (Mar. 1991): 54–55.

———. "A New Species of Man: *The Man of Feeling*." *Performing Emotions: Historical & Anthropological Sites of Affect. Historein* 8 (2008): 63–71.

———. "Re-Reading *Titus Amdronicus*." *Epistimonike Epetirida Philosophikis Scholis, Aristotle University* 2 (1990): 133–51.

———. *Shakespeare and Law*. Athens: Papazisis, 1979.

Prayag Magh Mela Research Group. "Living the Magh Mela at Prayag: Collective Identity, Collective Experience and the Impact of Participation in a Mass Event." *The Social Psychology of Collectivity*. Spec. issue *Psychological Studies* 52 (2007): 293–301.

Puchner, Martin. *The Poetry of the Revolution*. Princeton, NJ: Princeton UP, 2006.

Pynchon, Thomas. *Gravity's Rainbow*. Harmondsworth, Middlesex: Penguin, 2006.

Quiggin, John. "Economic Blogs and Blog Economics." *Uses of Blogs*. Ed. Axel Bruns and Joanne Jacobs. New York: Lang, 2006. 69–80.

Radhakrishnan, R. *Theory in an Uneven World*. Oxford: Blackwell, 2003.

Reddy, William. M. "The Textile Trade and the Language of the Crowd at Rouen 1752–1871." *Past & Present* 74 (1977): 62–89.

Rehling, Nicola. "Introduction." *The Individual and the Mass*. Spec. issue *Gramma: Journal of Theory and Criticism* 18 (2010): 7–28. http://www.enl.auth.gr/gramma.

Reich, Wilhelm. *The Mass Psychology of Fascism*. Trans. Vincent R. Carfagno. New York: Simon & Schuster/ Pocket Books, 1976.

Reicher, Stephen D. "The Battle of Westminster: Developing the Social Identity Model of Crowd Behaviour in order to deal with the Initiation and Development of Collective Conflict." *European Journal of Social Psychology* 26 (1996): 115–34.

———. "Making a Past Fit for the Future: Political and Ontological Dimensions of Historical Continuity." *The Psychology of Historical Continuity*. Ed. Fabio Sani. London: Sage, 2008. 145–58.

———. "The Psychology of Crowd Dynamics." *Blackwell Handbook of Social Psychology: Group Processes*. Ed. Michael A. Hogg and Scott Tindale. Oxford: Blackwell, 2001. 182–208.

———. "The St. Pauls Riot: An Explanation of the Limits of Crowd Action in terms of a Social Identity Model." *European Journal of Social Psychology* 14 (1984): 1–21.

Reicher, Stephen D., Clare Cassidy, Ingrid Wolpert, et al. "Saving Bulgaria's Jews: An Analysis of Social Identity and the Mobilisation of Social Solidarity." *European Journal of Social Psychology* 36 (2006): 49–72.

Reicher, Stephen D., and S. Alexander Haslam. "Tyranny Revisited: Groups, Psychological Well-Being and the Health of Societies." *The Psychologist* 19 (2006): 146–50.

Reicher, Stephen D., S. Alexander Haslam, and Nick Hopkins. "Social Identity and the Dynamics of Leadership: Leaders and Followers as Collaborative Agents in the Transformation of Social Reality." *Leadership Quarterly* 16 (2005): 547–68.

Reicher, Stephen D., S. Alexander Haslam, and Rakshi Rath. "Making a Virtue of Evil: A Five Step Model of the Development of Collective Hate." *Social and Personality Psychology Compass* 2 (2008): 1313–44.

Reicher, Stephen D., and Nick Hopkins. *Self and Nation*. London: Sage, 2001.

Reicher, Stephen D., and Jonathon Potter. "Psychological Theory as Intergroup Perspective: A Comparative Analysis of 'Scientific' and 'Lay' Accounts of Crowd Events." *Human Relations* 38 (1985): 167–89.

Reicher, Stephen D., Russell Spears, and S. Alexander Haslam. "The Social Identity Approach in Social Psychology." *The Sage Handbook of Identities*. Ed. Margaret Wetherell and Chandra Mohanty. London: Sage, 2010. 45–62.

Reid, Melanie. "Shannon Matthews is the New Face of Poverty." *Times Online* 17 Mar. 2008. 24 Apr. 2008. http://www.timesonline.co.uk/tol/comment/ columnists/ melanie_reid/article3564364.ece.

Rheingold, Howard. *The Virtual Community: Homesteading on the Electronic Frontier*. 20 Mar. 2009 http://www.rheingold.com/vc/book/intro.html.

Riewald, Paul de. *De l'esprit des masses*. Paris: Delachaux et Niestle, 1949.

Ritzer, George. *The McDonaldization of Society: An Investigation into the Changing Character of Contemporary Social Life*. London: Pine Forge P, 1996.

Roazen, Paul. *Brother Animal: The Story of Freud and Tausk*. London: Allen Lane, 1971.

Le Robert, Dictionnaire de la langue française. Revised Alain Rey. Paris: Editions Dictionnaire le Robert, 1986.

Robertson, Roland. *Globalization: Social Theory and Global Culture*. London: Sage, 2002.

———."Glocalization: Time-Space and Homogeneity-Heterogeneity." *Global Modernities*. Ed. Mike Featherstone, Scott Lash, and Roland Robertson. London: Sage, 1995. 25–44.

Roche, Maurice. *Exploring the Sociology of Europe*. London: Sage, 2010.

Roustang, Francois. *Dire Mastery: Discipleship from Freud to Lacan*. Baltimore: Johns Hopkins UP, 1982.

Rushdie, Salman. *Imaginary Homelands: Essays and Criticism 1981–1991*. London: Granta Books, 1992.

Said, Edward W. *Culture and Imperialism*. London: Chatto & Windus, 1993.

Sample, Ian. "Research Cuts will Force Scientists to Share Laboratories, Top Scientists Warn." *Guardian* 11 May 2011. 17 May 2011 www.guardian.co.uk/science/2011/may/11/cuts-endanger-science-research-teaching/.

Sandoval, Greg. "The New York Times Drops Online Subscription Service." 17 Sept. 2007. 29 Mar. 2011 http://news.cnet.com/8301–10784_3–9780063–7.html.

Santner, Eric. *My Own Private Germany: Daniel Paul Schreber's Secret History of Modernity*. Princeton, NJ: Princeton UP, 2006.

———. *On Creaturely Life: Rilke, Benjamin, Sebald*. Chicago: U of Chicago P, 2006.

S.B. "Web 2.0." *Neue Zürcher Zeitung* 25 Mar. 2008. 29 Mar. 2011 http://www.nzz.ch/nachrichten/kultur/medien/web_20_1.694446.html

Schaefer, Richard T. *Sociology: A Brief Introduction*. 7th ed. Boston: McGraw Hill, 2008.

Schiller, Herbert I. *Mass Communications and American Empire*. Boulder, CO: Westview P, 1992.

Schueller, Malini Johar, and Ashley Dawson. "Academic Labor at the Crossroads? An Interview with Andrew Ross." *Social Text 90* 21.1 (Spring 2007): 117–32.

Scott, Bonnie Kime. "Refiguring the Binary, Breaking the Cycle: Rebecca West as Feminist Modernist." *Twentieth Century Literature* 37.2 (1991): 169–91.

Self, Will. *Dorian: An Imitation*. London: Viking, 2002.

Shakespeare, William. *Coriolanus*. Ed. P. Brockbank. London: Methuen, 1976.

Sharp, Joanne P. *Geographies of Postcolonialism*. London: Sage, 2009.

Shelley, P. B. *Selected Poetry and Prose*. New York: Rinehart, 1951.

Shorter Oxford English Dictionary on Historical Principles, The. 2 vols. Oxford: Oxford UP, 1973.

Sklair, Leslie. "Social Movements and Global Capitalism." *The Cultures of Globalization*. Ed. Fredric Jameson and Masao Miyoshi. Durham, NC: Duke UP, 1998. 291–311.

Smith, Adam. *The Theory of Moral Sentiments*. New York: Prometheus Books, 2000.

Sobcheck, Vivian. *The Address of the Eye: A Phenomenology of Film Experience*. Princeton, NJ: Princeton UP, 1991.

"State of the Blogosphere." 29 Mar. 2011 http://technorati.com/blogging/article/state-of-the-blogosphere-2010-introduction/page-2/.

Stedman Jones, Gareth. *Languages of Class: Studies in English Working Class History 1832–1982*. Cambridge: Cambridge UP, 1983.

Steele, John. "Met Chief: Why the Fuss over Soham Murders." *Telegraph.co.uk* 27 Jan. 2006. 19 Mar. 2009 http://www.telegraph.co.uk/news /uknews/1508942/Met-chief-Why-the-fuss-over-Soham-murders.html.

Steinberg, Marc W. "When Politics Goes Pop: On the Intersection of Popular and Political Culture and the Case of Serbian Student Protest." *Social Movement Studies* 3.1 (Apr. 2004): 3–29.

Stern, Kathleen, and Martha K. McClintock. "Regulation of Ovulation by Human Pheromones." *Nature* 392 (Mar. 12, 1998): 177–79.

Sterne, Laurence. *The Life and Opinions of Tristram Shandy, Gentleman*. 29 Mar. 2011 http://www.gutenberg.org/etext/1079.

Stevenson, Nick. "The Future of Public Media Cultures: Morality, Ethics and Ambivalence." *Culture and Politics in the Information Age: A New Politics?* Ed. Frank Webster. London: Routledge, 2001. 63–80.

Stott, Clifford, and John Drury. "Crowds, Context and Identity: Dynamic Categorization Processes in the 'Poll Tax Riot'."' *Human Relations* 53 (2000): 247–73.

Stott, Clifford, and Stephen D. Reicher. "How Conflict Escalates: The Inter-Group Dynamics of Collective Football Crowd 'Violence'." *Sociology* 32 (1998): 353–77.

Strathern, Marilyn. "'Improving Ratings': Audit in the British University System." *European Review* 5.3 (1997): 305–21.

Surowiecki, James. *The Wisdom of Crowds*. New York: Anchor Books, 2004.

Tajfel, Henri, ed. *Differentiation between Social Groups: Studies in the Social Psychology of Intergroup Relations*. London: Academic P, 1978.

Tajfel, Henri, and John C. Turner. "An Integrative Theory of Intergroup Conflict." *The Social Psychology of Intergroup Relations*. Ed. William. G. Austin and Stephen Worchel. Monterey, CA: Brooks/Cole, 1979. 33–47.

Tausk, Victor. "On the Origin of the 'Influencing Machine' in Schizophrenia." *Sexuality, War and Schizophrenia*. Ed. Paul Rozen. New Brunswick, NJ: Transaction Publishers, 1991. 185–219.

Taylor, Alastair. "Estate is Like a Nastier Beirut." *The Sun* 9 Apr. 2008. 19 May 2008 http://www.thesun.co.uk/sol/homepage/news/article1018795.ece.

"Technorati Top 100." 29 Mar. 2011 http://technorati.com/blogs/top100/.

Thomas, Robert. *The Politics of Serbia in the 1990s*. New York: Columbia UP, 1999.

Thompson, E. P. *The Making of the English Working Class*. Harmondsworth, Middlesex: Penguin, 1976.

———. "The Moral Economy of the English Crowd in the Eighteenth Century." *Past & Present* 50 (1971): 76–136.

Thrift, Nigel. *Non-Representational Theory: Space/Politics/Affect*. London: Routledge, 2008.

Thurschwell, Pamela. "Ferenczi's Dangerous Proximities: Telepathy, Psychosis and the Real Event." *differences* 11.1 (1999): 150–78.

Todorov, Tzvetan. *The Fragility of Goodness: Why Bulgaria's Jews Survived the Holocaust*. London: Weidenfeld & Nicolson, 2001.

Tomlinson, John. *Cultural Imperialism: A Critical Introduction*. Baltimore, MD: Johns Hopkins UP, 1991.

———. *Globalization and Culture*. Cambridge: Polity, 1999.

———. "Globalization and Cultural Analysis." *Globalization Theory: Approaches and Controversies*. Ed. David Held and Anthony McGrew. Cambridge: Polity, 2007. 148–68.

Tremayne, Mark, ed. *Blogging, Citizenship, and the Future of Media*. London: Routledge, 2007.

Trotter, W. *Instincts of the Herd in Peace and War*. London: Ernest Benn, 1916.

Tumber, Howard. "Democracy in the Information Age: The Role of the Fourth Estate in Cyberspace." *Culture and Politics in the Information Age: A New Politics?* Ed. Frank Webster. London: Routledge, 2001. 17–31.

Turkle, Sherry. *Life on the Screen: Identity in the Age of the Internet*. New York: Touchstone, 1995.

Turner, John C. "Towards a Cognitive Redefinition of the Social Group." *Social Identity and Intergroup Relations*. Ed. Henri Tajfel. Cambridge: Cambridge UP, 1982. 15–40.

Turner, John C., Mike A. Hogg, Penny J. Oakes, Stephen D. Reicher, et al. *Rediscovering the Social Group: A Self-Categorization Theory*. Oxford: Blackwell, 1987.

Urry, John. *Global Complexity*. Cambridge: Polity, 2003.

———. *Sociology Beyond Societies: Mobilities for the Twenty-First Century*. New York: Routledge, 2000.

Van Doorn, Niels, et al. "Writing from Experience: Presentations of Gender Identity on Weblogs." *European Journal of Women's Studies* 14. 2 (2007): 143–58.

Van Ginneken, Jaap. *Crowds, Psychology, and Politics, 1871–1899*. Cambridge: Cambridge UP, 1992.

Veale, Jennifer. "South Koreans are Shaken by a Celebrity Suicide." *Time* 6 Oct. 2008. 29 Mar. 2011. http://www.time.com/time/world/article/0,8599,1847437,00.html.

Vertovec, Steven, ed. *The Multiculturalism Backlash: European Discourses, Policies and Practices*. London: Routledge, 2009.

Vertovec, Steven, and Robin Cohen. "Introduction: Conceiving Cosmopolitanism." *Conceiving Cosmopolitanism: Theory, Context, and Practice*. Ed. Steven Vertovec and Robin Cohen. Oxford: Oxford UP, 2002. 1–22.

Vojkovic, Sasa. "Factum Documentary Films: Searching for the Present." *Cineaste* 32.3 (Summer 2007): 41–44.

Volosinov, V. N. *Marxism and the Philosophy of Language*. Trans. Ladislav Matejka and I. R. Titunik. Cambridge, MA: Harvard UP, 1986.

Wallerstein, Immanuel. *Historical Capitalism With Capitalist Civilization*. London: Verso, 1999.

———."World-Systems Analysis." *The Essential Wallerstein*. New York: New York P, 2000. 129–48.

Waters, Malcolm. *Globalization*. London: Routledge, 1995.

Webster, Frank. "A New Politics?" *Culture and Politics in the Information Age: A New Politics?* Ed. Frank Webster. London: Routledge, 2001. 1–13.

West, Rebecca. *Black Lamb and Grey Falcon: A Journey through Yugoslavia*. Edinburgh: Canongate Classics, 1995.

———. *The Meaning of Treason*. London: Phoenix P, 2000.

Wilby, Peter. "The Nursery-Tale Treatment of a Real-Life Nightmare." *Guardian.co.uk* 14 May 2007. 24 Apr. 2008 http://www.guardian.co.uk/media/2007/may/14/mondaymediasection9.

Wilde, Oscar. *The Picture of Dorian Gray*. Ed. Donald L. Lawler. London: Norton, 1988.

Wilkes, David, and Venessa Allen. "Tapas Nine Witness Says 'Mediterranean Man Took Madeleine'." *Mail Online* 20 Nov. 2007. 28 Mar. 2009 http://www.dailymail.co.uk/news/article-495092/Tapas-Nine-witness-says-Mediterranean-man-took-Madeleine.html.

Williams, Jeffrey J. "Academostars: Name Recognition." *The Celebrity Culture Reader*. Ed. P. David Marshall. London: Routledge, 2006. 371–88.

Williams, Linda. *Playing the Race Card: Melodramas of Black and White From Uncle Tom to O. J. Simpson*. Princeton, NJ: Princeton UP, 2001.

Williams, Raymond. *Keywords: A Vocabulary of Culture and Society*. New York: Oxford UP, 1983.

Willink, C. W. Introduction and Commentary. *Orestes*. By Euripides. Oxford: Clarendon P, 2001.

Wilson, Rob. "A New Cosmopolitanism is in the Air: Some Dialectical Twists and Turns." *Cosmopolitics: Thinking and Feeling beyond the Nation*. Ed. Pheng Cheah and Bruce Robbins. Minneapolis: U of Minnesota P, 1998. 351–61.

Wilson, Samuel W., and Leighton C. Peterson. "The Anthropology of Online Communities." *Annual Review of Anthropology* 31 (2002): 449–67.

Withington, Phil. "Public Discourse, Corporate Citizenship and State Formation." *The American Historical Review* 112.4 (Oct. 2007): 1016–38.

Wolf, Christa. *Ein Tag im Jahr, 1960–2000*. Munich: BTB, 2001.

Woodward, Susan L. *Balkan Tragedy: Chaos and Dissolution after the Cold War*. Washington, DC: The Brookings Institution, 1995.

Wordsworth, William. *The Prelude. Major British Writers*. Ed. George Bagshawe Harrison. 2 vols. New York: Harcourt Brace, 1954. II, 42–80.

———. "I wandered lonely as a cloud." *College Survey of English Literature*. Ed. B. J. Whiting. New York: Harcourt Brace, 1951. 63.

Wright, Oliver, and Jerome Taylor. "Cameron: My War on Multiculturalism." *The Independent* 5 Feb. 2011 http://www.independent.co.uk/news/uk/politics/cameron-my-war-on-multiculturalism-2205074.html.

Wright, Susan, and Elisa Camahort Page. "2009 Women and Social Media Study." 29 Mar. 2011 http://blogher.com/files/2009_Compass_BlogHer_Social_Media_Study_042709_FINAL.pdf.

Wyatt, Tristram D. *Pheromones and Animal Behaviour: Communication by Smell and Taste*. Cambridge: Cambridge UP, 2003.

Wykes, Maggie. "A Family Affair: The British Press, Sex and the Wests." *News, Gender and Power*. Ed. Cynthia Carter, Gill Branston, and Stuart Allan. London: Routledge, 1998. 233–47.

Young, Robert J. C. *The Idea of English Ethnicity*. Oxford: Blackwell, 2008.

Žižek, Slavoj. *Looking Awry: An Introduction to Jacques Lacan through Popular Culture*. Cambridge, MA: MIT P, 1992.

———. "Multiculturalism, or, the Cultural Logic of Multinational Capitalism." *New Left Review* (I) 225 (Sept.–Oct. 1997): 28–51.

———. *The Parallax View*. Cambridge, MA: MIT P, 2006.

———. *The Sublime Object of Ideology*. London: Verso, 1989.

———. *Tarrying With the Negative: Kant, Hegel, and the Critique of Ideology*. Durham, NC: Duke UP, 1993.

———. *The Ticklish Subject: The Absent Centre of Political Ontology*. London: Verso, 1999.

———. *Violence: Six Sideways Reflections*. New York: Picador, 2008.

———. *Welcome to the Desert of the Real!: Five Essays on September 11 and Related Dates*. London: Verso, 2002.

FILMOGRAPHY

Before the Rain [*Pred dozhdot*]. Dir. Milcho Manchevski. 3DD Entertainment, 1994.

Cabaret Balkan [*Bure Baruta*]. Dir. Goran Paskaljević. Vans, Serbia, 1998.

Cordon [*Kordon*]. Dir. Goran Marković. Doriane Films, France, 2003.

Lives of Others, The [*Das Leben der Anderen*]. Dir. Florian Henckel von Donnersmarck. Lionsgate, UK, 2006.

No Man's Land [*Ničija zemlja*]. Dir. Danis Tanović. Momentum Pictures, 2001.

Pretty Village, Pretty Flame [Lepa sela, lepo gore]. Dir. Srđjan Dragojević. Fox Lorber, USA, 1996.

Professional, The [*Profesionalac*]. Dir. Dušan Kovačević. Vans, Serbia, 2003.

Ulysses' Gaze [*To Vlemma tou Odyssea*]. Dir. Theo Angelopoulos. Artificial Eye, UK, 1995.

Underground: Once Upon a Time There Was a Country [*Podzemlje:Bila jednom jedna zemlja*]. Dir. Emir Kusturica. New Yorker Films, USA, Artificial Eye, UK, Komuna, Yugoslavia, 1995.

Witnesses [*Svjedoci*]. Dir Vinko Brešan. Film Movement, USA, 2004.

Wounds, The [*Rane*]. Dir. Srđjan Dragojević. First Run Features, USA, 1998.

Index

T